Under the Old School Topee

Leslie James Goddard, OBE, MA (Cantab),
Rector of St. Paul's School, Darjeeling, 1934-1964

Under the Old School Topee

Hazel Innes Craig

First published in 1990 by BACSA
(The British Association for Cemeteries in South Asia.)
76½ Chartfield Avenue, London,
SW15 6HQ

Reprinted 1991

This revised edition published 1996 by the author

ISBN   0 9526997 0 2

Published by Hazel Innes Craig,
53 Hill Rise, Rickmansworth,
Hertfordshire,
WD3 2NY

Produced by Axxent Ltd
The Old Council Offices,
The Green, Datchet, Berkshire,
SL3 9EH

Contents

List of Illustrations

The author acknowledges and thanks all those who so kindly provided photographs and/or drawings, and in particular: Alan Craig; the Goddard family; 'Kim' Taylor; Theon Wilkinson; Jane Turner; the late Ted Coulby; Allan Hipwood; Janet Chapman; Denise and Colin Coelho; Barbara and Douglas Haye; Myrtle Forbes; Harold Pateman; Edith Stiffle; Foy Nissen; Dorothy MacNabb; 'Les' Paul; Ursula Townsend; Pat Hardie; Florence Booth; Frank Hippman.

Foreword
to first edition (1990)

"Under the Old School Topee" is the sixteenth in a series of books about Europeans in South Asia, written by a BACSA member, published by BACSA for BACSA members with a wider public in mind, and particularly for those who went to school in India or Pakistan and those with an interest in education in its widest sense.

The author has a strong personal interest in the subject having spent four years at a co-educational school in Darjeeling while her twin brother was at a neighbouring boys' school. After her early schooldays 'under the old school topee', Hazel Craig completed her education in England and trained as a secretary in a college in Brighton. She returned to India with her parents for a further three years during which time she worked as a secretary at 'The Statesman' in Calcutta and at the office of the British High Commission in Karachi. She continued her secretarial career in London until she married in 1959, after which she obtained her LRAM teaching diploma and taught the piano privately. She lives with her husband in Hertfordshire.

Hazel Craig has constructed an unique account of the growth and development of the British schools which were established in the latter half of the 19th century, first in the plains and later in the hills, to provide an English public-school style education for children from very mixed backgrounds of race, religion and economic circumstance, from all corners of the Sub-Continent. The first part of the book identifies the different kinds of school that emerged, with details drawn from a few in various hill-stations to typify many others. The second part of the book seeks to capture the spirit of these oriental schooldays, wherever or whatever the school through the reminiscences of a remarkably wide cross-section of erstwhile pupils and teachers.

Theon Wilkinson MBE
(Hon Secretary – BACSA)

Acknowledgements

I am very grateful to all the people named in the text who have so kindly allowed me to share their reminiscences of schooldays in India as students or teachers.

I would also like to thank the many others not mentioned in the text who helped me by answering my questionnaire or gave me their assistance in a variety of ways, all of whom contributed in painting the overall picture.

My grateful thanks must also go to the following schools, whose staff responded to my request for magazines, prospectuses or histories: Auckland House, Simla; Barnes School, Deolali; Bishop Cotton School, Simla; Goethal's Memorial School, Kurseong; Ghora Gali College, Murree; Hebron School Ootacamund; Jesus & Mary Convent (Chelsea), Simla; Lawrence School, Sanawar; Mount Hermon School, Darjeeling; Pine Mount Government Girls' High School, Shillong; St. Joseph's College, Darjeeling; St Joseph's College, Naini Tal; St. Mary's Convent High School (Ramnee), Naini Tal; St Mary's High School, Mount Abu; St. Peter's Boys' High School, Panchgani; Sherwood College, Naini Tal.

The India Office Library and Records provided much valuable information on European education in India, and I would like to express my appreciation to the staff for their patient assistance and unfailing courtesy during my researches.

Finally, I am indebted to Theon Wilkinson for his interest and encouragement, and to his co-editor, Rosie Llewellyn-Jones. Without them – and BACSA – this book would not have seen light of day.

This revised edition 1996

After publication of the 1990 edition of "Under The Old School Topee", I was taken to task by many disgruntled readers who felt that their old schools had been unfairly left out! It would be impossible to mention them all – so in this edition I have added eleven more schools which I feel deserve a mention. A flick throught the index will reveal the schools which feature to a greater or lesser degree – yours might just be there!

Schools on the plains of India and Pakistan do appear here and there but this book deals expressly with the boarding schools in the hill stations.

H.M.C.

Introduction

The advent of the 1970s heralded a resurgence of interest in British India, with a spate of books, television and radio programmes in the following decade about the lives of the British in that jewel in the Empire's crown, culminating in 1984 with the eponymous television series based on Paul Scott's, *Raj Quartet*. I was one of the survivors of the Raj who gobbled up everything the media had to offer on this fascinating segment of our history in the Sub-Continent, and was much struck by the insistence of some writers that all British children were sent 'Home' to school in England, there being no decent schools for them to go to in India. This may have been true prior to the opening up of the hill stations in the mid-19th century, when the white-faced offspring of the British community were forced to wilt in the sultry and debilitating heat of India's plains until they were packed off at the tender age of seven to live with relations, or suffer incarceration in one of the many 'prep' and public schools Home had to offer.

But by the late 19th century and indeed right up to India's independence in 1947, English schools did exist in India and Part I of this book is an attempt to set the record straight, with additional glimpses in Part II of the experiences of a number of ex-students educated there. With the establishment of the hill stations as sanatoria for government officials, the army and 'ordinary' civilians alike many of the British in India did not automatically send their offspring Home at a tender age. Some could not endure the dreadful partings and others could not afford the fees required to give their young a Home-grown education. From the 1860s onwards there were boarding schools in the Indian hill stations to which thousands of British, Anglo-Indian (in the sense Eurasian) and Indian children were sent.

The subject of European (Anglo-Indian) education is a vast one, and I am only too aware of many notable omissions in my own account. The charting of the history of the famous Indian public schools, Mayo College, the Doon School et al for instance, does not come within the scope of this book. In their own way, these schools, too, are monuments to the work of many eminent British educational pioneers of the late 19th century. They were, however, established with the primary objective of inculcating the public school ethos into the sons of India's princely families through the medium of the English language, and they still flourish today with a student body drawn from families comprising India's affluent middle class. In any event, much has already been written about these famous schools whereas the rich seam of information on boarding schools for the children of the Raj has scarcely been tapped.

As the daughter of a former 'imperialist' – if sweating it out for 25 years while working for what used to be called 'The Gramophone Company' ('His Master's Voice' records) marks my father as an imperialist! – I spent the early part of my childhood under the Raj. My twin brother and I were taken out to India at the age of 14-months and spent those early first formative years out there, interspersed with sojourns at Home with our parents. Later, my brother and I were among the boat-loads of 'evacuees' whose parents had been advised, if not positively encouraged, by the British Government to take their children out of war-torn Britain. So it was that in 1940 we were despatched as boarders to two old-established schools in Darjeeling, I to Mount Hermon, a co-educational school run by American Methodist missionaries and he to St. Paul's School for Boys. And there we stayed for the next four years for nine consecutive months of each year. The education we received was on a par with that of the day Grammar and High Schools we attended at Home for a further 18 months on our return from India, and we were both put into classes a year ahead of our English peers, finishing up with good School Certificate results.

The fact that these European, now called 'Anglo-Indian', schools are alive, well and still flourishing in today's India and Pakistan – albeit now catering mainly for indigenous pupils – is a testament to the strength of their foundations. Jingoism apart, their development and success is due in no small measure to the Victorian muscular Christians, the dedicated missionaries, the devoted religiosi and the courageous eccentrics of all nationalities with a passion for education who saw a need and decided to fill it, at whatever cost.

It is fascinating to speculate as to what kind of schools would have evolved in India had that sub-continent been successfully colonised by the Portuguese, the Dutch or the French instead of the British. The British public school ethos would have remained where it started, at

'Home', its attendant by-products of team spirit, character-building, chapel-going and games-playing denied to thousands of Indians and Pakistanis. (It must be said, however, that not all Indians and Pakistanis are in favour of the continued existence of what they term 'elitist' establishments.)

But what might have happened to us and thousands of our fellows? Without those hill boarding schools, we could have become Kiplingesque evacuees, lonely, homesick and strangers to our parents. We consider ourselves lucky to have experienced a major part of our schooldays under the old school topee.

Hazel Innes and her twin, Geoffrey, at Darjeeling, 1940

In affectionate memory of
Maisie and Leslie Goddard
who opened so many doors

Part 1

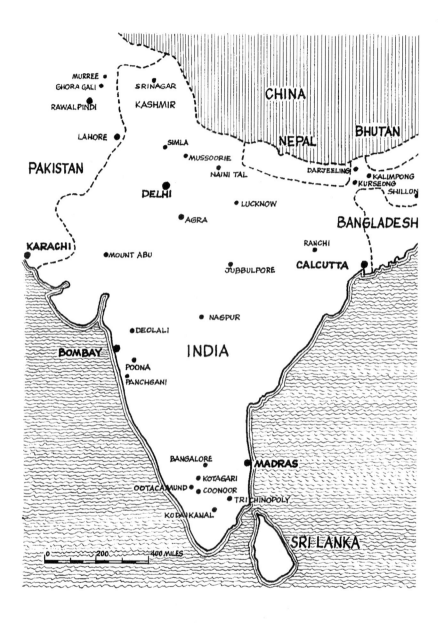

1

Early Days

When the East India Company was founded in 1600, its covenanted servants could not have foreseen how powerful the trading organisation was to become. By 1858 the Company ruled much of the vast Indian sub-continent – a far cry from those early traders in spice and indigo. A year after the Indian Mutiny, or the Indian War of Independence, as many Indians choose to call that holocaust in our mutual heritage, the Crown took over from the Company's Court of Directors and, in Disraeli's phrase, India became 'the jewel in the Crown.' The British had acquired it almost in a fit of aberration, their supremacy achieved through the vesting of commercial interests, bribery, treaty and victorious battles against the ruling Indian princes, successfully fending off Portugese, Dutch and – their deadliest enemy – French attempts at colonisation on the way. Bare faced annexation, too, played its sorry part in adding enormous tracts of Indian soil to Britain's rapidly developing Empire.

Gain was the primary objective in those early Empire-building days, but the profit motive gradually gave way to a sense of duty towards the conquered by the conquerors. The Victorian age, with its evangelistic fervour and sense of fair play, saw the reins of good Government being taken up by wise and able men whose tenure of office brought improvements in the lives of India's teeming millions: canals irrigated their parched earth; railways brought communication; schools and colleges brought the gifts of literacy; the British legal system forged a tortuous path through the alien maze of Eastern culture and – a mixed blessing – missionaries spread the Gospel. The seeds of evangelism had already been scattered however, with the arrival of Lord William Bentinck as

Governor General in 1828, an office he held until 1835. Out of this climate of evangelism grew the concern for social reform, resulting in the suppression of suttee, female infanticide and thuggee and, not least, the rise of feelings of cultural superiority by the British.

But these 17th century merchants were blissfully unaware of the seeds they were planting. As far as they were concerned, their sojourns in the trading posts established in Madras, Calcutta, Bombay and the minor settlements which sprang up in their wake were to be short ones. 'Get rich quick' was their watchword. As for the education of any children born behind the settlement walls, nothing could have been further from their minds. Women were not allowed to accompany their menfolk on the six to nine month journey in the old sailing ships. The Company's first writers (clerks) and factors were doomed to a monastic existence, their tedium relieved only by the weekly Sunday dinner at the President's table, when the homesick exiles raised their glasses to toast absent wives. Many were pious and god-fearing; some were remittance men sent out East by despairing fathers; others were just plain crooks. Gentlemen rubbed shoulders with men of humbler origins, greed their only bond.

As time passed it was realised that the wealth behind the primitive walls of the poorly defended settlements would have to be guarded from the attentions of the local banditry. The factories (as the trading posts were called) would have to become forts, arsenals built up and soldiers recruited. In Madras, the Company's largest and most important trading post established in 1639, soldiers were recruited from the Portugese mercenaries already ensconced as a result of their country's colonisation in the 16th century, and from the sons born to them through their marriages with Indian women baptised into the Roman Catholic faith by the Portuguese priests bent on spreading Catholicism all over India. (A dream never more than partially realised and hampered by the arrival of the British). Next, Company regiments were raised by the recruiting of British soldiers from home. Having no women of their own kind to marry, they naturally gravitated towards the only ones available. Seeking a Christian mate they did not marry Indian women, but sought wives from the Portuguese and Luso-Indian community, the name given to

2

the progeny from marriages between Portuguese men and Indian women. The newly-wedded Company soldiers, factors and writers then became Roman Catholics themselves and such Popish carryings-on caused consternation among the Court of Directors in London. These were intolerant times and England was experiencing a wave of puritanical zeal under Cromwell and his Ironsides.

The Company's Directors at home were accused by their more bigoted colleagues of undermining the Established Church by allowing such practices, and the repercussions in Madras led to the presentation of a petition to Mr Chambers, the Madras President, seeking the banishment of all Portuguese women and children from within the precincts of the fort in order to discourage this alarming spread of Roman Catholicism. The President declined the request, pointing out that if it was acted upon, all the Portuguese mercenaries engaged in its defence would resign in a body, leaving the settlement unprotected.

Further efforts were made to discourage this trend by despatching occasional boat-loads of Protestant women from home. These potential wives were sent out at the Company's expense and had to be models of sobriety and decorum. Naturally, some fell short of such virtuous expectations and scandals ensued, resulting in warnings that they would be put on bread-and-water and shipped back to England unless they toed the line. But there were never enough ladies to go round and in the 1670s only three unmarried women landed in Madras. Following the social order of the day, the female immigrants were divided up into 'gentlewomen' and 'other women' all of whom were provided with one set of clothes by the Company for up to one year's foray into the marriage market.

Despite such stop-gaps, the demand for marriageable women, Portuguese, Luso-Indian or English, eventually exceeded the supply. Worse, in the eyes of the bigwigs at home, overcrowding at the Fort compelled many of the Company's English soldiers to live in the native quarter of the town where they formed illicit liaisons with Indian women. Sex reared its ugly head again and was no respecter of race or religion. Realising that the sexual urge was stronger than any kind of legislation, the Court of Directors faced this new dilemma by issuing the following edict to the President of Madras. Dated the 8th April 1687, it ran:

'The marriage of our soldiers to the native women of Fort St George is a matter of such consequence to posterity that we shall be content to encourage it with some expense, and have been thinking for the future to appoint a pagoda (eight or nine shillings in those days) to be paid to the mother of any child that shall hereafter be born of any such future marriage, upon the day the child is christened, if you think this small encouragement will increase the number of such marriages'.

The Directors' offer was favourably received and acted upon forthwith. A momentous decision. Thus it was that the British themselves deliberately created a mixed population, and the 'Anglo-Indian' community became a reality. The designation 'Anglo-Indian' in this book refers to people of mixed race, sometimes called 'Eurasian', and not to be confused with the British who lived and worked in India and, at times, dubbed themselves Anglo-Indian.

However such children came into existence, the officials of 'John Company' of those early years paid scant attention to their educational needs. They and the few British children growing up in the Company's settlements, were introduced to a smattering of the three 'Rs' by such unsuitable tutors as factors, bankrupt merchants, disabled soldiers or old army pensioners. A very early number of 'The Calcutta Review' reveals the following illuminating scene:

'Let us contemplate him, seated in an old-fashioned chair, with his legs resting on a cane "morah" (cotton-reel shaped stool). A long pipe, his constant companion, projects from his mouth. A pair of loose pyjamas and a "charkana banian" (informal jacket) keep him within the pale of society, and preserve him cool in the the hot climate of this clime. His rattan – his sceptre – is in his hand; and the boys are seated on stools, or little "morahs", before his pedagogue majesty. They have already read three chapters of the Bible, and have got over the proper names without much spelling; they have written their copies – small, round text, and large hand; they have repeated a column of Entick's Dictionary with only two mistakes and are now working Compound Division, and soon expect to arrive at Rule of Three. Some of the lads' eyes are red with weeping, and others expect to have a taste of the ferule. The partner of the pensioner's days is seated on a low Dinapore matronly chair, picking vegetables, and preparing the ingredients for her coming dinner. It strikes twelve o'clock and the schoolmaster shakes himself. Presently the boys bestir themselves; and for the day the school is broken up.'

Poor little boys! The heat must have been intolerable, the perspiration running down their puckered brows. Their contemporaries in England were not faring all that well either, the education they were receiving in the miserably furnished one-room dame schools not much better than that doled out by the old army pensioner. Illiteracy was the order of the day in England and many years were to elapse before the great Education Act of 1870 enabled local authorities to establish the School Boards providing elementary education paid for from rate aid for children from humble homes. So perhaps the little Company boy in India wasn't doing so badly. His sister would have fared no better in England either. Girls in England were expected to confine themselves to learning how to sew and cook in preparation for marriage to a poor man, or domestic drudgery in the house of a richer one.

The Company's laissez-faire attitude towards the education of the children of mixed as well as 'pure' British parentage continued until 1670 when they bestirred themselves sufficiently to set up an official inquiry into the subject. As a result of their findings they brought out a Scottish preacher named Pringle to Fort St George as Headmaster of a school for the children of Portuguese and British fathers, also admitting a few children of the Company's Indian subordinates. A major reason for the school's inauguration was the age-old fear that so many of the Company's children were being educated in schools run by French and Portuguese priests of the Roman Catholic faith. Mr Pringle's school started in 1673 and he was succeeded in 1678 by Mr Ralph Ord, an ex-soldier. In 1692 the school's supervision became the responsibility of the Chaplain of Madras and, with the arrival of a Mr Stevenson in 1715, it became the St Mary's Church Charity School for orphan and destitute children with 18 boys and 12 girls on its rolls. Thirty pupils in an area which must have had hundreds of such children makes one wonder if the dreaded Catholic priests hadn't made a much deeper mark than that envisaged by the Company authorities.

St Mary's Church Charity School has the distinction of being recognised as the first European school in India. But not to be outdone, the Roman Catholic Capuchin Fathers started another English medium school in the Black Town of Madras where European and Anglo-Indian boys were taught with boys of Indian communities.

Madras continued to be in the forefront of the educational field in the 18th century and can claim further distinction by the establishment of the first girls' school in India in 1787. This was the Madras Female Asylum Orphanage which came about as a result of the 'poor peopling' – Florence Nightingale's immortal description for the devoted philanthropy of her upper class contemporaries – of Lady Campbell, wife of the Governor of Fort St George. The Orphanage was a refuge for the daughters of British soldiers killed in the defence of the newly emerging Indian Empire, or taken off by the dreadful scourges of cholera, typhoid and the many other tropical diseases prevalent in those days of primitive hygiene and ignorant doctoring. Some were left totally destitute when their mothers, too, went to early graves.

Lady Campbell's appeals for funds were generously met, with all ranks below Field Officers contributing two days' pay with larger amounts donated by Generals and Field Officers. Her efforts led to the expansion of the original St Mary's Church Charity School into the Madras Male Orphanage under Dr Andrew Bell. As a result of his tours of Indian village schools where he observed the practice of older pupils drawing in the sand to assist in the instruction of their younger fellows, Bell founded his monitorial or pupil-teacher system of education in the Male Orphanage. His young monitors, some of them not much older than 12 years of age, would write out exercises for their slower companions to copy and learn by rote, freeing the teacher for work with other pupils. Teachers were hard to find in those pioneering days and not many made the long voyage from England to India. Bell's monitorial system was later adopted by the Quaker, Joseph Lancaster, in the English schools of the early 19th century.

Regarded as one of the great educationists of his day, Andrew Bell was appointed to a prebend's stall in Westminster Abbey. After his death in 1832 a tablet was placed in the Abbey in his honour, stating that he founded

> 'the Madras system of education and discovered and reduced to successful practice the plan of mutual instruction founded upon the multiplication of power and division of labour in the moral and intellectual world which has been adopted within the British Empire as the National system of education of the children of the poor in the principles of the Established Church.'

As the oldest presidency to be established under the British in India, Madras had a head start in the founding of Church schools and orphanages. Still surviving in Trichinopoly is the St John's Vestry School established by the Society for the Propagation of Christian Knowledge (SPCK) in 1773 for the orphans of soldiers of the Company's artillery killed in an explosion of the powder magazine at the Trichinopoly Fort.

Apart from the work of the Church in Madras, the 18th century saw the setting up of many schools by private individuals where Eurasian boys and girls were educated side by side with Indian children. The education they received would not have been very advanced, but such schools helped to fill the gaps left by the indifferent officials of the East India Company.

ಞಞ

After many vicissitudes, Bengal achieved permanence as a British possession after the Battle of Plassey in 1757, when the British were surprised to find themselves owners of nearly 900 square miles of Bengal. But Calcutta, the Company's important trading post on the banks of the River Hugli, was originally founded by the Company's agent, Job Charnock, in 1690. Destined to become the capital of British India until it was superseded by Delhi in 1912, Calcutta was guarded by Fort William, erected in 1696 and named three years later after the Dutch King of England.

The children born to the British and Eurasian settlers there in the late 17th century would have suffered the same fate as their fellows in Madras: a cursory acquaintance of the scriptures and a smattering of reading, writing and arithmetic through the doubtful ministrations of the untutored pensioners and other well-intentioned individuals working as Company servants.

Again it was the Church which took the first steps in bringing a glimmer of light into the lives of the poorer children of the community in Calcutta. In 1713 the Rev Samual Briercliffe, a zealous member of the SPCK and later Trinity College, Cambridge, to boot, landed in Calcutta determined to promote the establishment of charity schools in the settlement. His efforts were rebuffed by the Company, who refused to pay for a schoolmaster. It was not until eighteen years later that the project was successfully launched, this time through the munificence of Robert Bourchier, later to become Governor of Bombay, who paid for the building of a school-house. The school was opened by the Rev Gervase Bellamy in 1731, and its first schoolmaster was a Goan friar named Aquiare, conveniently received into the Church of England by Bellamy a year before. The unfortunate Gervase Bellamy was to perish in the Black Hole of Calcutta in 1756. The school eventually came under the supervision of the Rev John Maplecroft of Clare College, Cambridge, who considerably raised its standards. Following the policy of creating little English corners in India's foreign fields, it was modelled on the Bluecoat School in London, its eight foundationers clad in blue cassocks but, in consideration, no doubt, of the miseries of Calcutta's humid climate, spared the constriction of the yellow stockings and buckled shoes of their English counterparts.

Records show that this establishment can rightly claim the distinction of being the first European school in Bengal. In 1789 Calcutta's wealthy merchants gave it generous financial assistance and it merged with another charity school started by the Rev Zachariah Kiernander to become the Calcutta Free Schools for Boys and Girls. Located as they were in the parish of St Thomas, the schools were later re-named the St Thomas's Schools for Boys and Girls, the Clewer Sisters taking charge of the girls' department. Starting as charity enterprises, the schools eventually emerged as secondary institutions specialising in various vocational fields in the 20th century.

The Church in Calcutta was not alone in its efforts to care for the children orphaned by the deaths of their fathers in the service of the

Company. In 1783 The Military Orphan Society founded the Upper and lower Military Orphanages under the auspices of Colonel William Kirkpatrick, secretary to General Giles Stibbert, Commander in Chief of the Bengal Army. The Upper Orphanage was for the children of officers and the Lower Orphanage for children of other ranks. Upper Orphanage children received a good preliminary education before being sent to England to complete their schooling, the boys returning to India in senior positions in the Company's service. The elementary education given to the Lower Orphanage children enabled the boys to take up employment in the Company's junior ranks but, unlike their fellows in the Madras Orphanage, they were not taught trades which would enable them to take up work outside the company. Further education at Home was not deemed appropriate for them.

But apart from providing schooling for these unfortunate orphans, the Asylums as they were called, provided, according to WH Carey in his book, *The Good Old Days of the Hon'ble John Company,*

'a harbour of refuge for bachelors in want of wives. Balls were given expressly for the purpose of securing proposals of marriage for the young ladies. Persons in want of wives frequently made their selection of an evening. Officers in the Upper Provinces sometimes travelled a distance of 500 miles to obtain a wife in this way. The suitors had to satisfy the authorities of the school that they were men of good character and in a position to support a wife. The girls were left entirely free to accept or reject their suitors and were never forced into marriage.'

Marriages to child-brides were commonplace among the officers and other ranks in the Company's regiments of the 18th century and later, as many a marriage registration in the India Office Ecclesiastical Records in London bears witness, some of the girls were as young as 12 years of age, and the permission of the groom's Commanding Officer was necessary in such cases. These orphanages prospered until 1846 when both were closed, the remaining children being absorbed into other institutions.

Following the Madras pattern, three types of school: charity, military and private were established in Calcutta during the 18th

9

century. The philanthropic and missionary societies were hard put to cater for the ever-increasing Eurasian population, to say nothing of the Indian children whose parents wanted them to have a 'European' education, and this led to the mushrooming of numerous private schools. A Mr Archer opened a boys' school in 1789, and newspapers of the day reveal many others. The schools lasted for as long as their founders did, dying with them in many cases.

Several Eurasian ladies started schools for 'young ladies', the first among them a Mrs Hedge, who taught French and dancing in 1760, retiring with a 'snug fortune' in 1780. These private schools sought to cater for children from a higher social order than those who filled the charity and military schools. Reports state that the girls were taught the three 'Rs', needlework, lace-making and so on – subjects destined not to transform the young ladies into 'blue-stockings'. As the education of girls was never considered as important as that of their brothers, some of the few 'pure' British parents of children born in India may have sent their daughters to these glorified 'dame schools', rather than pack them off on the long and hazardous voyage to England as they did their sons. But there cannot have been many such pupils in the 18th and early 19th centuries. Women were still in the minority in India and until the 1833 Charter Act which did away with many restrictions on entry into India, the Company would only admit travellers, particularly women, on board the Indiamen, who had been granted special permits. And in the Bengal of 1816, according to the Company's official guide book *The East India Vade Mecum*

> 'the number of European women to be found in Bengal and its dependencies cannot amount to 250, while the male population (European) of respectability, including military officers, may be taken at about 4,000.

ଓଽୠ

The East India Company's policy of masterly inactivity in the field of European education was as prevalent in Bombay as in the two other Presidencies. As we have seen, they took some initiative in the 17th century but were content to shift their educational responsibilities on to the shoulders of the few missonaries who were arriving in India at the beginning of the 18th century.

Acquired from a Gujarat Sultan by the Portuguese in 1534, Bombay was ceded to Charles II in 1661 as part of the dowry brought to him by his wife, Catherine of Braganza. He transferred it to the East India Company in 1668 for £10 a year 'in free and common soccage' and after fending off the Marathas and Mughals the British were finally left to trade in comparative peace by the end of the 18th century.

The first school of any note to be established in Bombay was again the result of missionary zeal. In 1718 the Rev Richard Cobbe, an East India Company chaplain, founded a small free school for twelve poor boys in a building near the present Cathedral of St Thomas, in the Fort. One master had the responsibility of feeding, clothing and educating them. This small school continued to cater for only a dozen boys until 1815 when another Company chaplain, Archdeacon George Barnes, appealed for funds to enlarge the school to meet the needs of the increasing number of poor children in the area. The Bombay Education Society was formed, the first small school taken over and new premises opened at Byculla on a site donated by the Government of the day. Girls as well as boys were admitted and by 1818 numbers had increased from 12 to 25. This doubling of the school population led to the resignation of the Headmaster, a Mr MacVeigh, who protested that such a number was unmanageable! But other dedicated souls came forward to work for the school's continuation and from such small beginnings emerged the famous Barnes School, which moved to Deolali in 1925 and still flourishes today.

ᎠᏛᎧ

The history of the schools for Eurasian and European children in the three main Presidencies of Madras, Bengal and Bombay during the 17th and 18th centuries has touched only briefly on the general education scene. As already mentioned, the schools fell under the headings of charitable (the Churches), military and private and, in the main, catered for the poorer children of the community.

The Church played the greatest part in European education in India throughout the period of the British Raj. The first step towards this dominant trend was taken in 1698 when a Company Charter decreed that chaplains appointed to the three Presidencies were charged with the spread of education and Christianity among the children of its employees. Many of these chaplains augmented their paltry salary of £50 a year by indulging in commercial deals and eschewing their true responsibilities. Some returned to England considerably richer than when they first left its shores. The neglect suffered by their flock led to the lowering of educational and religious standards, some of the Company's servants joyfully going native, adopting the wearing of Indian clothes and converting to Indian religions. Thus it was left to the few conscientious clergymen and the more pious souls in the settlements and factories to keep up a semblance of church-going and teach the children a smattering of scripture and the three 'Rs'. Thanks to them and the old war-pensioners, many of their erstwhile pupils became sufficiently literate for posts in the Company's early business houses and in the army as clerks.

Non-conformist missionaries, too, worked devotedly to improve the lot of the needy children, and many Roman Catholic priests, both French and Portuguese had already established schools and orphanages. The Danes and the Dutch were also spreading the Christian gospel in their settlements, although they were more concerned with the conversion of the Indian population. (The British East India Company was not at all keen for their missionaries to come to India with the intention of converting the 'heathen' natives and was bent on pursuing a policy of religous neutrality). It was not until 1813 that an East India Company Charter allowed a Bishop to be appointed to the Indian Church, also permitting British missionaries to work in India under licences granted by the Company. This and the later Company Charter of 1833 opened the floodgates of evangelism and laid the foundations of the many famous European schools on India's plains and, later, in her hill stations, with the Governments of the day providing grants-in-aid to many approved schools.

2

The Plains Schools

Before lifting our eyes unto the hills whence came the majority of boarding schools run on English public school lines – some lines more wavy than others – for European and Anglo-Indian children, we must briefly pick up the threads of the progress of European education on India's sweltering plains before the hill stations were discovered in the 1820s and developed as havens of rest and recuperation first for the soldier, then for the government official, the 'box wallah' (the pejorative description given to Englishmen earning their living in trade or commerce, probably a reference to itinerant Indian pedlars who carried their wares in boxes), their memsahibs and children.

As we have seen, apart from the charitable orphanages set up in the 18th century by both the Anglican and Roman Catholic churches as well as the military in the Presidencies of Calcutta, Bombay and Madras, many individuals had also established private seminaries for the children of middle-class parents who could afford the fees. With the establishment of Archer's School in Calcutta in 1780, the early years of the 19th century saw more private schools springing up in Calcutta, notably Drummond's Dhurrumtollah Academy, Farrell's Seminary, Ardwise's Calcutta Academy, and others started by similar academically orientated gentlemen.

Girls' schools, too, began to proliferate in Calcutta, their owners quick to emulate the redoubtable Mrs Hedges. who retired with her snug fortune in 1780 after running her school for 20 years. Other Eurasian ladies such as Mrs Pitts, Mrs Savage and Mrs Durrell opened their own institutions, and Mrs Durrell's school in Clive Street 'enjoyed the most extensive support' according to contemporary records.

These private schools catered for the growing number of European, Eurasian and, in some cases, Indian children whose parents wanted them to have a European education, and standards no doubt varied. But the redoubtable Captain Thomas Williamson, author in 1810 of two volumes of *The East India Vade Mecum* after fifteen years service in India, was in little doubt as to the questionable educational standards of such schools. His adverse opinions were echoed by later generations of British parents and did much disservice to the many well-run boarding schools established in the mid and late 19th century, some of which still survive in modern India. The antipathy towards the education of British children in India persisted right up to the 20th century and resulted in the heart-breaking separations between parents and children which were a predominant feature in the lives of the exiled British.

Of those early private schools, Williamson says:

'Whatever may be the merits of teachers, nothing would reconcile me to bringing up a child in India. All so educated are rendered unfit for the society of gentlemen who have been brought up in Europe; they know nothing of the world, but while imitating the manners and customs of those they term their countrymen, exercise all that craft which peculiarly characterizes the native youths. In a moral point of view the detention of a child, particularly a female, in India, is highly culpable; and when treated as a matter of economy, will, in the end, be found to be equally objectionable. That the disadvantage under which parents labour, is considerable must be fully admitted... (but) they can rarely have a child creditably schooled in Calcutta for less than £75 per mensem, all charges included.'

He maintained that for half that sum, say for £40, much better education was available at home, and that although girls could learn the 'accomplishments' taught in a school such as the one run by Mrs Hedges 'they know nothing of the world.' Williamson's preoccupation with pupils' lack of worldly knowledge seems misplaced. In those days, surely the most important reason for sending children home for their education was because of the debilitating influence of India's climate?

If a knowledge of the world in the English public schools of the day was to be gleaned from the brutal flogging of little boys, sparse and usually disgusting food, bestial and ill-educated masters, then

Williamson was right. And, in the case of the daughters of the English middle classes, their only means of education was in the confines of the home-based room under a sparsely qualified Governess. Hardly a suitable background for knowledge of the world. Miss Buss and Miss Beale were still waiting in the wings...

He might have revised his opinion if he had still been in India when David Drummond took over the Dhurrumtolla Academy in 1813. The school had a high reputation because of his insistence, as Headmaster, on holding an annual examination at which prominent ladies and gentlemen were invited to attend. These worthy voyeurs are said to have been deeply impressed by the silent, crowded hall full of eager and serious pupils and the school's popularity soon increased, with places much sought after. One of its most famous pupils was the Eurasian poet, Henry Derozio, who became Drummond's favourite scholar.

On Drummond's retirement in 1823 his school was merged with the Verulam Academy. New methods and progressive ideas were instituted; no classics were taught, but particular attention was paid to English Literature, Science and Natural History. The dreary repetition of lessons by rote was abolished and the cane was swished neither in anger nor in cold blood, an innovation contrasting strongly with the obsessive beating practised in the school's counterparts in England. One wonders what careers the Academy's pupils were eventually fitted for after a diet consisting of English Literature, Science and Natural History? But vocational training was rare in such educational establishments of the early 19th century, and certainly not envisaged for the middle classes.

Such schools had to be financially self-sufficient as the Government of the day made no grants-in-aid to the so-called European schools, concentrating on those set up for Indians, which were to be secular in character, with aid granted to religious institutions only for the secular results achieved.

Anglo-Indians and Europeans continued to pursue the policy of self-help and one of the major steps they took towards the education of their own community was the establishment of the Parental Academic Institution in 1823. This was the brain-child of Mr J W Ricketts and his fellow 'East Indians', the term used to describe people of mixed parentage in those days. On a Saturday evening on the 1st March 1823, while the more frivolous of the European community were enjoying themselves at cards or consuming mountains of food washed down with vast quantities of claret and going on to dance at one of Calcutta's regularly held balls, where their heavy, English clothes became – like their wearers – limp with perspiration, Ricketts was installed as Secretary of the Institution. Exactly two months later, on the 1st May, the school began to function in a small two-storied building at 11 Park Street – 'an excellent house in the best part of town', according to Bishop George Cotton, who was himself to become famous on the educational scene in India.

But all was not well. Within a month of opening, the members of the Management Committee were quarrelling among themselves about religion and ecclesiastical supervision. As a result, five committee members broke away from the Institution and enlisted the help of a Mr William Sinclair, who was running a private school in Calcutta's Wellesley Square East. His school now formed the basis of the splinter group's new non-denominational establishment with 52 pupils on its rolls. Numbers increased and by 1839 had reached 215, with the new school now housed at 53 Park Street, later to become Park Mansions. In 1855 the school's financial difficulties were resolved by the receipt of a legacy of Rs 230,000 from the will of Captain John Doveton, an Anglo-Indian officer in the army of the Nizam of Hyderabad. A year later the school was raised to the status of a College affiliated to Calcutta University and re-named the Parental Academy and Doveton College. Although its pupils were instructed in the Christian doctrines, its doors were open to children from all religious backgrounds, and the Principal's Report of 1862-3 reveals that some 10 to 15 per cent of the total enrolment was made up of students of the Hindu, Muslim and Buddhist faiths.

The College imparted a very progressive education, its curriculum embracing the teaching of scriptures, English Literature and English grammar, an Indian vernacular, geography, Roman and Indian history, astronomy, natural philosophy, Latin, mathematics including geometry and algebra, and political economy. The wise inclusion of an Indian vernacular in the course of instruction lapsed in many of the European schools set up in later years, particularly after the Indian Mutiny, which resulted in universal antipathy amongst the British towards all things Indian. Nonetheless, Carey, in his *Good Old Days of the Hon'ble John Company*, published in 1882, gives the College a typically Victorian pat on the back when he says: 'To the Parental Academy must be given the tribute of having raised the tone of Christian education in Calcutta, and directed attention to the study of the History of India and its vernaculars.' The institution lived on until 1916 when it finally closed its doors for lack of pupils, leaving a valuable legacy in the form of the Doveton Trust, the income from which would pay for post-school scholarships for Anglo-Indian children proceeding to higher academic, professional or technological education. During the College's lifetime, the high quality of its instruction also earned it affiliation to Oxford University.

Meanwhile, the remaining members of the original committee had re-established themselves at the Parental Academy's first premises at 11 Park Street, and in June 1823 started their own school called the Calcutta Grammar School. Rivalry naturally ensued between the two. But both organisations were having teething troubles. In its early days, the Parental Academy was having to cope with inefficient teaching standards and the Grammar School was heading for dissolution despite its strong ties with the Anglican Church. Leading members of Calcutta's Anglo-Indian and European community endeavoured to act as peacemakers by exhorting the two schools to amalgamate and form an undivided national institution for the education of the Christian youth of the community, but, as we have seen, the Parental Academy would have none of it.

In 1830 the new Calcutta Grammar School closed down briefly, but help was at hand in the shape of Archdeacon Daniel Corrie under whose efforts the school was re-opened in June 1830, this time as the Calcutta High School. Daniel Corrie was the forerunner of that other eminent pioneer in the field of European education, Bishop George Edward Lynch Cotton, founder of Bishop Cotton's School for Boys in Simla in 1863. Under Corrie's leadership the High School flourished and standards improved. He was aided by Bishop John Matthias Turner who played a large part in raising subscriptions and engaging the services of an experienced Rector, the Rev John

McQueen. With McQueen's departure in 1833 the boarding establishment came under the charge of a Clerk of the Treasury and his wife, with a Mr James Graves overseeing the pupil's education. A contemporary Government report on education comments that the 'strange separating of the institution into two parts seems to have been one cause for its want of success.' For in 1846 the school again fell into financial difficulties and was only saved from disaster by a donation of Rs 10,000 from another Daniel – Bishop Daniel Wilson, the first Metropolitan of India, leading to the purchase of better premises, the one-time home of St John's College, on Chowringhee.

At the instigation of Bishop Wilson, the Calcutta High School was re-named St Paul's School, the change of nomenclature no doubt due to the Bishop's desire to connect it with Calcutta's St Paul's Cathedral Church, then nearing completion.

Nearly 20 years later, the school was transferred to Darjeeling, one of the most popular hill stations in India's Himalayan mountain range, where it still stands and flourishes, a monument to the dedication of those early pioneers and known to many as 'the Eton of the East.'

Another famous name in the annals of European (or, as it eventually became known, Anglo-Indian) education, is that of Claude Martin, founder of La Martinère Colleges in Calcutta and Lucknow. Martin was the son of Fleury Martin, a cooper in the French city of Lyon. Born in 1735, he had some of his education at a School in Lyon where he revealed a taste for mathematics and science. As a young man he joined the French East India Army, arriving in India in 1752 and rising to become an officer. After the fall of Pondicherry in 1760 he threw in his lot, with other deserters and prisoners, with the victorious British in whose army he took up an appointment as Ensign in 1763, eventually rising to the honorary rank of Major General.

In his varied career his scientific and mathematical aptitudes led to his engagement as a surveyor in Bengal and soon after, he was put in charge of the Nawab of Oudh's arsenals. He remained in the Nawab's service while still attached to the East India Company's Bengal Army. Martin lived the life of a Nabob in Lucknow and amassed his wealth in a variety of ways. The Nawab paid him a monthly salary of Rs 1,860 per month and, as superintendent of the arsenal, he naturally followed the custom of taking a commission on all the purchases he made for his master. In addition he cultivated indigo which also brought him handsome dividends. He also took commissions on the purchase of curios from Europe and collected insurance for looking after clients' valuables at 12 per cent. He was a man of diverse interests and on his death in 1800 a sale of his effects lists 4,000 Latin, French, Italian and English books, Persian and Sanskrit manuscripts, pictures by such famous painters of Eastern scenes as Zoffany and the Daniells and 150 other oil paintings.

Martin built himself a magnificent palace in Lucknow which he named 'Constantia', and in which he incorporated his own tomb. Travellers to Lucknow were entertained at 'Constantia' in great style, and his household consisted of seven Eurasian concubines, a staff of eunuchs and slaves, and several adopted children. These were the abandoned off-spring of Europeans who had left Lucknow, taken in by the kind-hearted General as his own and for whom he even made provision in his Will. Although it is said in some circles that he died after the battle of Seringapatam in 1799, this is incorrect. He died of bladder stones, in his own home on the 13th September 1800. Towards the end of his life he was saddened by the fact that, as a Frenchman, he was unable to contribute to the English war fund during the war raging between England and France since 1793.

Though by no means a particularly religious man, he was always charitable especially where children were concerned – indeed, his name figures regularly on the subscription list of the Calcutta Military Orphanages – and he bequeathed £160,000 to the Government of India for the founding of schools for European and Anglo-Indian children. His Will decreed that when the children had completed their education they should be apprenticed, and

> 'that every year a small premium and medal [should be given] to the most deserving or virtuous boy or girl; that at an annual public dinner the toast [should be] drunk in memory of the founder; that on each anniversary of his death a sermon should be preached to the children in the Church, and that the institution should be called La Martinière' (wishes still carried out to this day.)

His Will also called for the inscription of a foundation stone with his name, the dates of his birth and death.

La Martinière College, Lucknow
From a turn of the century postcard

The investment of the money and the organisation of the curriculum he left to the discretion of the Indian Government and the Supreme Court. With their customary procrastination in matters concerning European education, the Government did nothing towards fulfilling the terms of his bequest. They woke up thirty years later when, under the influence of Sir William Russell, £17,000 was spent on the building of La Martinière College in Calcutta, together with the erection of a chapel for Divine Service. The Governing Board was made up of members of the Church, the Supreme Court and the Governing Council together with other prominent citizens, and it was laid down that 20 girls and 30 boys should be maintained, educated and started in life. Martin's splendid home, 'Constantia', became La Martinière College in Lucknow, and another La Martinière school was established in his native city of Lyon. The Lucknow La Martinière became famous for the part played by the older boys during the Mutiny of 1857 in the defence of the Lucknow Residency – 'the only public school in the Empire with a record of active military service' according to Bishop Eyre Chatterton in his pamphlet *Our English Church Schools in India*, published by the SPCK in 1934. In common with the Doveton College, La Martinière Colleges received no financial aid from Government. Claude Martin's schools still flourish in Calcutta and Lucknow and Lyon today, the majority of pupils in India drawn from Indian familes, with a sprinkling of Anglo-Indians.*

With the arrival of Daniel Wilson in Calcutta as the Church of England's first Metropolitan Bishop in India in 1832, there was a move to affiliate the Calcutta La Martinière to the Church of England. Such a step met with violent opposition and it was decided that the school was to be Christian and undenominational with Church of England standards of worship and doctrine being observed, and a layman appointed as Head Master. Bishop Wilson played his part in this diktat with his customary goodwill and he was joined on the managing committee by the Vicar-Apostolic, a Jesuit, as well as by Calcutta's Presbyterian Chaplain. A very ecumenical arrangement, indeed, in those religiously intolerant times.

Numerous other schools for boys and girls sprang up all over the plains and plateaux of India before the development of its hill stations. Most of them were started by the Protestant and Roman Catholic churches, as well as the nonconformist missionary societies. There was constant rivalry between the Protestants and the Catholics, leading to much wasteful duplication and a consequent dilution of good educational standards. It must be said, however, that the Catholics had the edge over the Protestants as the nuns and priests of the Catholic schools would work for nothing, and, even more significantly, were often highly-trained educationalists from well-known teaching orders, whereas the Church of England was often hard put to find well-qualified teachers to come out to India and work for low salaries.

A distinct pattern of religious 'tit-for-tat' emerged in Calcutta during the first half of the 19th century, with schools popping up side by side to compete with those of rival denominations. The St James School for Boys was established in 1823 with the aid of funds

* The story of La Martinière College, Lucknow, is told in *'Bright Renown: La Martinière College, Lucknow 1845-1995'* by Satish Bhatnagar (See Useful Addresses)

from the English SPCK, assisted by Bishop Middleton, followed by the opening of a girls' school of the same name under the patronage of Lady Auckland in 1830. Not to be outdone, the Roman Catholics established St Xavier's College in 1834 under the auspices of a band of English Jesuits. But after many vicissitudes the school failed and the English Jesuits returned home in 1843, leaving it to be run by the local Diocesan clergy in Calcutta. Nothing daunted, a group Belgian Jesuits sailed out to Calcutta bent on bringing the College back to life in 1859, which they did with considerable success. The school magazine of St Joseph's College, Darjeeling, an offshoot of St Xavier's College administered by the Jesuits and established in 1888, records that the re-born St Xavier's was re-opened in January 1860 'in the teeth of the fiercest opposition. Despite the enormous difficulties before them, these heroic men unflinchingly faced their gigantic task, and after years of gruelling toil and painstaking effort, brought the barque of their ideals to port, there to securely anchor her. It was thus from being a sad memory, St Xavier's College became a living reality, pulsating with the richness of Catholic life and energy'.

Rivalling the Church of England St James School for Girls was the Roman Catholic Loreto House established in Calcutta's Middleton Row in 1842. Eminent Roman Catholic parishioners raised funds and a committee of ladies known as the 'Ladies of the Nun Committee' approached nuns from the Institute of the Blessed Virgin Mary in Ireland to come out and run the school. Contemporary reports reveal that a very good education was offered, including writing, arithmetic, grammar, geography, history, French, and plain and fancy needlework. Drawing, music and dancing were extras. The school was a day-cum-boarding establishment and a significant example of religious tolerance is revealed in the prospectus with a sentence stating that 'Catholic pupils only will be required to attend Divine Service and Religious Instruction'.

The degree of religious tolerance exercised in the schools established by Christian bodies in India seems to have depended upon the particular order running the school. Nonetheless, the intense rivalry between Catholics and Protestants for the souls, let alone the academic instruction, of the young in India during the 19th century strikes a jarring note in the burgeoning ecumenical climate of the 1990s. But a mere 60 years ago it still flourished; for in 1934 Bishop Eyre Chatterton was busily fanning the flames of dissent in his polemical pamphlet, *Our English Church Schools in India*, and made no bones about his dismay at the growing number of Catholic schools springing up in opposition to those of the Church of England. He speaks of Roman Catholic nuns promising not to 'interfere' with Protestant pupils and then obliging them to attend their services and receive religious instruction (an accusation not always borne out in the many reminiscences I have received from Protestant pupils about their schooldays in Catholic convents). 'Naturally,' notes the good Bishop, 'girls are attached to their teachers by ties of personal affection, and after leaving school frequently pay visits to their old schools for the annual school festivities' and – *horrors!* – 'some, I know from personal experience, join the Roman Church in later days.' Worse, in his opinion, was the fact that such Roman Catholic incursions were dangerous in that children passing under their influence would be removed from their allegiance to England, leaving aside the Church itself.

To support his xenophobia, he quotes Sir Andrew Fraser, who, in an article on European education in India in *The Contemporary Review* of April 1911, wrote:

'The members of French, Belgian and German Brotherhoods are not qualified to represent before the people of India the characteristics and traditions of the race to which the Anglo-Indians belong nor the country which they still desire to regard as their Mother Country.' *(Not only were they Catholics, but Frogs and Huns to boot ...)*

In his summing up, Bishop Chatterton delivers his final riposte:

'If our great missionary societies can give thousands a year towards missionary schools and colleges in India, can we not give liberally to the education of the children of our own race and that of the Household of the Faith? It is to the boys in our church schools that the Church of India must look more and more in the future for fit men for the Sacred Ministry. Are we going, through our want of foresight and generosity, to allow all the splendid material to gradually drift away from us into the hands of

foreigners [my emphasis] who care little for our great English
traditions and still less for our Mother Church?'
*[We can almost hear his ringing tones as the split infinitive rolls off
his tongue...]*

In no way seeking to denigrate the devoted work of Bishop
Chatterton for the Church and its less fortunate adherents
throughout his lifetime, one cannot help but gain the impression that
he was a prey to misplaced jingoistic fervour, as witness the
following passage from another SPCK pamphlet entitled *The Anglo-
Indian Community and their Romantic History* published in 1937.
Presenting the Anglo-Indian plight and launching an appeal for
funds for the Church Missionary Societies' work in education, the
Bishop quotes the message given to the Anglo-Indian Community
by the Prince of Wales during his visit to India in 1921:

> 'You may be confident that Great Britain and the Empire will not
> forget your Community who are so united in their devotion to
> the King-Emperor, and who have such unmistakable tokens of
> attachment to the Empire by their great sacrifices in the war.'

As events were to prove, the Bishop was backing the wrong horse.
Great Britain and the Empire did forget the Anglo-Indian Community,
as did King Edward VIII, for the royal pending file must have been
washed away in the waves of consternation which engulfed both
Royal and government circles at the time of his Abdication in 1936.
Not to put too fine a point on it, the passage seems strangely out of
place in a tract which was published a year after the Abdication.

It must be acknowledged, however, that even if Royalty deserted
the Anglo-Indian Community, the Church of England continued to
render devoted service to its children through the hundreds of
schools it founded all over India in spite of the religious bigotry
which seemed, at times, to play its sorry part. And, as we have seen,
the Roman Catholics as well as the non-conformist missionary
societies were equally devoted to the cause of education in the vast
sub-continent.

But to return to the 19th century. The Church was as active in
Madras as it was in Calcutta and, with the appointment of the first
Bishop of Madras in the early years of the century, a number of

schools sprang up in that Presidency. Bishop Corrie took over the Madras Parental Academy in 1834 which was on the point of closure through lack of funds, remodelling it along the lines of a British Grammar School and renaming it the Madras Grammar School. On the Bishop's death the school became the Bishop Corrie Grammar School opening its doors not only to Europeans and Anglo-Indians but also to the children of Indians who could afford the fees. At the same time a Bishop Corrie High School for girls was established.

In Bombay a similar pattern was established with the formation of the Bombay Education Society in 1815 leading to the taking over, as we have seen, of the first little school founded by East India Company Chaplain, the Rev Richard Cobbe, in 1718, to become, under the auspices of Archdeacon George Barnes, the famous Barnes School at Byculla which eventually moved to Deolali in 1925. Another notable school was founded in Bombay in 1860 – the Cathedral Grammar School. With the formation of the Anglo-Scottish Education Society in 1922, this school amalgamated with the Cathedral Choir School of St Thomas's Cathedral (established 1878) forming the Cathedral Boys' School and the Cathedral Girls' School. (To-day these schools go under the names of the Cathedral & John Connon Boys' School and ditto Girls School, with a separate Kindergarten School). As a modern footnote, Booker Prize Winner, Salman Rushdie, was a pupil at the school in the 1950s and early 1960s, going on from there to Rugby. Despite the jumbling of names and locations, his erstwhile Headmaster, Bernard Gunnery, recognises some of the incidents described in Rushdie's prize-winning novel *Midnight's Children.*

Apart from the various orphanages established for the children of soldiers in the Company's and British armies, there were, in the 19th century the little garrison schools which followed the regiments to the various cantonments all over India, offering education at an elementary level to the offspring of other ranks which continued well into the 20th century. It was not until 1846 that Sir Henry Lawrence founded his first military 'asylum' at Sanawar in the Simla Hills followed during his life-time by a similar establishment at Mount Abu in Rajputana. Similar Lawrence boarding schools were set up in his memory at Lovedale (Ootacamund) in 1858 and Ghora

Gali (Murree) in 1860. Here children could leave the vicious atmosphere of the barracks to lead healthier lives away from the punishing heat of the plains and the ever-present dangers of disease. To-day the three Lawrence schools at Sanawar, Lovedale and Ghora Gali still exist, albeit with pupils mainly from Indian families. (Ghora Gali is, of course, in Pakistan and composed of Pakistani boys from army as well as civilian families.) And after the advent of the Railways in the 1850s, various schools sprang up in the many railway colonies on India's plains for the children of Anglo-Indian Railway employees.

From the time of the arrival of the British in India until the mid-19th century everyone, Europeans, Anglo-Indians and Indians alike, lived, worked and sometimes died in the dreadful climate of the plains, only the very rich being able to find some relief in the 'garden houses' they built in the surrounding country away from the sweltering confines of the cities. The popularity of these garden houses reached its apogee in the 18th century, by 1800 their owners' lives made more bearable with the introduction of 'kus-kus tatties', the bamboo-framed matting draped over open doors and drenched in water, thus cooling the evening breezes which blew into the houses or bungalows as they were called. With the improvement of the 'punkah', basically a swinging fan made of paper or cloth which was suspended from the ceiling and worked by a cord on a pulley, and the introduction of the flat-roofed bungalow with its verandahs, some relief was obtained from the stifling heat. The only other means of recuperation was a sojourn on the coast with its cooling sea breezes. It was not surprising, therefore, that most English parents, and the more privileged Anglo-Indians, sent their children on the long sea journey to England to escape the rigours of the climate. However, the prime motive for such enforced separations, was usually a social one. In many cases, 'Home' was considered the only place in which to educate one's children.

But the opening up of the hill stations as sanatoria for the military and civilians alike was to bring about revolutionary changes in the lives of many children.

3

To the Hills

Apart from Kashmir, the Mughal rulers of India were content to leave the foothills of the Himalayas, the Nilgiris in the south and many other of the country's mountain ranges undisturbed and unexplored. They found their repose in their gardens of their elegant palaces, lolling beside the fountains in enclosed courtyards, their languid existence enhanced by the ministrations of their nubile concubines. It was left to the robust British to make forays into the cool and healthy heights in search of relief from India's ferocious sun.

Most of India's hill-stations were discovered and developed in the 1820s and 1830s by the British army as sanatoria for their sick and debilitated officers and men, and the military term 'station' has stuck ever since. By mid-Victorian times these oriental spas were patronised not only by the military but also by Government officials and box-wallahs, their jaded memsahibs and peaky offspring where the very 'Englishness' of the climate encouraged them to create a way of life as close to that of their homeland as possible.

The first hill-stations to be established in Northern India were Simla in 1819 and, 146 miles south-east, Mussoorie in 1826, as a result of the British acquisition of territory conquered in wars with the native princes in adjoining states. The expertise of the army was used in the hewing out of roads and, later, of railways for its own use, and it is true to say that if there had been no British Army there would have been no hill-stations. Simla was India's most popular resort, due, in no small measure, to the fact that it became a summer residence for the Governor-General for six months of the year. Further north in the Punjab stood the little hill-station of Muree, where the residents of Rawalpindi were wont to go for recuperation and refreshment: Mr Dyer ran his famous brewery in nearby Solan, although he and his family chose to reside in Simla in a house called 'Ladyhill', with its beautiful English fruit and flowers. Generations of British exiles were to be grateful to Mr Dyer for his Murree beer. His son Rex, grew up to become the controversial Brigadier General Dyer, reviled by some and revered by others for his role in the Amritsar Massacre of 1919.

Murree's other claim to fame was that until 1876 it was the summer residence of the Punjab Government. In his *Guide to Murree* of 1883, Mr E P Peacock, the station's Assistant Commissioner, plaintively records that,

> 'in that year the Lieutenant-Governor changed his residence to Simla, and up to the present his successors have followed his example. Hopes are, however, still entertained that the local Government will again make Murree its summer residence. It has never flourished since Government withdrew its patronage.'

He notes that there was a move afoot to establish a Lawrence Asylum for the orphans of British soldiers similar to that in Sanawar, financed partly by subsciptions and donations. (This was the Lawrence school established at Ghora Gali).

The assistant Commissioner paints Murree as a kind of mini Simla, with its club and Assembly Rooms tennis, skating, balls, concerts and amateur dramatics. Sportsmen, too, were catered for with the promise of pheasant, partridge, hare, pig, black bear, barking deer and leopard shooting. A further image of mid-Victorian Murree is gleaned from the Rules for the Sanatorium of Murree framed by an earlier Municipal Commission in 1867. Among the 30 rules set down there was to be,

> 'no public bathing, no tom-tom beating, blowing or sounding of instruments, no slaughtering of animals except at the public slaughter house and no begging or exposure of bodily deformity, etc.'

In common with the municipalities of other hill resorts, such sentiments sought to create a little Heaven away from the real India, where the British could imagine they were in England. Despite Mr Peacock's dismay at the withdrawal of Government patronage, Murree prospered and became a very popular resort.

Another of Murree's rivals was Mussoorie. Almost 100 years after Peacock's *Guide to Murree*, we find the Mussoorie Tourist Board's 1977 Guide extolling that hill station's delights in the most purple of prose. Waxing enthusiastic about picnics by the falls, pony-trekking, the cinemas, the dancing and the skating, it splurges:

> 'Mussoorie, where the mountains go gay and the nobility mingles with the elite, when they sojourn there for the summer as they did in the past and as they shall continue to do so in the future...post independent Mussoorie, unlike some other resorts, still maintains the old world charm and way of life, the gay camaraderie of kindred souls mixing in a mental free-masonry, of the Maharajah, sportsman or business man making the town gay, friendly and cosmopolitan. Such was the town in its glittering past and such it still remains.'

Gay's the word. We meet it again as 'gay, friendly and cosmopolitan...the spirit of gaiety prevails everywhere in this 25 sq.mile area, making the town a good mixer' (?) But in 1838 it reminded that indefatigable traveller, Fanny Parkes, of the back of the Isle of Wight...

Mussoorie's big sister, Simla, too, was relentlessly gay in mid and late-Victorian times, such gaiety providing much gossipy grist to Kipling's mill. The upper echelons of British pleasure-seekers were amply rewarded with the balls, concerts, picnics and amateur dramatics abounding in the little station, even the sometimes acidulous Emily Eden waxing enthusiastic in 1838 when she was ensconced with her brother, Lord Auckland, the Governor-General in their 'jewel of a little house' which she ingeniously decorated by tearing up red and white 'country cloth' into strips and sewing them together. One evening when we 'dined at six, then had fireworks, and coffee, and then danced till twelve' she mused that

> 'Twenty years ago no European had been here, and there we were with the band playing the Puritani and Massaniello and eating salmon from Scotland and sardines from the Mediterraneon (sic), and observing that St Cloup's potage à la Julienne was perhaps better than his other soups, and that some of the ladies' sleeves were too tight according to the overland fashions for March.'

Emily also enjoyed the performances she witnessed at the 'little theatre'. But Anthony D King observes in his paper, 'The Hill Stations in Colonial Urban Development' published in New Delhi in 1976, that Simla was avoided by those wishing to be free of the constraints imposed by their social position, and alleges that Mussoorie, more tolerant of deviant behaviour, provided an alternative setting. A quaintly apposite observation if one applies to-day's interpretation to the word 'gay', so innocently employed in the Indian writer's eulogy to Mussoorie!

One of the most famous of the Indian hill-stations was Darjeeling, 7,000 ft up in the Himalayan foothills of north east India, and said to have derived its name from Dorje Ling, 'the land of the thunderbolt'. It is often called 'The Queen of Hill Stations', a royal accolade claimed with monotonous frequency by many of the major mountain resorts.

In 1835, after a period of settling internal strife between Nepal and Sikkim, the British were given a strip of hill territory by the aged Rajah of Sikkim which included the villages of Darjeeling and Kurseong 'as a mark of friendship' for the Governor-General (Lord William Bentinck) for the establishment of a sanitorium for the invalid servants of the East India Company. In return for this favour the Rajah received an allowance of Rs 3,000/- subsequently revised to Rs 6,000/- per annum.

Jan Morris in her book *Heaven's Command* paints a vivid picture of Darjeeling, praising its elegant plan and rejoicing in its sparkling air, with

> 'bright crowds hastening arm-in-arm along the Mall or clattering hilariously about on mountain ponies... [We used to call them 'tats' in the 1940s]... [where] hoots shouts, axes, hammers, bugles or even bagpipes sounded... It was the belvedere of a ruling race, obedient to no precedent, subject to no qualm, from whose terraces as from some divine gazebo the British could look down from the cool heights to the expanses of their unimaginable empire below.'

'Darj' was also the stronghold of the tea planting fraternity, the other most sizeable group of Europeans in India, as distinct from the army and civilians. A law unto themselves, the planters worked hard on their plantations and played even harder at their own Club in Darjeeling. In the 20th century, when not refreshing themselves at the Club bar, they were to be found in their own cricket and football teams in matches against neighbouring schools.

Another popular hill resort discovered by the British in 1841 was Naini Tal in the Kumaon foothills of the Himalaya range, south east of Simla and Mussoorie. Unlike the other Himalayan resorts, Naini was built round a lake – Tal. Every paradise has its serpent and, in common with many other hill towns, Naini Tal experienced disastrous landslides when the monsoon was at its height. In 1880 a landslide submerged its Victoria Hotel and even while soldiers were rescuing casualties, a second fall hurtled down to bury rescuers and rescued alike, sliding down to wreak further havoc upon the remainder of the town.

Down south in the Nilgiri Hills is Ootacamund, affectionately known as 'Ooty', to inhabitants and visitors alike, the happy hunting ground for Madras dwellers in search of holidays out of the heat. Ooty was discovered in 1819 when John Sullivan, the Collector of Coimbatore, the plains district south of the Nilgiris, despatched two assistants to capture a gang of smugglers who had fled into the hills. The smugglers escaped them but the two young men discovered a vast plateau at about 8,000 feet where the countryside was lush and the air refreshingly cool. Sullivan grasped the nettle and resolved to claim the area for the British. He went up himself the following year with a French botanist who was very ill with a fever. The Frenchman recovered and made some important botanical finds, and Sullivan hastened to report to the Madras Government that Ooty and the surrounding district could be developed as a sanatorium for British soldiers and civilians. Land was acquired from the Todas, an ancient race living in thatched huts dotted about the rolling slopes of Ooty's downland – those downs which came to remind many a British exile of Sussex and Surrey while riding to hounds with the Ooty Hunt. Others were struck by similarities to other British counties, while one threw Portugal in for good measure. In 1877 Lord Lytton records,

'Having seen Ootacamund I affirm it to be a paradise. The afternoon was rainy and the road muddy, but such beautiful

English rain, such delicious English mud. I imagine Hertfordshire lanes, Devonshire downs, Westmoreland lakes, Scottish trout streams and Lusitanian views'.

The Government moved swiftly after Sullivan's glowing report, and the little resort was soon established. For seekers after a way of life still lived at a Edwardian, even Victorian pace, Ooty must be their goal and represents the very summit of the British obsession with recreating England abroad. It was at 'Snooty Ooty' that Sir Neville Chamberlain introduced the game of snooker in 1881. He was far from his knighthood in those days and was on the staff of Commander-in-Chief Madras, repairing to Ooty during the hot weather. Six years previously, as a subaltern in the Devonshire Regiment stationed at Jubbulpore, while playing black pool in the officers' mess he enlivened the game by experimenting with additional coloured balls. On noting that one of his party had failed to hole a coloured ball close to a corner pocket, 2nd Lieutenant Chamberlain shouted, 'Why, you're a regular snooker,' a reference to the name given to raw, first year cadets. In order to soothe his fellow player's feelings he added that the party were all snookers at the game and it would therefore be appropriate to call the game snooker. But although the game was conceived at Jubbulpore in 1875, it never really 'took on' until played of the Ootacamund Club during Chamberlain's leave in 1881. The original rules were hung on a wall in the Club and are there to this day. (There is a touching insistence in some parts of India upon the preservation of British Raj relics and customs.)

As a teenager (not a term we were familiar with at the time), I spent three unforgettable months in Ooty just before Partition in 1947. The British Army had not yet left India and young females were much in demand at various social activities to be had in the company of young officers and men up on leave there. A young lieutenant named Browne, who formed part of our happy-go-lucky group, showed me a poem he had cut out from 'The Onlooker' magazine which pretty much describes those halcyon days. The author, Michael Charlesworth, a wartime army officer, wrote it while on leave in Ooty. Later he returned to Pakistan and was Principal of Lawrence College, Ghora Gali, in the 1960s. In 1966 he was awarded the OBE for services to the British Community in Pakistan.

NILGIRI DESPERANDUM – by Michael Charlesworth

To relax from your duty
To up where it's snooty
Where there's plenty of beauty
Where the ground's 'tutti phuti' -
Put on your new suity,
Pick a promising beauty
If her parents are snooty
Just don't care a hooty
Though you're only a Lieuty,
Blow your trumpet, toot-tooty,
When she gives you the booty
You've had it! – that's Ooty

Ooty May 1944

Published by July 'Onlooker' 1944
(for which the author received the
handsome sum of Rs 10/-)

The better known hill stations of both Northern and Southern India have been relentlessly written up, but although most of them retain their early charm to-day despite chronic overcrowding, deforestation and 'over-building', there is one hill station in Southern India which seems to have remained comparatively unspoiled with the passage of time, and this is Kodaikanal in the Palni Hills, part of the Western Ghat mountain range which runs north-south along the west coast of S. India, in Tamilnadu state, bordering Kerala. Apart from its delightful climate giving relief to the throngs of holidaymakers up from the plains, 'Kodai', nestling 2,133 metres up in the Palni Hills, seems to have a special appeal. In her excellent handbook *'Hills In The Clouds'* A Guide to Kodaikanal published in 1993 by Zai Whitaker, the author reveals that 'it wasn't the British civil servant as much as the American missionary who laid the foundations of modern Kodai.' These were the missionaries of the American Madurai Mission who built two bungalows on the southern edge of the plateau which is Kodaikanal in 1845 where their hard-pressed workers could enjoy some rest and recreation from their labours in the unbearable climate of the plains.

Over the years they were joined by other missionaries, both British, American and of other European nationalities as well as by British Government officials, coffee planters, army and civilian families. Mrs Whitaker writes, 'There were bitter opponents to this rival of established hill stations such as Ooty... and perhaps a touch of chagrin about Americans invading the hill domains of the British.' 'Kodai' comes over to-day as a little paradise with its lake and waterfalls, its hill walking, its lush countryside and its vibrant community life, including several important schools.

Presentation Convent, Kodaikanal, in the 1940s

The famous Presentation Convent was founded in Kodaikanal as a Roman Catholic boarding school in 1916 and lasted until well into the 1980s. There is still a PCK in Kodai but to-day it is an English-medium day school for Indian children up to Standard VI with a Junior School for Tamil-speaking 'littlies'. The nuns are all Indian, the last of the Irish nuns having left India in the 1980s when the original boarding school closed. In its heyday the school also took boys of prep school age. During the Second World War, however, when some parents kept their children with them in India, older boys joined the girls in the higher classes, and their letters in old school magazines of the wartime period and later reveal that they were as fond of the nuns as the girls were.

'Little swans' of the Presentation Convent, Kodaikanal – Dance Competition, 1955

One of the foremost boarding schools still flourishing is the Kodaikanal International School founded by American missionaries in 1901 and previously known as Highclerc School. The school is a Christian, co-educational, English-medium boarding school with multi-national students and staff. It offers an international college-preparatory curriculum in 12 'grades', with students prepared for entrance to Indian and world-wide colleges and universities via the Kodaikanal School Diploma, with selected students sitting the external examinations of the International Baccalaureate, based in Geneva. During my schooldays at Mount Hermon in Darjeeling I vividly remember some of my American classmates talking about 'Kodai', and I used to wonder what was so special about it. Would that my parents had known then about such an enlightened example of boarding school education! I have since learned that the sons and daughters of some of the Americans I went to school with were specifically sent from the States to the Kodaikanal International School for their education. Fifty years ago such 'unnecessary' transplantation of the young *from West to East* would have been viewed with utter disbelief and amazement, especially by the British. To most of them 'Home' was the only possible place at which to be decently educated.

As well as the hill stations, there were the plateau towns of India at lower levels such as Poona, Mahableshwar and Bangalore, where relief could be had from the heat. Bombay people patronised Poona and Mahableshwar, and Poona was the official resort of the Army. The Penguin *Encyclopedia of Place Names* gives its height as 1,850 feet and notes with some asperity that 'it came to be a symbol of what was most superficial and reactionary amongst the British community in India'. The sarcastic rejoinder 'When I was in Poona' became a phrase I used to dread if ever I let drop that I had been brought up in India, so much so that I have always kept quiet until recently, when Indian connections have become respectable in the light of a resurgence of interest in our 'colonial' past.

Bangalore was the plateau resort for the Madras wallahs and much patronised by the military. Situated west of Madras, this pleasant and well laid out city is 3,000 feet above sea level and under British rule had the largest cantonment in South India. It became a very popular place in which to retire, and even to-day retired British and Anglo-Indians are to be found there. According to J C Maitland's *Letters from Madras by a Lady* published in 1843 before hill stations were well-established, Bangalore's military wives rode about.

> 'in habits made according to the uniform of their husbands' regiments... The more superior, senior ladies never seem to become Indianised. Some of them keep up schools for the English soldiers' children, girls especially – superintend them, watch over the soldiers' wives, try to keep and encourage them in good ways, and are quite a blessing to their poor countrywomen'.

We are not told what Judy O'Grady thought about the philanthropic ministrations of the Colonel's Lady, but we may be sure that Victorian snobbery and muscular Christianity were doled out in equal measure.

There is no doubt that but for the recuperative effects of sojourns in the hill stations and plateau towns of India, the British Army would have lost many more of its men, their wives and families. And it is thanks to the few energetic and more compassionate men and women who came to India during the mid-19th century and after that such lives were saved and their existence improved. Dr Julius Jeffreys, FRS in his book *The British Army in India* published in 1858, advocated that children 'of the soldiery of European blood should be reared on the Himalaya, Neilgherry and similar hills with holidays once a year during the two coldest months'. He observes that 'the mortality of barrack children is appalling especially in the months of June, September and October. At Cawnpore from twenty to thirty have died in one month. In short, the soldiery leave no descendants of unmixed blood. Of the half-million of soldiers who have gone out to India, where are all their legitimate descendants of pure English blood, who by this time would have multiplied into a numerous population if born in New Zealand, Canada or Oregon, reciprocating industrial advantages with the mother country of their parents, how much more secure and durable than the military tenure of India can ever yield? Let myriads of feeble voices from little graves scattered through her arid plains supply the melancholy answer – "here!"'

Despite the throbbing violin obligato we can just hear rising above that last impassioned sentence, a lump does come to the throat at the thought of the hundreds of touching little gravestones left all over India. We cannot doubt the doctor's sincerity, and he goes on to press for changes in such conditions, adding a footnote to the effect that 'since these pages were written, public attention has been drawn to Sir Henry Lawrence's humane and munificent effort to provide for the rearing of European children in the hills'. He adds the hope that the Court of Directors will continue to aid this institution morally and financially.

'Maddocks' School, Mussoorie, the first hill 'Public School', Founded in 1835

4

The Hills Schools

The title for the very first European school of any standing to be established in the hills must go to the Mussoorie School. India's future Empress, the young Victoria, was two years away from her coronation when John Mackinnon, a retired Army schoolmaster brought up his private boys' school from Meerut to Mussoorie in 1835. On Mackinnon's retirement, the Chaplain of Mussoorie, the Rev H Maddock, invited his brother, the Rev Robert North Maddock MA (Oxon), to come out to India and re-establish the school in 1849. Although officially known as the Mussoorie School, from then on it was always known as 'Maddocks'. The Rev Maddock retired as Headmaster in 1864 and decided to sell the school. The fees he had been charging had remained unchanged since 1849 and Maddock had beggared himself by pouring his own savings into the venture. In a letter to the Bishop of Calcutta offering to sell the school to the Diocese he was at pains to stress that 'Maddocks' should be a public school for *boys of the upper grade,* adding that boys of the lower grades could be admitted via scholarships. Whether the word grade refers to academic or social standing is not clear, but we might assume that in the Victorian vocabulary of the day he was referring to the latter. Fees were very high and 'Maddocks' was considered a very *pukkah* establishment indeed. A note from a Lucknow Diocesan Board Report states that 'the school was founded by the Rev R N Maddock in 1849 and in his hands became a school second to none in India'.

On his retirement, Robert Maddock advocated that the new Principal should be appointed in England, bringing out staff with him. He let go of the reins of his Headmastership with difficulty, offering his further assistance during the new management's first year – 'for I would not wish to be separated in thought from the school.' He went down to the plains in 1866, returning to

Mussooorie in 1867 to initiate the new Headmaster. Tragically, he died of smallpox in March 1867 at St Helen's, the Headmaster's house adjoining the school.

The first Headmaster of the new Diocesan school was the Rev A O Hardy, an MA of Trinity College, Oxford, and a Domestic Chaplain to the Bishop of Calcutta, who persuaded him to take on the Headship. An old Rugbeian under Dr Arnold, Hardy remodelled the school on public school lines. But the parents and boys missed their well-loved former Headmaster and did not care for the school's new look. Hardy remained undaunted, and during his tenure as Head from 1867-69 he came to be appreciated by boys and parents alike. He inaugurated the idea of a school chapel and donated generously towards the project. Ill health forced him to retire in 1869.

The school's next Head was the Rev A Stokes BA, who stayed at the school until 1899. Under his leadership the school improved in every way. New buildings sprang up and educational standards rose. Boys leaving 'Maddocks' went regularly to the Thomason Engineering College in Roorkee. Some obtained places at Calcutta University and many resumed successful scholastic careers at school in England. Stokes built the chapel his predecessors had envisaged and was also personally involved in fund-raising for the project. During his time too, a cadet corps was formed. Stokes was very keen on 'volunteering' and became known as 'the Mud Major'. The school motto was Promite Vires, which the boys translated as 'Promote your Men'.

In 1872 a Report on the state of European Hill Schools by Mr A J Lawrence, an indefatigable Bengal Civil Servant who conducted a long and meticulous survey on India's European schools reveals that the school staff consisted of six masters, three of them clergymen all out from England. At that time the fathers of the boys were listed as PWD officers, Police Officers, Assistant Commissioners, Government servants, employees of the Survey Department, apothecaries, planters, merchants, hotel proprietors, surgeons, veterinarians, bank managers, a College Principal, an NCO and persons of private means. Such a varied list of professions even as long ago as 1872 gives the lie to the oft-repeated assumption that all children were sent 'Home' for their education. The school fees were high and if we assume that most of the above professions were sufficiently well-paid to enable parents to send their boys to Britain for their education, it would appear that they preferred not to be separated from them and found 'Maddocks' suitable as a boarding school.

The boys played cricket and fives as befitted a school run on English public lines, and A J Lawrence is moved to observe in his Report that there used to be a good deal of dandyism on the part of the elder boys, but that this had given place to an interest in 'manly games'.

All still seemed well with the school financially in the 1870s, and when Archdeacon Baily visited it in 1876 he found the school in such a flourishing condition that he did not recommend any grants-in-aid. For by this time the Government of India had roused itself sufficiently to offer such schools financial assistance in the form of payments-by-result and later grants-in-aid towards new buildings.

In 1893 the school's management became the official responsibility of the Lucknow Diocesan Board of Education and in a fit of grandeur the Board decided to launch out by bringing more graduates from England as masters, but the venture was a failure resulting in considerable financial loss. In 1896 the Rev Stokes published a pamphlet entitled 'Remarks upon the prospects of the Higher Classes of Europeans and Eurasians in India' in which he ascribed the falling off in attendance of a school like Mussoorie to the lack of good government positions open to Anglo-Indians (Eurasians), resulting in a lack of desire for a good education. He noted, 'With the absence of professional prospects in India and the boycotting of the Anglo-Indian in his native land, parents do not care to spend more on their sons' education than they can help.'

There was worse to come. In 1899 Calcutta's newspapers were flooded with letters from parents worried by rumours of the school's closure, which led the Government to initiate an enquiry. Several alarming facts came to light: the school's endowment had been diverted from the legitimate purpose of paying the headmaster's salary in order to meet an overdraft with the Mussoorie Bank, and the school was heavily in debt. To make matters worse, school premises were in a very bad state of repair.

The writing was on the wall. Mr Stokes retired in 1899 with a bonus of Rs10,000 and no deputy was appointed. In 1900 the school closed and the site and property were sold in 1901 and the Savoy Hotel built in its place. 'Maddocks' had lasted for 51 years. To-day its 'old boys' must all be dead, but a fascinating souvenir of this early monument to the English public school system remains in the archives of the Society of Genealogists in London.

In the Journals and Registers of 'Stokes School', Mussoorie, we find various references to the school's daily life. The Head's Journal for 1858 records that of the five Willcocks brothers studying there, W J and A Willcocks headed the prize list, with their efforts rewarded by first prizes for Maths, Literature and Drawing respectively. W Willcocks became Sir William, the well-known engineer, and one of his brothers was the General Sir James Willcocks who commanded the Indian Corps in France during World War 1. That year's prize list included such stirring volumes as Hayes's *Indian Heroes,* Tennyson's *Idylls,* Dasent's *Popular Tales from the Norse,* Kitto's *Scripture lands,* Coleridge's *Poems,* Smiles's *Self Help,* Macaulay's *Essays, Naval & Military Heroes* and *Schoolboy Honour.* Lucky Willcockses.....

The 1869 Journal reveals that the school was divided into Classical, Mathematical, Drawing and Music schools, that it became affiliated to 'the University' (presumably Calcutta) from 1st January, that the Viceroy, Lord Mayo, visited the the school with a holiday declared, when 'we beat the Manor House boys at football'. (This was the unfortunate Lord Mayo assassinated in 1872 on a visit to the Andaman Islands, when he was stabbed in the back by an escaped Pathan convict). In the section giving reasons for boys leaving the school, we find that one was expelled for being absent without leave for a week and who subsequently went to England – others left for University and one left due to a reduction in his father's pay. The Johnson brothers were recorded as having been removed because of their father's objection to the Head's report!

Much later, in 1881, the then Headmaster (Rev Stokes, 'the Mud Major') indulges in uxorious praise for his wife's devotion to her duties as Housekeeper, and lists parents' occupations as

Superintendent, Salt Revenue Department, civil engineers, railway employees, Conductor, mechanical engineer, merchants, RA Officer, barrister, policeman, surveyor. A column headed 'Object of Education' lists boys intending to enter the public services in India – engineering, medicine, the Army and the Navy.

A sad little note in 1882 refers to S W Patton as 'the chap who accidentally shot and killed his sister in a gun accident at Landour'. Stokes goes on to chronicle old boys' successes noting that:

> 'one passed with Honours fourth out of Sandhurst; one passed with Honours into the Indian Medical Department; three passed with Honours into the Survey Department; one passed with Honours into the Thomason Engineering College at Roorkee; one was prizeman at Selwyns College, Cambridge; one passed his preliminary examination into Sandhurst; 19 passed their lower standard Hindustani'.

It is interesting to note the reference to success in the study of Hindi. Every Government Report on Education, from A J Lawrence's made in 1872 right up to the 20th century, stresses the need for the European schools to include the study of Indian vemaculars, but very few of the schools complied with this recommendation. Indeed, at my own school in the 1940s, the study of Hindi was perfunctory to say the least. During the few lessons we had, chaos reigned with the Hindi master unable to keep order and leaving his classes bespattered with the ink we had shot at him from our fountain pens. Other schools, notably girls', eschewed vernacular studies altogether, reasoning that as burgeoning memsahibs their young charges would be perfectly well-equipped to deal with 'the natives' via the Hindi or Urdu or Tamil they had learnt at their ayahs' knees, and that many would be going 'Home' anyway.

The Rev Stokes went on to record that the latrines at 'Maddocks' were remodelled 'with privacy, ventilation and cleanliness being secured'. One wonders what they were like before...

The Head's Journal for 1867 records the full names, birth dates and attendances of 904 pupils with the initials and occupations of fathers alongside, but by 1899 when the school was near to closing down the picture is very different, with only 28 senior day boys plus

41 junior boarders and two junior day boys. A sad end to India's first *pukkah* boarding school in the hills. There was a school magazine called 'The Maddock' published at Mussoorie between 1894 and 1899, but sadly no copies have come to light.

The next oldest hill school to be established was the Convent of Jesus and Mary in Mussoorie in 1845, the Order having arrived in India in 1842. As far as education for girls was concerned, the Roman Catholics were by far the first in the field.

While the nuns were welcoming their first young ladies to the Convent in 1845, Sir Henry Lawrence, then plain Major Lawrence and British Resident in Nepal was conducting a vigorous correspondence with the Government of India's Military Department outlining his scheme for the setting up of an 'asylum' boarding school for the children and orphans of soldiers of the British Army, with a site proposed at Sanawar in the Simla hills. Senior officers did not like his proposal and their first salvo could not have given him much encouragement. It thundered:

'The Regulations in both the Queen's and the Company's Service for Regimental Schools, and for educating the offspring of soldiers, being well adapted to the purpose, the Commander-in-Chief sees little chance that parents would avail themselves of Major Lawrence's proposed institution in the Hills.'

The Adjutant General added that parents would not part with their children 'with the climate of the Hills being the only advantage'. But his Excellency the Governor on hearing of Lawrence's proposal declared that those children not having the advantage of attending the Regimental Schools would indeed benefit from such an asylum, and therefore proposed that details of Lawrence's scheme and appeal for funds should be circulated to the Commanding Officers of Artillery and Light Infantry Regiments of the Company's Army. He agreed that any appeal for funds to the Queen's Regiments would breach HM Regulations and recognised the 'positive prohibition' by the Commander-in-Chief British Army of any creation of funds from that quarter.

Accordingly, the Company regiments were circularised, with mixed results. It transpired that Lawrence's initial proposal was only for children of European born soldiers and their European wives – a strange requirement from so upright a Christian. The CO of the Artillery Company in Dum Dum pointed out that were 181 'East Indians' – the term in those days for people of mixed parentage – whose children needed such an asylum, as well as 268 Europeans. Another CO, Lieut Colonel Orchard of the 1st European Light Infantry, reported very little support from his men in the way of donations or subsciptions and registered the strongest disapproval of the prejudice against the 'East Indians' as well as Lawrence's insistence on receiving children of both the Protestant and Roman Catholic faiths. On top of these objections he added that some of his soldiers felt that their children would get no better an education at such an asylum than at the Regimental Schools available. Others objected to the low number of teaching staff proposed, and the keeping of scholars at the school until the age of 17.

Lieut Colonel Orchard pointed out that many parents relied on their sons for contributions towards the family purse. The Government allowed 30 half pay Buglers to his Regiment who entered at the age of nine, becoming full pay Buglers at 15, and this extra source of income would be denied to parents if boys were sent away to school in the hills until the age of 17. On a placatory note he adds that such limitations would not apply to girls and orphans and that Lawrence's scheme should be supported by 'these Classes'!

In his concluding remarks this particular CO agrees with his soldiers that 'if distinction of blood was to be made, this would foster jealousies and bad feelings and must be very hurtful to the feelings of some of the best soldiers in Army.' As to the financial support to be expected from his Regiment, he felt that the Officers of his Regiment would support it, even more so if the distinction of blood were removed. But he was doubtful about monetary support from the other ranks as many of them had contributed generously eighteen months ago towards the building of a church at Sabathu, with no signs of its being built, and they wouldn't want a second disappointment.

Support for Lawrence came from Lieut Colonel Trushard, CO of the 2nd Regiment, Karachi. He thought that Lawrence's scheme promised advantages, particularly for girls, but doubted if it would receive financial support from the Army at large. While high-grade officers could afford to contribute, junior officers could not, and

NCOs would start well but drop off later and privates would never be able to afford the Rs 2/- asked for per month. As for children living away from their parents, soldiers would object greatly to such partings, fearing also that they might never see them again.

On the religious question, he felt that Roman Catholics must be assured of no interference in their children's religious instruction, adding that 'this sect' formed the majority of every Corps.

On the 10th January 1846 the Officiating Secretary to the Government of India Military Department delivered the final blow to Brevet Major H M Lawrence of the Artillery Regiment and now Governor's Agent North West frontier. After referring to the adverse reports received from the majority of those Regiments circularised, the Secretary's letter ended by stating that Lawrence's 'philanthropic scheme' was of too unfavourable a nature to hold any prospect of success.

But officialdom was proved wrong. Lawrence persevered and subscriptions came pouring in, with the founder himself contributing Rs 80,000/-. Not only did the scheme receive generous support from many Regiments, but also from the European community of Bengal as well as from Civil Servants in general. The eventual site chosen was near Kasauli 'the hill of Sanawar', with Mr Hodson of the 1st Europeans at Sabathu acting as architect. Supplies were easily obtainable from Kasauli and the Garrison stationed there could give protection if needed. By 1847 the first building housed 30 children and a second much larger building was erected from plans furnished by Colonel Napier of the Engineers. Numbers of pupils rose steadily and by 1853 there were 195 pupils at the school, all of whom proudly took part in the ceremony at which the Marquis of Dalhousie donated a pair of colours to the school, which officially became the Lawrence Royal Military School. In 1858 the 'asylum' was transferred to the Military Department of the Government of India and was conducted as a Government institution of British India, and in 1949 it became the responsibility of the newly-independent Government of India.

From contemporary reports of the school's first ten years of existence we learn much about the rules and regulations laid down, and the support Lawrence received for his philanthropic ideals. H B Edwardes made an impassioned plea for financial support, claiming that Lawrence gave as much every year to the project 'as the whole of the officers in the Hon'ble Company's service put together'! He eulogised that Lawrence,

'with the strong faith of a good man fixed his eye on the snow-clad peaks of the Himalayas and saw there in the distance towering above all obstacles, a happy, healthy home where hundreds of little boys and girls upon a green mountain side should run about without hats and bonnets and catch butterflies instead of deadly fevers; where they should grow up straight and strong, to be hale, hearty useful men and women, instead of dying at the age of two or three, or dragging on a pale and sickly existence; above all where they should be well educated, where they should see no drunkenness and hear no oaths, and where all the impressions of their childhood should be those of religion and not those of vice.'

The institution had over 50 rules and by 1858 was run on military lines with boy NCOs and girl orderlies. Children were divided into companies with five companies forming one division. An adult Sergeant supervised the boys and a Matron the girls. Pupils paraded to the sound of bugles and learnt obedience by carrying out their various duties with military precision. 'Little officers' saw that the regulations were carried out with supervision from the adult Sergeants who reported any deviations to the Principal.

Boys wore the uniform of the artillery as a compliment to the founder: a blue coatee with red facings, grey trousers and a 'leathern' helmet. The girls wore a jacket of 'drab' edged with scarlet (over a long skirt, no doubt), white bonnets and tippets.

Account had been taken of the Commanding Officers' objections to the 'distinction of blood' and the asylum was open to children of mixed parentage upon application to the Management Committee. But preference was given to children of 'pure European parentage' as they were deemed more likely to suffer from the climate of the plains than their Anglo-Indian fellows.

The rules laid down that no child should be admitted under three years or over 10 years of age, except in special cases to be decided on by the Committee. Another rule gave grounds of ineligibility of entrance as

i illegitimacy

ii being idiotic, or subject to some disease or infirmity which would render education impossible or very difficult

iii not being the child of a soldier serving or having served India.

The school leaving age was 16 if the father was living, but destitute orphans would be maintained 'until provided for in life'. Education consisted of religious instruction inculcating all the leading truths of Christianity, 'without unnecessary allusion to disputed points of faith and practice' the three 'Rs'; 'elements' of history, singing, drawing, land surveying, linear drawing, Merchants' accounts and 'Oordoo'. The religious instruction referred to the lessons given in open school, and another rule allowed that accredited Ministers of the Roman Catholic and Evangelistic denominations could give instruction 'to the children of their respective persuasions in places set aside for that purpose.'

Older pupils were to be given suitable instruction for entry into various Government Departments such as the PWD, Survey and Telegraph departments. There was also provision for instruction which would lead to careers in the Sub-Medical Department, a reference to the Indian Medical Department as distinct from the renowned Indian Medical Service which could only be entered by the passing of exams in England. In addition, where practicable, boys were to be taught printing, bookbinding, practical building, carpentry, turnery, plain drawing and mapping.

It was intended that the girls should be employed 'in such occupations as will tend to occupy them for becoming wives of working men, plain needlework, housewifery, attention to the sick, management of children, etc. etc.' The needlework and housewifery were put to good practical use by the girls performing many of the chores involving the mending of pupils' clothes and tidying of dormitories.

A system of pupil teacher training was advocated in Rule 43 for promising boys to follow eventual careers as schoolmasters in Regimental Schools. They would be maintained and clothed in the institution, receiving a monthly allowance in their 2nd, 3rd and 4th years, having signed an engagement with the Guardians for a four year period.

The school did not lack visitors during its first ten years. The Rev Dr Duff was moved to write an article in 'The Friend of India' setting out his impressions. He praised the improved personal habits of the pupils, commenting on their mental and moral attainment. He found the accommodation ample and airy noting also that 'every pupil was neatly and warmly clad and each had a separate couch, with abundance of clean bedding.' 'Suddenly arriving as I did from among the languid forms and pale faces of the southern plains, ' says the good doctor,

'I felt as if I had dropped from the clouds among groups of children on the breezy, heather slopes of the Grampians ... Ah, thought I, how might the British mothers of Calcutta and elsewhere – encompassed though they be with all the elegancies of art and all the luxuries and comforts which ingenuity can contrive – how might they envy the sturdy, robust forms and rosy cheeks of those hill-reared orphans and children of the common British soldier!'

While waxing very complimentary about the running of the school , other visitors' remarks reveal an obsession with the children's clean appearance – the next best thing to godliness in most Victorian hearts. 'The boys and girls were most *cleanly* in their persons' enthused one; 'their *cleanliness* equalled any school frequented by gentlemen's sons at home' remarked Mr Arthur Cocks, Chief Assistant to the Resident of Lahore on his visit in 1849. So pleased was he the general tenor of the institution that he doubled his annual subscription. In1852 Lieutenant Basil Bacon of the Quarter Master General's Department (aptly named for his post) noted 'the absence of constraint in the children's demeanor in the presence of and when addressed by the Superintendent' and – better still – 'all looked healthy and *clean*'. Similarly, Lieutenant Alexander Johnson of the 5th Native Infantry Regiment declares, 'Nothing is more striking than the peculiar *cleanliness* of both the boys and girls'.

Those clean little boys and girls in the 1850s rose to the sound of a bugle between 5 and 6 am, breakfasted at 7, with lessons from 9 to 12 and dinner at 1 pm. Lessons continued from 2 to 4 pm with supper from 5 to 6. They 'retired to rest', again to a bugle call, between 7 and 8 pm after a 14-hour day.

The cleanliness of souls was, of course, built into the time table with daily prayers held every morning and a Church of England Divine Service in the Chapel twice on Sundays.

In true army tradition, any offenders had to report to the Orderly Room at 12.30 midday and take their punishments. Offenders were given from one to twelve cuts on the hand for 'obstinacy' and flogging was reserved for the more heinous crimes such as stealing or indecency. The flogging ceremony was administered by one of the School Sergeants in the presence of the Principal at a special parade of all the boys.

The Sergeant Major was allowed to carry a rattan and use it if necessary, but the rules stated that 'he is required to be very sparing in the infliction of blows – not as a punishment, but solely to enforce discipline.' All punishments and serious offences were recorded in a log book.

As for the school 'grub', the rules laid down that the daily diet was to consist of 8 ozs of meat, 16 ozs of bread, 8 ozs of rice and vegetables, 16 ozs of milk, $1/_4$oz of sugar. Puddings were extra treats twice a week. An observer noted that older children

'who are engaged in school or industrial departments as assistants in carrying out domestic routine are indulged with a separate table, on which, besides the ordinary diet, some little extra is always to be found.'

Even today, this diet would be considered a very healthy one for growing children except for the $1/_2$ lb a meat a day. The little Sanawarians seem to have eaten like fighting cocks and the Rev J Barker, Chaplain of Kasauli in 1852, found the children in good physical condition although he thought the food of unexceptional quality but plentifully supplied. (The old story of good raw materials being ruined in the cooking).

Three years later in 1855, girls' prospects are reviewed, and after making approving comments about the girls' prowess in needlework, knitting and crochet, and their 'training' in looking after the younger children and the sick, and generally making themselves useful about the place, the writer notes that 'for girls marriage seems to be almost the only satisfying provision which can be made. At home many would be sent out as household servants;

but Indian life and habits are unfavourable to the exercise on the part of superiors of that superintendence and control which are indispensable to young females' and he comes to the comfortable conclusion that the older girls 'marry advantageously when so disposed.' Nonetheless he was obliged to note that three girls had been trained at the Female Normal School which was attached to the asylum to qualify as schoolmistresses of Regimental Schools; one becoming a mistress in an Artillery School, one a salaried assistant to the Matron and one teaching in the Sanawar school itself.

The scale of fees paid by parents was extremely reasonable with privates and corporals paying nothing for their first three children. Sergeant Majors paid Rs3/- for the first, Rs2/- for the second and nothing for the third child. Sergeant Majors paid on a sliding scale for all their children, as did soldiers on the staff. Pensioned soldiers whose pay did not equal those of a private or a corporal paid nothing, and the better paid pensioners paid on a sliding scale.

The parents' fears that they would never see their offspring again were groundless. The school holidays, although sparse compared with the generous school holidays of today, were adequate. There was Founder's day, the 28th June, one week in June, three weeks at Christmas, the Queen's birthday, Good Friday, Easter Monday and Tuesday and Whit Monday.

As to the academic progress of the pupils, reports were mixed during the first ten years. In 1853 the Guardians' Report states that results in English Grammar were not all they should be, with pupils poor at parsing and explaining the construction of a sentence. (Nothing new today, with some educationists maintaining that this is unnecessary anyway.) The Guardians expressed their surprise that history in the upper classes extended only to the reign of Henry IV, with the Roman and Saxon invasions touched on up to the Battle of Hastings and the Norman conquests. However, they could not fault the training of the children in vocal music and praised their performance of hymns and glees. The Infant Class examined 'passed with great 'eclat'. They knew their Old Testament and were proficient in the rudiments of Geography, Spelling and Singing.

The report from the Principal in 1858 states that he found all of the children excessively ignorant. Some could write and read tolerably 'but none had been taught to think'. Surely this was asking a lot of children reared on a curriculum built on very basic requirements? The worthy man decided to institute a Pupil Teachers class (apparently not yet started despite Rule 43) who kept a little ahead of their young charges, and things began to improve. He found the masters of a very low standard, but with his guidance progress was gradually made.

Some of the blame for the low state of pupils' academic progress in 1858 could have been laid at the door of the local Gurkha Battalion stationed at Simla who, during the Great Mutiny the year before, robbed the Government Treasury at Kasauli and forced the school authorities to evacuate the children, causing great unrest. A contemporary report states that the mutinous Nusseree Battalion decamped to Hurreepore on the road to Simla, insulting travellers, stopping the Daks (mails) and 'committed some depredations'. Sanawar prepared to defend itself, with the boys' school room converted into a Guard House and officers' wives and children lodged in the girls' house, where they spent an anxious night. The defending force managed to muster 25 bayonets but the buildings were not in a very good defensive position, with little refuge for 400 women and children. Their fears increased when they heard the next morning that a massacre had taken place at Simla. The Sanawar community made their way to Kasauli along the hastily constructed mountain road. They were housed in two barracks 'and the little people breathed more freely protected by the stout English hearts and strong arms of its garrison of the gallant 75th Foot consisting of 100 men. All however remained quiet.'

The local Rajas remained loyal during the flare-up with some of them actively engaged in the defence of the garrison, and a fortnight later the Nusseree Battalion and its officers moved to the plains, and the Sanawar contingent went back to school. The writer of the report notes that the sympathy of the hill population was manifestly on the side of British rule. But it seems that their confidence had been shaken for they stopped giving the school credit for supplies as had been their wont. Despite this setback the children continued to receive their full rations 'thanks to the pinching and contriving of the officers.'

As a result of the Mutiny, many more orphans were received into the school resulting in a considerable strain on the funds. This led to an appeal for funds which was met not only by contributions from all over India, but also from London. Such was the response that every debt run up by the school was paid in 1858. A contemporary subscription list reveals help from 'A Friend', Colonels, Majors and Padres, 'A Missionary', 'A Lady', 'A Soldier', 'A Soldier's Son', Captain Lewis (proceeds from a box of clothing) Sergeant-Majors, some Indians, Murree Fair (proceeds from various ladies' stalls) and, not least, 'Proceeds of a performance by the the 60th Royal Rifles at the Theatre, Kussowlee'.

The last word on this renowned establishment must come from one of Lawrence's champions, Lieut Colonel H B Edwardes, who revisited the school in 1857, just before the Mutiny, and ten years after his initial visit when he made his plea for support for his friend's idealistic dream of a haven for the children of soldiers in India.

'A Report from a Gentleman well-known to fame in England and India
It is about 10 years since I visited the Lawrence Asylum. It consisted then of a large barn; now it is grown into a small parish – School houses, workrooms, play rooms, sleeping rooms, eating rooms and washing rooms for the children and dwelling houses for the Officers of the Institution, all clustered round the most English Church I have seen in India. I went through them all and can only add my own testimony of satisfaction and respect to that of so many other visitors. The Boys and Girls are real English Children – well grown, well filled out, rosy-cheeked and high spirited.... well-fed and finely cared for... with good religious principles prevailing generally.. pupils who have been entirely raised here, who will be going out into the world, will prove in the practical business of life, what a real blessing the Lawrence Asylum is to the European Soldier in India... they must surely carry into their future home order, discipline, cleanliness and a right minded sense of duty to God and their neighbours.

SANAWAR, 2nd April 1857
Signed: H Edwardes
LIEUT COLONEL'

The Sanawar LRMS continued to prosper and Lawrence's next venture was the setting up of a smaller institution at Mount Abu in Rajputana. After his death during the seige of Lucknow on the 4th July 1857, two more Lawrence schools were established in his memory, one at Lovedale in the Nilgiri Hills near Ootacamund in 1858 and the other at Ghora Gali, Murree, in 1860. The Mount Abu school closed down after the last war, but the other three continue to prosper, Ghora Gali as a boy's public school in Pakistan, and the other two run by the Indian Government. (The Ghora Gali Girls' School was discontinued in 1947 when Pakistan was created.) In the 20th century the Lawrence schools continued to cater for children of the British soldier in India, and educational standards were high.

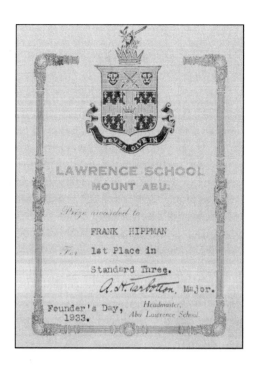

Lawrence School, Lovedale, Ootacamund

Lawrence Military School, Mount Abu
(Now a Police College)

57

Bishop Cotton Boy's School, Simla – Viceroy's inspection of cadets in 1926 when Rev W S O'Neill was headmaster

5

Enter Bishop Cotton

George Edward Lynch Cotton is held by many stalwarts of the Anglican church at Home and in India to have been the originator of the idea of hill schools for Anglo-Indian and British children domiciled in India. As we have seen, this is not strictly true if we acknowledge the work already done for European hill school education by the Reverend Maddock and his successors, Sir Henry Lawrence and the Roman Catholic religiosi in the 1840s and 1850s. But there is no doubt that as the second Metropolitan Bishop of Calcutta, to which post he was called in 1858, Cotton provided the stick with which to prod the Government of India into realising its own responsibilities in the education of such children. The scheme he proposed for a dual role between Government and Church was to make him famous as an educationalist in the sub-continent.

Born in Chester on the 29th October 1813 at the house of his grandmother, widow of the Dean of Chester, the young Cotton was educated at Westminster and went up to Trinity College, Cambridge in 1832. Here he obtained his BA and stayed at the college to read for his Fellowship. He became an assistant master under the great Doctor Arnold at Rugby, and is said to have been the original for Thomas Hughes's 'model young master' in his classic *Tom Brown's School Days*.

Cotton taught at Rugby for fifteen years and during this period drew up and published manuals of devotion for school boys known as his 'sermonettes', which were widely used in preparing many of them for confirmation. In 1852 he was elected to the Mastership of Marlborough College, when, says his biographer,

> 'an empty exchequer, an increasing debt, a community of boys still agitated by the recollection of an exciting conflict with authority' [the great Marlborough Rebellion of 1851]...... 'an

absence of healthy public school feeling and falling numbers seemed to present all the elements of disastrous failure.'

G E L Cotton's six-year tenure as Master altered this woeful situation, and Marlborough became one of England's foremost public schools. It was Cotton who used games as an organised instrument of control, after the Marlborough rebellion, to reinstil that healthy, public school feeling.

Arriving fresh from England in 1858, the Bishop was concerned that the Government of India had not played its part in providing education for its poorer European and Eurasian subjects.

'The first great practicable step,' runs an early report of the Calcutta Diocesan Board of Education, 'towards the removal of the great educational destitution which prevailed throughout these parts of India may be dated from the 28th July 1859, the day appointed for a general thanksgiving for the suppression of the mutinies. On the day, in consequence of a pastoral letter from the Bishop, a collection was made in most of the churches of the diocese for the foundation of a public school at the station in the Himalayas, as a thank-offering to God and permanent memorial of the great deliverance then commemorated.'

A year later Cotton followed up this eloquent appeal in a letter to the Viceroy, Lord Canning, outlining his grand plan:

(1) A school must be found at a central station in the Himalayas 'with building and endowments provided by private liberality and assisted, we may hope, by a Government grant-in-aid, so as to receive a certain number of children at a low rate of payment.... '

(2) Day schools of a humbler kind must be founded for the children of Christian residents in the great cities of the plains, with scholarships for promising scholars to the central institution in the hills, and

(3) Other schools might then be founded at hill stations 'at two extremities of our Empire – at Darjeeling probably and Murree – just as the Lawrence Asylums at Ootacamund, Murree and Mount Aboo are the daughters of Sir Henry's parent foundation at Sunawar.'

Lord Canning responded enthusiastically to Cotton's proposals. His historic Minute of the 29th October 1861 was to be dubbed, with customary Victorian grandiloquence, 'The Magna Carta of European Education'. While agreeing whole-heartedly with the Bishop that the Government had a duty towards the education of the increasing numbers of children born to the less affluent European and Eurasian residents in India, he had two reservations about the scheme in its present form. First he felt that schools should be founded on the plains 'as soon, at least, as schools in the hills' and feared that by beginning with the hill schools 'the error into which we are most likely to fall is that of constructing a scheme above the reach of those whom it is most necessary to benefit, and this being so, we ought not to begin to construct from the top only.' Secondly, he felt that the Government of India could not with justice limit its support to Church of England schools alone and recommended that grants-in-aid should be extended to any Roman Catholic or Presbyterian schools founded in the hills or on the plains.

The Secretary of State concurred with his Viceroy's recommendations and as a result Cotton's scheme, slightly revised, was put into operation. Government agreed to match any sum collected by private subscribers as a building and foundation fund; that each school would receive a grant-in-aid from the time it first opened, and, where possible, that any Government-owned land would be given free. Over the years, successive Governments made modifications to the original scheme, but it was under Lord Canning's viceroyalty that European education became a priority. When he left India, a broken-hearted widower, to die at Home in 1862, some of the impetus for completing the task he had started died with him. Nonetheless, the next ten years saw the establishment of many new schools at 'stations' (the quaint appellation given to towns and cities during the British Raj), on the plains and plateaux and in the hills all over the subcontinent. And Roman Catholic and non-Conformist schools were also entitled to receive Government aid of one kind or another.

Cotton's dream was realised by the founding of his memorial school at Jutogh, near Simla, on the 15th March 1863. First known as Simla Public School, then Bishop's School, it was moved from Jutogh to Simla as Jutogh was considered too far from medical assistance, the bungalows used were unsuitable for the school's requirements and the Headmaster thought that the ground on which the boys played was objectionable, being an orchard of bad fruit trees. The foundation stone for the new building was laid by the Viceroy, Sir John Lawrence, on the 26th September 1866.

Old school archives reveal that the original school at Jutogh got off to a very slow start. No boys arrived on the first day, but the next day heralded the arrival of one Frederick Naylor, joined on the 17th March by three more snail-like scholars. (It seems strange that the school seems to have opened without any 'advance booking'. Such touching trust seems out of character in an enterprise connected with an individual as dynamic as George Cotton, but his Christian faith no doubt played its part, and in the event was rewarded.) By 1864 the pupils numbered 65, the highest number which could be accommodated until the school moved to its new site at Knollswood, Simla, in 1868.

Bishop Cotton threw himself whole-heartedly into the organisation of his new school despite his arduous and time-consuming responsibilities as India's Metropolitan Bishop. Sadly, he never lived to see the total realisation of his grand plan. Ten days after the laying of the new school's foundation stone he died in a tragic accident. After a nine-week pastoral tour of Assam and Cachar, the Bishop returned to Kushtia in the Government's yacht 'Rohtas', where he was due to consecrate a cemetery. He performed the ceremony on the evening of 6th October 1866 and returned to the landing stage in the fading light. While crossing the narrow planks from the river bank he lost his balance and fell into the Gorai river and was drowned immediately. The river was in full spate after the rains and his body was carried away in the rushing waters. The news of the Bishop's untimely death was received with deep sorrow all over India and to perpetuate the memory of its founder, Bishop's School became Bishop Cotton School in 1867, known with affection as BCS by scholars and public alike ever since.

The school had its share of teething troubles in those early years. A Government Report in 1873 reveals much heart-searching from the school governors as to 'the status of the lads for whom the school was intended', and how best to fix appropriate fees for the 'middle and lower classes'. Bishop Cotton had himself been in no doubt:

'The general object is to found a school for what may be called the middle classes of European and Eurasian residents in India. It is not designed for such boys as now go to Mr Maddock's at Mussoorie, still less to supersede or discourage the practice of sending boys for education in England. Hence it is a great object to have the charges as low as possible'.

The compiler of the 1873 Government report on the school received a return from the Headmaster, the Rev Slater, headed 'Social status of parents' which listed one Colonel, two Deputy Commissioners, two Police Superintendents, one Pleader, three Uncovenanted Civil Servants, two Customs Officials, ten Clerks in Public Works, Canals and Sub-Engineering Departments, twenty Widows and seven Traders, from which he deduced 'that the classes contemplated by Bishop Cotton are most largely represented – classes who ought to get a fair education for their sons and cannot afford to send them to England.' However he expressed his disapproval at the number of Simla residents who had managed to get their boys in at reduced fees as 'foundationers'. In his opinion their sons should have attended the school as day boys or weekly boarders.

The question of day boys was a nasty thorn in the flesh of the school governors and staff alike. Between 1870 and 1872 there was much heated correspondence between the Government of India and the Provincial Government in the Punjab concerning allegations that the Headmaster of BCS was refusing to admit day scholars. The school governors were rapped on the knuckles several times by successive Government officials, and one officer in the Department of Public Instruction, Punjab, received his share of the general castigation. His suggestion that the reduction in fees for day scholars would result 'in the admittance of the children of European or Eurasians in indigent circumstances [which] might prove injurious to the school' earned him a furious reprimand.

It was pointed out that

'it was presumably for the education of children belonging to Europeans and Eurasians in indigent circumstances that Bishop

Cotton's Schools were designed... It is clear that Major Holroyd [the unfortunate DPI official] has entirely lost sight of this policy, and the Governor General in Council trusts that the Lieutenant-Governor [Punjab] will lose no opportunity of insisting that the true object of Bishop Cotton's School is more faithfully carried out for the future than appears to have been hitherto the case.'

Day scholars and weekly boarders thus became a part of the school, but it was noted in the same Report that Masters in other schools also objected to day scholars:

'They are not as amenable to discipline as boarders are; they are less regular in their attendance; they carry home school tales... And I can quite believe that in this country these difficulties are much increased. Eurasian mothers are especially weak; houses in the hills are small; literary habits are as a rule not cultivated; the boys have no special room to study in; the distances in Simla are great, and heavy rains fall at school-going as at other times. Still the benefit of the greatest number is sought, and even the feelings of the school masters must give way when a clash occurs.'

(By the time of the Second World War when I was at school in Darjeeling, day scholars in most hill schools were a fact of life – and how we envied them. What bliss it must have been to go home after school, even in the pouring rain!)

But for all the Government of India's pious admonitions regarding the carrying out of the Bishop's expressed intentions, it must have been difficult for those early schoolmasters and their successors to tread the thin line between the wish and the fulfilment. In many a pedagogic mind in those early hill schools was the conviction that 'public schools' were the prerogative of the more affluent classes. They lost sight of the fact that their English counterparts, upon which they modelled themselves so assiduously, had originally been founded for 'poor scholars'. Not so Bishop Cotton, whose original scheme allowed for the admittance of a certain number of children at a low rate of payment, under which heading day scholars would be included. Undoubtedly, further confusion arose by the apparently neat division of 'posh' education for the middle classes in the hills and a humbler kind down in the plains for the 'lowest and the poorest', an arrangement which came unstuck when the latter seemed unaware of their socio-geographical standing and elected to live in the hills! On the other side of the coin, fortunately for those 'middle class' European and Eurasian parents who kept their children down on the plains, several excellent boarding and day schools were eventually founded on the plains which provided a good secondary education for boys as well as girls, in addition to the elementary schools intended for the 'lowest and poorest.'

Setting aside the social nuances operating during the school's infancy, what were those fortunate BCS boys learning in the second half of the 19th century? Bishop Cotton, reviewing the progress of his scheme in 1866, expressed himself thus:

'Our desire is that the boys should be instructed in Christian knowledge, in Latin, English, one Indian vernacular, a short course of mathematics, history, geography, and either music or drawing, with certain optional studies according to their various tastes and inclinations.'

This dictum was faithfully carried out, with a greater emphasis placed on English 'than the Bishop, from want of acquaintance, no doubt, with the deficiencies of Indian boys in this respect had contemplated' runs a note from the Government report. (The reference to Indian boys is puzzling as the school at that time was not structured to admit Indians. This might be the writer's way of translating 'Eurasian born'. It was not until the 1920s that an intake of 25 per cent of Indian students was mandatory in the Government's Code for European Education, although a small percentage of Indian parents did succeed in placing their sons in such schools from the outset, and Headmasters were only too glad to receive their fees).

The reports from the Education Inspectors in the early 1870s were, if not exactly fulsome, satisfactory. BCS had been in existence for only ten years, during which time it had been affiliated to Calcutta University, for which a few boys had passed the entrance, with others passing the Entrance Exam for the Roorkee Engineering College. They must have been well schooled by the Headmaster, the Rev Slater, and his four assistant masters. Two separate inspectors however were moved to use the same phraseology in their assessment of the boys' progress in Latin: 'the false quantities made by the boys in reading the Aeneid were so numerous and ingenious as to be absolutely wonderful' and 'the construing was on the whole creditable, though the false quantities were simply wonderful'! But they could not fault the students on their knowledge of the Hindustani idiom and grammar, a result to be applauded especially when the imperative tense, then, as in the twilight years of the Raj, was the one most frequently employed by Europeans and Anglo-Indians alike when using the vernacular.

One Inspector praised the school's 'institutions' which included a cricket club, libraries and 'similar institutions.' The school had one holiday from 1st December to 1st February, 'and Mr Slater is of the opinion that the longer they are, the worse it is for boys and masters.' Other occasional holidays, not counting Sundays, brought the total up to 102 in the year and the boys worked at their lessons for six hours a day. Their maximum pocket money allowance was Rsl/-, with the minimum set at 2 annas.

By 1904 there were 112 boys at the school, 19 of them day boys (the prejudice against the latter apparently still as strong as it had been 30 years earlier). The Rev H M Lewis as Headmaster had three assistant masters, one lady teacher and a Munshi (Indian language teacher). In common with other hill schools at the turn of the century, BCS had its share of financial difficulties. In 1900 the school had been forced to apply to Government for a loan. Over thirty years earlier Bishop Cotton's appeals for funds had resulted in thousands of rupees being collected for St Paul's School, Darjeeling, the Mussoorie School and BCS Simla. These amounts were doubled by an equivalent contribution by Government and were considered as the schools' endowment funds. They were invested in 'Government paper' and the income derived was intended for the payment of the Heads' salaries and, if possible, towards the salaries of assistants. Unfortunately, the trustees used the money for other pressing expenses and a horrified Civil Servant was moved to report in 1903 that 'there is not one of the Church of England endowments which has remained intact for so much as twenty-five years'. Unlike their Roman Catholic fellows, some of whom had even been able to decline Government aid, the Church of England schools were in no way self-supporting and appeals to the public at Home very often fell on deaf ears.

The Government Committee set up to report on the financial position of the hill schools in Northern India in 1903 recommended that BCS Simla should raise its fees and stop taking in orphans and wards at reduced rates, a proposal which would not have pleased its illustrious founder. They also recommended a firmer hand from Government in administering the school's finances, with Government paying off its current debt. In addition they proposed that there should be three graduate assistant masters on the staff, with two English-trained elementary teachers, two Indian-trained teachers, a Drawing Master and the indispensable Munshi, all at increased salaries. In its summing up, the 1903 Committee commented that

'the total disappearance of the type of school established in India by Bishop Cotton is threatened, and the chief cause of this danger is that the schools are almost entirely dependent upon the payments made by scholars and Government grants, which are together insufficient to maintain them.'

The solution to this disastrous situation would be the granting of greater financial aid; a few subjects well taught rather than many taught badly, and better pay and provident schemes for teachers.

Bishop Cotton would have approved of many of these proposals some of which did become law in the fullness of time. But, as we have seen, European education (to become Anglo-Indian Education in 1932) was never very high on the Government's list of priorities, and it was not until well into the 20th century that the schools were placed on a firm financial and educational footing. And right up to Indian Independence in 1947 the Heads of schools all over the sub-continent fought a constant and unending battle to maintain standards with insufficient funds at their disposal.

On the 27th September 1923 'The Pioneer' newspaper in India carried a report of the BCS Diamond Jubilee celebrations in Simla on the 25th. The speech of the Headmaster, the Rev W S O'Neill, touched on the school's progress since 1863, revealing that it was totally destroyed by fire in 1904, 'but phoenix-like it rose from its ashes stronger and finer than before.' (That was all they needed in that particularly shaky period in the school's finances. We can only hope that the buildings were insured, and that the insurance payment enabled the phoenix to become airborne again.) Mr O'Neill reported a student roll of 206,

'very near our maximum. With the great increase in numbers we are, however, faced with an increased need for accommodation and for additional equipment and though this need has been realised as urgent for some three years past, owing to financial stringency it has been impossible to do much to remedy matters.'

'Plus ça change...' In common with Headmasters' speeches the world over, having passed the metaphorical hat round he stiffened his quivering lip and looked on the bright side:

'...we are not pessimists. Rather are we fully confident that no boy who passes through this School and takes full advantage of the corporate life, the games, and the course of studies provided will be at any disadvantage in the great game of life... I have no hesitation in saying that this School compares most favourably with many of the lesser English public schools.'

Today BCS is flourishing, with Indian students under an Indian Headmaster. There are over 750 students on the rolls with 50 academic staff and 90 on the administrative and domestic side. The school is divided into four houses, Lefroy, Ibbetson, Rivez and Curzon, with sports such as cricket, basketball, hockey, soccer, boxing, athletics and tennis all contributing towards the retention of the public school ethos.

A recent school magazine, still called 'The Cottonian' since its inception in the 19th century, reveals that BCS is as strong in its Christian ideals as it ever was, with Chapel services and the annual Carol Service playing a major part in school life. The annual school play, too, is a highlight in extra-curricular activities, and in 1983 the then Headmaster's wife directed 'A Pound of Flesh' in one act, which that indefatigable lady had abridged from Shakespeare's 'Merchant of Venice'. The creative section of the same magazine carries some highly creditable articles and poems on a diversity of subjects, which indicate great teaching strengths from the English Department, whose pupils of all ages demonstrate an excellent command of the language. Also, in common with most of modern

India's hill schools, the school magazine devotes a section to articles in Hindi. One is left with the impression of a happy fusion of East and West, revealed in another aspect by the inclusion of 'bhajans' (Indian hymns), which, according to the Carol Service notes, 'lent the traditional Indian touch, their blending melodies and lively beat brightening up the Service'.

* Mr Ronald Hakim MA, who became Headmaster in 1986, affirms that BCS is one of the most flourishing schools in the country, adding that it is self-supporting and rated as 'one of the best institutions in the world.' In his 1987 Speech Day address he concludes, 'This is not an ordinary school and the staff and boys who went before were no ordinary people. The School is based on historical facts and rich traditions. To this time from its foundation in 1863, this School has sent out about 11,000 Cottonians into the service not only of this country but of the world. They are settled in different walks of life holding the highest positions with honour and integrity. In India they are found playing vital roles in the Defence Services, in Parliament, in business, in law, in administrative and foreign service and in Medicine.' George Cotton would have been proud.

He would also have approved of the simple name chosen for his first school. His dislike of humbug and pretentiousness of any kind is demonstrated in an article attributed to him in an issue of 'The Calcutta Review' in the early 1860s on colleges and schools in India.

'Such appellations as "Parental Academy" and "Young Ladies Institutions" tend to foster the faults of vanity and puffing. We do not want to train girls to be young ladies, but useful Christian women; and while it is most important for a master to be parental in his care of his pupils, he need not proclaim this in the name of his school, any more than he should call it the "Virtuous Academy" or "Pious Academy", however much he may foster piety and virtue. Nor shall we substitute *sesquipedalia verba* like institution or academy for dissyllabic "college" and the good old downright "school".'

---

* Mr & Mrs Hakim were tragically killed in a car accident in 1993. The incumbent Principal at BCS is Mustaffi Kabir, an ex-student of St. Paul's School, Darjeeling.

On Headmasters he is equally explicit:

'We are glad to see that in the Simla and Darjeeling schools, and in the reports of the Diocesan Board, the word Head Master is always applied not to the second, but to the first officer, and we accept this as a pledge that he is really to teach the boys and move among them, instead of sitting aloft in some remote Olympus, adding up accounts, arranging the dietary, receiving reports from subordinates, and drawing up returns for the Director of Public Instruction. We do not mean that the Head Master should have nothing to do with such details; we trust that under his auspices the acquisition of habits of neatness, order, cleanliness, and punctuality will be among the chief benefits conferred by everyone of these schools; we only mean that, among the details which he personally concerns himself, the largest share of his time and attention should be devoted to teaching.'

Before his death in 1866, Bishop Cotton saw further evidence of the success of his scheme in the setting up of two more Bishop Cotton Schools in Nagpur and Bangalore in 1863 and 1865. His proposal for the inclusion of a school in Darjeeling resulted in the removal of St. Paul's School in Calcutta to that hill station in 1864, and Auckland House for Girls, founded in Simla in 1866, was also a beneficiary in the scheme, as was Caineville House School for Girls, established in Mussoorie in 1864.

The ball was rolling and Cotton's example was followed by other religious bodies such as American missionary societies, as well as private individuals. The Roman Catholics, first in the field, continued to set up excellent schools both in India's hill stations, and in cities on the plains. By the turn of the century and into the 20th century, thousands of European and Anglo-Indian children were being educated – most of them thanks to George Edward Lynch Cotton.

St Paul's School with Darjeeling below and the Snows beyond.

6

St Paul's

St Paul's School for Boys, Darjeeling, also owed its existence to Bishop Cotton, who had always intended that another such school should be established in the Eastern Himalayas. He had spent the summer of 1862 in Darjeeling, during which time his duties took him to Jalapahar, above the little town of Darjeeling, where he was to superintend a soldiers' Bible class. So taken was he with the charming little station that he decided that this should be the site for another boys' boarding school.

Thus it was that in 1863 St Paul's School, Calcutta, was sold to the Government as new premises for the Indian Museum, and with the proceeds a fine site was purchased in the 'best part' of Jalapahar. (In 1868 St Paul's received its share of the endowment fund inaugurated by Cotton, and swelled by the tireless fund-raising exertions of Archdeacon Pratt of the Calcutta Diocese – the fund which, unhappily, was encroached upon in later years in order to shore up the school's shaky financial foundations instead of being used to pay staff salaries.)

But all this was in the future, and in 1864 St Paul's was ready to receive its first pupils in buildings making up the estate purchased from Mr Bryan Hodgson, a Bengal Civil Servant. Hodgson's house, 'Bryanstone', (later to become the Rectory) and two adjoining bungalows comprised the major part of the teaching and boarding accommodation. The school opened with only 31 boarders and a few day scholars under the Rectorship of the Rev J C Nesfield, who was brought out from England to take up this post. In due course more buildings were constructed, with accommodation for 100 boarders, but pupils were slow in coming and all was not rosy in those early days. Jalapahar was inaccessible. There was no mountain railway at that time, and boys had to travel from all over India on horseback, by river boat and bullock cart, sometimes taking months to arrive. There were many changes of Headmaster with no less than eight different Rectors and four acting Rectors during the period 1864-1870. Three Rectors gave up the unequal struggle and became HM Chaplains in other parts of India; one became Headmaster of the Simla school; one joined the Additional Clergy Society; one joined Government service; another returned to England and one, according to a Government Report on European education in Hill Schools of 1872, 'is now labouring devotedly to raise the school from the depths of dejection into which it had fallen. Although there is accommodation for 150 boarders, only 26 were present in 1870.'

During the early 1870s, apart from the fees received from pupils, the school's financial position was determined by the availability of subscriptions raised, to which Government added an equivalent grant-in-aid. The management of the school was in the hands of a committee in Calcutta, which, according to a Government Inspector, was inadequately represented in Darjeeling itself The staff consisted of three masters with the Rector always, and the others as a general rule, university men. The Inspector's Report records the expensive domestic arrangements and the need for 23 servants. (With only 26 pupils boarding, his complaint is understandable.) The Inspector grieved at 'the tendency of the Headmaster to make the school pleasant by giving an abundance of food and agreeable surroundings'. From our modern standpoint, this deplorable tendency would seem eminently desirable, but to a man who was probably an ex-public schoolboy from a great Victorian establishment at Home, must have smacked of downright wasteful indulgence.

A table drawn up in the Report revealed the social position of pupils' fathers: Seven in Government at salaries of Rs 400/- to Rs 800/- per annum; six at the lower rate of Rs150/- to Rs 400/-; three land owners with incomes from Rs10,000/- to Rs 20,000/-; two merchants; two railway officials; three indigo planters; one captain of a river steamer; one civil engineer; two retired Indian Army officers; two tea planters. And nine of those early Paulites were orphans. Nationalities were listed as 20 of pure English extraction; two Italians; five Armenians and 11 Eurasians. Of these eight were from Darjeeling and the rest came from Dacca, Calcutta, Rangoon,

Monghyr, Benares, Shahabad, Agra, Hazaribagh, Chittagong, Bhagalpore and Assam.

Amongst this heterogeneous bunch must have been the boys encountered by Sir Edmund Cox who, as Mr Cox, late of Marlborough and Trinity College, Cambridge, joined the staff of St Paul's in 1877 as Classics Master. Arriving in India with the intention of making his fortune as a tea-planter, he was soon disabused of this romantic ideal by his brief sojourn in the uncomfortable domestic bosoms of his tea-planter hosts. In his book *My Thirty Years in India*, he graphically describes the rugged lives they led, rising early and standing drenched in the ceaseless rain. Such discomfort was not for Mr Cox and he was saved from a similar fate by the intervention of the Rev G Mathias, Rector of St Paul's. This gentleman also owned several tea-gardens. Cox wonders at his dual role: 'I never saw his gardens, and I can only hope that they were more efficiently managed than the school was.' He accepted Mathias's offer of the post of Classics Master 'on a salary of Rs120/- a month, with furnished rooms and food at the boys' table.'

The Rev Mathias was an eccentric who took a pride in telling his fledgling Classics Master that the natives considered him mad. Cox had arrived during the annual school holiday, at the end of which Mathias was to go Home on a year's leave. Appointed to act for him in his absence was the Rev B Warburton, an assistant master from a school in Simla. On his arrival the two reverend gentlemen were immediately at loggerheads, with Cox playing an unwilling pig in the middle.

His first encounter with his new charges filled him with distaste: 'I shall never forget the sight of the fifty boys who constituted the school. Some were pure Europeans, in appearance at least, but they varied in colours from white through various shades of brown to something pretty near black.' Cox was a man of his time and such indications of Victorian white supremacy are a predominant feature in the narrative of his long sojourn in India. Happily, it does not seem to have been evident in the life of the school itself, particularly in later years. He continues... 'they straggled in during the course of an afternoon, some riding ponies, some sitting in bullock carts, and some walking, all more or less disreputable... a nice prospect for me, fresh from an English public school and university, to have to look after such a rabble.' He found St Paul's 'an amazing specimen of a collegiate institution', deeming the whole tone of the school most objectionable, with an educational standard beneath contempt, the boys without the faintest idea of discipline. However, with the assistance of another Master, the redoubtable Edmund Cox threw himself heart and soul into teaching and organising cricket, football, riding and swimming; and order emerged out of chaos. Boys were expelled, there were letters in the press from indignant parents, and a special commission of inquiry into the state of St Paul's was set up. The indiscipline was blamed on the absence of the mad Mathias (who finally retired) and parents were assured that with the assistance of the worthy and competent masters then at the school, all would be well. Cox left towards the end of the school year to take up another teaching post on a much higher salary at a college in Moorshedabad and, despite the vicissitudes of his first foray into schoolmastering, reveals that he was truly sorry to leave the school. He ends on a self-congratulatory note, referring to a complimentary article in the 'Darjeeling News' about the school and taking credit for the reported

> 'thorough shaking-up and revision which the school has undergone. The present staff is a strong one and all that could be desired in every respect... the boys are no longer the ill-dressed nondescripts of former days, but well-mannered, well-conducted gentlemanly lads. The standard of education has been also raised and improved.'

A new era was ushered in by the appointment of the school's first lay Rector in 1878. He was Mr Richard Carter, educated at King Edward's School, Birmingham, and Queen's College, Oxford, one time Assistant Master at Cheltenham College and for some years Headmaster at the Cathedral School, Allahabad. An accomplished musician and a scholar in the Classics and English Literature, Carter proved remarkably popular with both masters and boys. During his time new buildings were added, trees planted, a cricket pitch laid and a chapel built, with a great improvement in educational standards. His was no easy task, with money always in short supply and masters constantly moving on to better paid posts. Besides teaching, he had to keep accounts and dispense medicines. He also played the organ at Darjeeling's parish church to which the school went on Sundays, St Paul's boys forming the choir. Carter had the additional burden of re-building school premises, including the Rectory and a new hospital after a five-minute earthquake in 1897 had wrecked them.

Fortunately there was no loss of life as the disaster occurred at 5 pm when the boys were out of doors.

The education the boys were receiving in the late 19th century under Richard Carter prepared them for the High, Middle and Primary examinations laid down in the Government's Code of European Education and for entrance into Calcutta University, as well as for the London Matriculation Exam, later abolished in India. The school took boys from the age of seven, rising to some as old as 20 when they left school, with many hulking young men in the College Department.

Many old Paulites in Carter's day and well into the 20th century became tea-planters. To digress for a moment, some of India's best tea-planters were made up of men who had been born and bred in India, their education spent in one of the hill boarding schools. Some were made to feel inferior by ex-public schoolboys out from 'Home' for not having had a 'Home-grown' education as they had. This legacy from the socially compartmentalised Victorian era manifested itself in every corner of the business and professional world in India. But as far as the tea-planters were concerned, the sons of parents domiciled in India had the edge over the 'Kid Glove Planters', as they dubbed their 'Home-educated' colleagues; they spoke the language, knew the terrain and, in the main, treated their workers humanely. This is not to impugn the integrity of English ex-public schoolboys turned tea-planters, but the sad fact remains that some of them did affect lofty attitudes towards their India-educated fellows. Be that as it may, St Paul's maintained a connection with the tea-planting fraternity from its inception until the Raj had packed up its tents and gone. But the one thing they all had in common was their obsession with games. There was always a Planters XI of cricketers and footballers in Darjeeling, mostly old Paulites, who would go back to the school to take part in matches against the boys and other visiting teams. And, no doubt, it was his prowess at sport which tipped the scales in a St Paul's boy's favour when he went for interviews with the managers of the many tea gardens in the Darjeeling district.

To return to the running of the school under Richard Carter, the following extracts from his school diary reveal some aspects of his own, the staff's and the boys' daily lives:

1895

Mr Barnes applied for leave to be married. I replied that I must consult the Bishop. The Bishop declined to accede to the request without consulting the Archdeacon, being averse himself on the ground that there was no good accommodation for married assistants and that he preferred celibate masters, the probability also of a young family would add many difficulties.

The drain of the new school dormitory was found to have in it mangoes, knives, forks, etc. A stringent order was given to the whole school that the severest measures would be taken against the whole dormitory if this dangerous practice were not discontinued.

Received a complaint from a Durji that a long needle had been driven into his hand by J Tweedie. Made enquiries and found that affair to have been an accident. Gave Durji Rs 2/- and some medicine. Admonished Tweedie.

Wrote to Mr Barnes regarding a remark he made to me saying that if masters were allowed to marry they would not (implying that some did) 'go into the highways and hedges'. I asked him to circulate my letter to him among the other masters in which I stated very strongly that discovery must come sooner or later and that besides the scandal in the school it would mean immediate dismissal.

1896

The college class came before me (monitors excepted) to present a series of complaints against the treatment they received from Mr Harris. I sent for Mr Harris and they openly accused him of partiality in allowing privilege of leaving the room, using oaths, of not returning examination papers for many weeks, of setting lessons which he never heard. There was exaggeration but some truth. I had a very serious interview with Mr Harris who promised to remove all cause of complaint.

Issued a circular to the masters requesting them that as we have numerous big boys and that as it was not unknown that bad women had been seen coming into the School at night, and as I heard in Calcutta that a boy had gone wrong when at home in Burmah, the masters on duty and others should keep a sharp look out and all co-operate for the detection of vicious propensities which would in so large a company as ours be inevitably bound to exist.

1897

Circular issued to the masters about playing billiards on Sundays at the Club. This was done at the instigation of the Offg. Inspector of Schools who reported that the DPI had mentioned it as a gossip he had heard.

June 12 – A severe earthquake at 5 pm lasting 5 minutes. (a) Gable of old school came partly into dormitory and partly through verandah, nothing more. (b) The hospital was cracked and the chimneys loosened making it necessary to remove them. (c) My house was cracked all over, the drawing room being much damaged, the front walls bulging and the whole house unsafe. Many shocks more or less severe occurred during the night. Telegrams were sent to Calcutta papers assuring people of the safety of the boys.

Discovered that Bury had run up a bill of Rs 6/- at Maratta's: caned him and took the money from his pocket money.

Mr Clarke informed that his connection with the school must cease if he persists in marrying Miss Collingwood. Wrote to Mr Brittain to know if he would be willing if elected to succeed Mr Clarke next year. [*India Office marriage records reveal that Mr Clarke did indeed marry his Louisa*].

Wrote to Inspector regarding the expulsion of a boy from the HS Examination for taking a book in his pocket into the room. He had not intended cheating – that was obvious from its being in his overcoat. But he was of course not allowed to appear any more. The boy's name was Cyril Myers.

There is a sad little entry during the journal for 1898 reporting on a meeting at Carter's house to look into the financial position of the school. Various resolutions were passed regarding reduction of staff and raising of fees, including Carter's own suggestion that he should resign on a pension of Rs 300/- a month. Much haggling ensued and a lower figure was offered. Despite Carter's request for time to consider, the committee took their offer as accepted by him and he was told that a withdrawal would be practically not considered. He continues:

'I afterwards asked for 12 months notice or 12 months pay: refused; also to stay one more year: also refused ...

General Wodehouse and the Rev H 0 Moore came round the school. I was struck with the want of courtesy shown by the General to the masters and myself. We were treated as if we were his military subordinates.

Mrs Hewett wanted her son and also the son of Mr Tweedie (both former pupils of St Paul's who had left to go to St Joseph's and who had lately been expelled from there on account of a trivial offence connected with their refusal to play football against St Paul's) to return to this school. The matter was referred to the Honorary Secretary (the Archdeacon) and at my suggestion transfer certificates were asked from St Joseph's.

Mr Burnett having written the most grossly insulting letters to me, containing shameful falsehoods I dispensed with his services. Correspondence may be inspected. He ought never to be employed in school again under any circumstances. I took him on when he was in destitution. He has been a veritable snake in my bosom: repeating astounding falsehoods regarding myself, masters and boys. He wore his hair long, was very weak, was much chaffed, absolutely tactless and so very unpopular.'

In 1895 Richard Carter went to England on leave having been presented with a purse of Rs 730/- by masters and boys to help him with his expenses. In what seems an underhand way, an inquiry was held in his absence upon the finances and general state of the school. During the next three years, as witness the above paragraph written in his journal of 1898 about the meeting at his house, numbers decreased, debts piled up and there were complaints about slackness of work and discipline. Thus, in 1898 he was virtually forced to resign on a pension of Rs 250/- a month, which was continued after his death as payment to this widow for twenty years. Sadly, the disappointment at the treatment meted out to him in conjunction with private financial troubles led Carter to commit suicide in England soon after his return in 1898. A pitiful and apparently senseless end (brought about by the crass behaviour of the school's governing board) for a man who had contributed so much good to the school he loved.

His successor was the Rev E A Newton MA – Winchester and King's College, Cambridge, who arrived in 1899 with his elder brother, Mr C W Newton MA – Charterhouse and Trinity College, Oxford. The new rector although a fine scholar, preacher and conversationalist, had little experience in school work and knew little and cared less for India. His brother's aloof manner, too, did not endear him to pupils or staff alike and Newton Senior left the school for health reasons in 1901. The brothers Newton strove to improve the school by running it along the lines of their respective alma maters of Winchester and Charterhouse and there were many staff sackings, with only one member of the old staff remaining in 1901. Discipline was tightened up, leave from school premises discontinued and work timetables and meal times altered to match the English system. The square college caps were replaced with cloth school caps and there was a greater insistence on proper games equipment and neatness. The Newton brooms were determined to sweep clean.

One of the Bishops instrumental in getting the new Rector out from England to run St Paul's had assured him that the school, as far as he knew, was well-conducted and contained 150 boys. But Newton received a rude shock when he found only 43 boys on the rolls, 'the school staff impossible, the buildings deplorable and the finances of the school in a state of hopeless confusion'. What he no doubt did not realise was that many parents had removed their boys from the school on Mr Carter's retirement, and that Carter had been working against the impossible odds not to be found in the English public school system used by Newton as a yardstick. On his first day, the new Rector walked into a classroom and was appalled to discover the master with a cheroot in his mouth, his topee on his head and his legs upon a table, reading out translations of Caesar to the Middle School standard.

Under Newton's reign from 1899 to 1906 numbers were doubled and fees raised, with a Government grant of Rs 20,000/- in 1904 allowing for the lowering of fees again. Newton and his brother erected an Eton Fives Court and a Gymnasium out of non-school funds, in all probability paying for these innovations out of their own pockets. He changed the boys' diet and meal times with breakfast of porridge and eggs, or dhal and rice, taken at 8.15, bread and butter at 11, dinner with meat, pudding and water at 2, and tea the last meal of the day at 6, with bread and butter and, occasionally, jam.

He informed a Government Committee in 1903 that St Paul's was doomed to failure unless greater Government grants-in-aid were paid annually, with the security of tenure, regular salary and pension increments for staff, pointing out that the staff's feelings of insecurity had led to the employment of 25 different masters in five years. He added that the school's two functions were to educate 'the best class of boys who cannot go home to England for their education, and to give preparatory education to boys who go Home at the age of 12 or thereabouts'. St Paul's was one of the first European schools in India to install the Cambridge Local Examinations in the curriculum under Newton's tenure in 1901. These were set by the Cambridge Board in England with pupils sitting for their Junior Cambridge at 13, and older pupils, aged anything from 16 to 18, sitting for their Senior Cambridge, the school leaving exam. Newton felt that the use of these exams would enable English heads to place the boys correctly when they returned 'Home', as well as providing a sound education for boys domiciled in India. These Cambridge exams eventually became the norm in all European hill schools in India, with the Senior Cambridge being equivalent to the English School Certificate.

In further answers he gave to the Government Committee, Newton revealed himself as an educationist with revolutionary ideas before his time, some of which must ultimately have influenced European educational standards in India. He advocated that the lower schools should confine themselves to sound education in the three 'Rs' with a start made in French, German, history, geography and maths at the age of 10, with Latin and Greek at 11. At 16 he thought a boy should choose between a classical and a modern course, with science offered instead of a language in the modern course, and suggested that more time should be spent in the study of mathematics. In one astonishing revelation he pointed out that no science was taught at St Paul's in 1903. And he must have raised Governmental eyebrows with his assertion that he was not particularly worried about the lack of much teaching of Indian history and geography in the Cambridge local syllabus. His views on the teaching of English were equally provocative – he did not believe in English being taught as a separate and compulsory subject and it was not offered by St Paul's in the early 1900s for the Senior Cambridge exam. In his opinion, English was taught individually every hour of the day! He added that the school had a good library as well as a debating society and a school magazine, from which his questioners were to infer that English as a special subject was quite unnecessary.

In his book, *Indian Travels*, published in 1903, Oscar Browning is fulsome in his admiration of the Rev E A Newton. He goes to stay at school as Newton's guest and gives us the following insight:

'The Rector, as he is styled, is Mr E A Newton, some ten years ago one of the most eloquent speakers of the Cambridge Union. Brought out to India by Bishop Welldon, in three years he has created an English Public School in the heart of India. The boys wear Eton jackets, play games in flannels, and even submit to being flogged. These reforms were not introduced without difficulty, especially the last. An indignant parent wired, "Is it true my son has had to remove his trousers in order to submit to corporal punishment?" The Rector replied, "Perfectly true, results excellent." The telegram and the reply flashed like wildfire over India, and the results were more excellent still.'

Browning's starry-eyed assessment of his hero was not borne out however, by Newton's suggestions to the Government Committee for the future of St Paul's and parents, too, would have been alarmed to hear them. In Newton's view there were two alternatives available: (i) that the school should remain where it was and be worked as an English public school on lines suggested by him, or (ii) that the school should unite with Bishop Cotton's School, Simla.

Eventually, despite Newton's many reforms, both educational and domestic, which placed the school on a firmer footing, such dissatisfaction was expressed 'from certain quarters' at some of the Rector's actions, that the Governors called upon him to resign in 1906. He had done his best according to his lights but he never earned the affection held by pupils, parents and staff for his predecessor, Carter, and the greatest stumbling block towards his total acceptance must have been his lack of sympathy for India and things Indian.

Newton was succeeded by the Rev E E Benson MA, 27th Wrangler, Trinity College, Cambridge, Rector from 1908 until 1922. Under his tenure electric lighting was installed, followed by an electric pumping station and water tower, new school kitchens and playing fields. Most importantly, Benson brought science into the curriculum with a properly equipped laboratory. During the 1914-18 War he had to cope with shortages of supplies, not least Fives-gloves which he philosophically deemed 'a mere luxury, and no difficulty has been found in playing with the bare hand'! And a major shortage was masters, with so many called up. The School Chronicle of the time is full of sad little lists of names of masters and old boys who lost their lives or were wounded in the war to end all wars. St Paul's boys joined the IDF (Indian Defence Force) at the school, with instruction from Sergeants seconded from British Regiments and war games, as we call them today, were played with great enthusiasm by the young recruits. A paragraph from IDF notes in the School Chronicle of December 1918 sums up the keenness and derring-do:

'During the Muhurrum (religious festival/holiday) from October llth to 17th, we received instructions to take special precautions about our armoury. In consequence of this order we mounted a guard every night from 9.30 pm to 5 am. The guard consisted of a Sergeant, 8 men and the bugler. The sentries were posted every two hours but to our great disappointment no raid was attempted on the armoury. The only duty the sentries were called upon to perform, and which caused some excitement, was to give chase to a small boy who was suffering from a bad fit of home sickness, and made an attempt to run away from school. He was caught and brought back in triumph, but alas! the sentries were rewarded with 14 days CB for deserting their posts... We were to have had a Camp-of-Exercise at Jalpaiguri from the 9th to the 16th, but owing to the prevalence of so much sickness it was thought advisable to abolish it much to our disgust and disappointment...'

Numbers on the student rolls rocketed during the Great War, with parents loath to send their sons home to England on ships open to enemy action. Numbers rose to 275 by 1918 and remained over the 200 mark until 1923. The Rev Benson, who was forced to retire for health reasons in 1922, referred in his farewell speech to his excitement on enrolling a new boy when the student roll was under 100, and his consequent dismay when the same boy fell ill and left the school a week later!

Benson's successor was the Rev F V Dawkins MA, of Selwyn College, Cambridge, and former Headmaster of Bishop Cotton's School, Bangalore, who served as Rector from 1922 – 1928, and was renowned as a musician. He trained the SPS choir to a high standard and they won many inter-school music competitions under his direction. In 1927 he led the choir on a tour of the Darjeeling and Calcutta districts where they performed at schools, churches, Homes and Institutes, with a broadcast on Calcutta Radio in an effort to raise funds towards the building of a new chapel. As a result the Chapel Fund was considerably increased and although not built under Dawkins's Rectorship, he had the satisfaction of having played a major part in its firm financial foundations.

Dawkins resigned in 1928, 'as I do not think it is good to remain too long in the same work' and was succeeded by the Rev R L Pelly, MA (Cantab), who stayed from 1928 to 1933. Unlike some of his predecessors he was no great believer in the use of the cane, and was renowned for his gentler approach towards erring boys. Masters and boys were amazed at his treatment of a homesick five year old who had run away from school. The little lad had seen a signpost to Calcutta when he had wandered into town on his first night at school, and trotted off in what he thought was the right direction towards home and mother. He got as far as Ghoom where he was befriended by some lady missionaries, who alerted the school. Prefects were despatched to fetch him back and on his return he was mothered by Mrs Pelly, given chocolates and put to bed.

Pelly was also responsible for abolishing preps on Saturday nights in favour of entertainments and during this time photographs appeared in the School Chronicle and volleyball was added to the school's sporting activities. In 1929 he introduced carpentry, gardening and poultry-farming to the boys' hobbies clubs, and decided to revive the sport of Eton Fives at his very model of an English public school in the foothills of the Himalayas. On the academic front St Paul's Junior School 'developed into the equal of the best private schools in England which prepare boys for the English public schools' Common Entrance examination' a distinction proudly recorded in the SPS Commemorative Volume 1823-1973. Also under Pelly the study of Hindi was added to the curriculum in accordance with the requirements of the Government of the day.

The Reverend Pelly arrived in India at a stormy point in her history. There was much political unrest with strong anti-British feeling from Indians. Pelly was surprised to find boys with hockey sticks by their bedsides one night 'as we want to be ready in case old Gandhi comes up the hill!' He also had a visit from two army officers who informed him that the school campus had been chosen as a mustering point for Europeans in case of trouble. An armoury of rifles was deposited in one of the classrooms with a squad of soldiers under a British sergeant to guard them. The drunken sergeant later terrified some boys by pointing his rifle at them out of the window and threatening to shoot anyone who came within range. Pelly bravely seized the man's rifle and called to some soldiers, who quickly disarmed him.

The Governor of Bengal and his entourage used to spend the summer in Darjeeling and on one occasion HE was a guest at the school's sports day. Because of the Civil Disobedience movement which was manifesting itself all over the sub-continent, Pelly experienced the unwelcome presence of officialdom on this important day in the school's calendar with the grounds crawling with plain clothes policemen prior to the great man's arrival, adding to the tension already present on such occasions.

In common with many of his predecessors, Pelly, too, experienced the hazards of living in a country prone to earthquakes. He and his wife had to snatch their baby daughter from her cot in the middle of the night during a small but nonetheless alarming earthquake. In the courtyard they found the whole school standing miserably in the rain, too frightened to go back into the buildings for their coats. The tremors eventually stopped with no serious damage done to the buildings and the bedraggled boys sent back to their dormitories.

A more devastating earthquake occurred in January 1934 while Pelly and his family were on the high seas en route for England after his resignation due to ill-health. His successor, Leslie Goddard MA (Cantab), his wife and baby son also escaped its immediate effect as they, too, were on the high seas, en route for India.

So it was that the Great Earthquake of 1934 heralded the arrival of a man who was to cause a few tremors of his own as Rector of St Paul's School, tremors which cut a swathe into all that had gone before and left an unforgettable mark. In February 1934 St Paul's was entering into the 'The Goddard Era' which was to last until 1964, the longest Rectorship in the history of the school.

Leslie James Goddard was born in June 1900 and educated at Brentwood School, Essex. Leaving school towards the end of World War 1, he gained his commission in the Artists Rifles in 1918 by which time hostilities had ceased. In 1921 he went up to Trinity Hall, Cambridge, where he took both parts of the History Tripos, gaining his BA in June 1924. He went on to study theology at Westcott House, Cambridge, and passed both parts of his General Ordination Exam. A keen sportsman, he captained both cricket and football XIs during his final year at Cambridge and, although passionately fond of cricket, considered himself better at football.

On leaving Cambridge, Goddard took the first step towards his lifetime commitment to schoolmastering in India. In 1926 he became an assistant master at Bishop Cotton School, Simla, and returned to England in 1929 to spend one more term at Westcott House. By this time he had decided to continue schoolmastering as a layman and spent the summer of 1929 teaching at his old school, Brentwood, going on in September 1929 as Housemaster of Tower House, St Lawrence College, Ramsgate. He married Maisie Fox in 1931, herself a teacher at BCS Simla, where the couple originally met. In October 1933 he was appointed by his guide and mentor, Bishop Foss Westcott, to the post of Rector of St Paul's, only the second layman Rector in the school's previous history.

The Goddards arrived in Darjeeling with 29 pieces of luggage and their baby son in a Moses basket. They found three masters living in the Rector's house as their own quarters had been wrecked by the earthquake. Goddard was amused by the antics of one of the three, who rushed out of his bedroom into the hall brandishing a revolver every time there was another tremor. The scene that met Goddard's eyes was not a pretty one. Buildings had been torn apart and the resultant chaos would have daunted a lesser man. His load was lessened when it was learnt that the Government of Bengal had agreed to bear the whole cost of repairs, but the ensuing disruption after an earthquake of such magnitude must have made his task as the new Rector an exacting one. Stifling a desire to return to England and take up the offer of the Head Master of St Lawrence College, who had assured him that his old job was secure if he felt that conditions at St Paul's were intolerable, Goddard turned his thoughts to the discipline and actual running of the school.

His first task was to let staff know how they stood with their new Rector. Realising that some of them were inevitably older than his 34 years and that there could be some embarrassment in choosing a suitable mode of address when speaking to their new young Head, he soon put them in the picture. He informed them that since the Governors had given him the perfectly good title of Rector, they might as well use it when addressing him. In his own words,

'I could never run a school in which all the staff including the Head were "Tom", "Dick" and "Harry" to each other. These things play their part in the kind of orderliness one wants in a school.'

An erstwhile staff member was to experience this kind of orderliness only too soon. On receiving a telegram from this master, who was on holiday in Rangoon, informing the new Rector that he would not be returning to school until ten days after the start of term, Goddard shot back a telegram by return informing him that he need not bother to come back at all and that other arrangements would be made. The effect on the staff was electric.

'I soon saw that, whether one was dealing with staff or boys, it was essential never to say a thing unless one meant it 100 per cent. You've got to be trusted implicitly, and there is no way of getting this over except by consistent behaviour.'

Leslie Goddard was just as much a humane Head as his predecessor Pelly, but with the important difference that he ran a tight ship. He eventually became known as 'Pa' to the boys, behind his back of course, but an affectionate term which summed up his attitude to them and theirs to him. On a personal note, I remember how impressed my mother was at the Rector's way of dealing with my brother's nervous bed-wetting. He told the homesick little new boy not to worry about it and merely to come along to his study and tell him each time the unfortunate occurrence took place. My poor little 'bra' (the name given to brothers by us children in India and nothing to do with female underwear) did just that, and when he realised there were no unpleasant repercussions apart from the ignominy of letting 'Pa' know, the bed-wetting phased itself out.

Under 'Pa Goddard' numbers on the student rolls steadily increased, although he, too, had a funny story to tell about the numbers he found on taking up his new post. On his arrival in 1934 the authorities informed him that the total number of pupils was 101. When he carried out a head count he found 102 and decided not to bother about where the extra one had come from! By 1936 the total had risen to 192, increasing to 268 by 1943, no doubt due to boys staying on in India during the war or being 'evacuated' there. By 1962, two years before Leslie Goddard's retirement, there were 300 boys at the school, now mainly Indian. Today, over 30 years since 'The Goddard Era' came to an end, the school is completely Indianised and the student roll has more than quadrupled.

Another highlight under the Goddard era was the building of the new chapel, for which Mr Dawkins had worked so hard to raise funds. Designed by W I Keir, Senior Architect to the Government of Bengal, the chapel was completed in 1935, together with the school's new quadrangle and grass plots, and Leslie Goddard had close consultations with the architect throughout the designing stage. The famous weather vane over the entrance to the Rectory depicting a boy being chased by a schoolmaster complete with mortarboard and gown was also designed by Keir, and he modelled the master on L J Goddard.

To Leslie Goddard the Chapel represented the focal point of the life of St Paul's and he placed great emphasis upon the boys worshipping together. But he was no dogmatist and recognised that many of his scholars came from a wide spectrum of religious backgrounds, largely Eastern. His sermons emphasised the brotherhood of man and he defined a Christian as 'Christ-like' in his daily life. He believed that there must be some universal religion behind all the various creeds of mankind and that this is what should be instilled into boys and girls in any vital school, whether in India, Britain or anywhere else in the world. These precepts are not unusual in a man who decided not to become ordained as he found it difficult to believe that Christ was the only son of God: 'if it happened once it could go on happening.'

Ten years after Goddard's departure, a young master from England was moved to include a reference to his antipathy for compulsory Chapel attendance at St Paul's by staff and boys in an article in the Commemorative Volume of 1974, the publishing of which does credit to the tolerance which abounded, and probably still does, towards views not always in line with school policy. The master in question reflected that as only about three per cent of St Paul's boys were Christians, he found it 'impossible to evoke any tenable argument in favour of compulsory Sunday Christian Service for the other 97 per cent, whether they be boys or members of the teaching staff.'

In common with some of his predecessors and depending on how much money was available, the new Rector did his share in adding extra classrooms, music rooms, staff quarters, dining hall, kitchen and extra playing fields, to name just a few improvements, and maintained a high standard in the recruitment of well-qualified staff during his 30-year tenure.

During the last war, St Paul's played its part in providing amenities for the troops stationed in Jalapahar, a leave centre for the army. Goddard gave two football grounds for the use of the troops, and the staff common room with a billiard table was also open to them. Maisie Goddard ran a canteen and organised dances every week, with girls invited from neighbouring girls' schools such as the Loreto Convent and St Michael's Diocesan School.

Leslie Goddard also found time in his busy life as Rector to take part in the broader spectrum of academic life in India. Already a member of the Headmaster's Conference in England, he was Chairman of the Conference of Anglo-Indian Schools soon after the war, and an associate member of the Indian Public School's

Conference. He also took an active interest in the local affairs of Darjeeling, becoming Municipal Commissioner and serving on several local committees, notably that of the Dooars and Darjeeling Nursing Home and Medical Association where he was responsible for starting medical and dental insurance. He became revered and respected in Bengal Government circles and both they and the public realised the St Paul's School was in excellent hands, with the result that the school rejoiced in one of the highest reputations in India and at Home.

As a former captain of his college's Cricket and Football XIs at Cambridge, the Rector took a keen interest in the sporting activities of the school. He himself captained the school Cricket XI in many an important match and often played for the school in soccer matches. He became persona grata with the Darjeeling tea-planters – to some extent because of his excellence as a cricketer and a soccer player – the more athletic of whom would have found little in common with a mere academic! This enthusiasm for sport resulted in Goddard's obtaining the services of some excellent coaches, and he was jubilant when the England cricketer, Joe Hardstaff, then an army sergeant, spent a week at the school in 1942. And he came to know the legendary Emmett brothers, Syd, Bill, Arthur and George, Old Boys of the school from the 1920s. All were excellent cricketers and no mean footballers, Syd and Bill Emmett playing for many years in the Planters' Cricket XI and their younger brother, George, going on to represent Gloucester in County Cricket and selected to play for England in 1948.

And what of his daily life with the boys of St Paul's? In his own words,

'I think the regular contact I valued most of all was the one I had every Sunday morning at 9.30. I inspected the whole school; I saw (it may have been for only a second or two) every single boy in the school. It gave me the opportunity of saying a word or two where I felt it was necessary ... I always had my Estate Manager, Dormitory Master and Matron with me. I found I looked forward to this more than anything else in the week.'

Later he added a half-hour chapel service immediately after the inspection with a ten minute talk from him, after which the boys were free until 6 o'clock in the evening.

91

In the words of one of his young masters of the 1940s, Leslie Goddard was colour-blind. As far as he was concerned all boys, whatever their nationality or religion, whether wealthy or poor, had to be treated alike. 'As they had to be uniform in appearance, so – as far as I was concerned – there should be uniformity of treatment.'

This passion for equality led him to assume the role of a latter-day 'Robin Hood' in that he managed to distribute the finances of the school in such a way that in many instances the poor were educated at the expense of the rich, and he ensured that boys from needy families obtained scholarships.

There is so much more which could be written on the career of Leslie Goddard, the longest serving Rector of St Paul's to date, but space does not permit this. In 1956 he was awarded the OBE for the work he had done in India in the field of education, and in 1958 his quarter-century of devotion to his beloved school took its toll. He had to be flown to England, unconscious, for brain surgery. Even such a serious health set-back could not deter him from returning to the school in 1959 for a further five years work until he retired in 1964.

For twenty years after Goddard's retirement from the school he loved, Old Boys from all over the world as well as ex-staff members made their pilgrimage to see 'Pa' at his house in Penn, Buckinghamshire, and after his death in 1984 continued to visit his widow, Maisie, until her death in 1991. 'The Goddard Pavilion' at the school commemorates his name, and a memorial to the life and work of this great educationalist is to be found in the school's Commemorative Volume 1823 – 1973, in the many pages devoted to his Rectorship, with many articles from his own pen. In the section 'The Goddard Era' compiled by Mr James Clarke MA (Oxon), and Head of the English Department from 1960 – 1966, one paragraph stands out as a fitting epitaph to the man considered by many as the greatest Rector of St Paul's:

'His energy, courage, wisdom and foresight, his tenacity and combination of idealism and realism were responsible for transforming a crumbling monument to inefficiency and woolly-mindedness into one of the finest educational institutions in Asia. Renowned for its academic and athletic achievements, for its highly-disciplined, well-mannered boys and its healthy cosmopolitanism, St Paul's survived, during his rule of three decades, natural calamities, landslides, cyclones and fires, grave financial crises, and disruptions caused by wars and political upheavals. A weaker man would have retired from the struggle long before the end, but Mr Goddard persevered, staunchly supported by a loyal staff, a sympathetic Government and Governing Body, and a host of friends and admirers all over Bengal and India.'

After Goddard's departure, the Rectorship was assumed by Mr David Gibbs MA (Cantab), who came to the school from Repton and stayed from 1964 to 1972. In 1973 he, too, was awarded an OBE for services rendered to the cause of public school education in India.

At this point in its history it was decided that the school should have an Indian Rector and Mr R S James MA, an Indian Christian from Southern India, served for only one year from 1973-1974, probably the shortest tenure of a Rector since the to-ing and fro-ing of Rectors in the early 1860s. James was replaced by Mr Michael Cross MA (Oxon), previously a master at Ampleforth and his old alma mater, Shrewsbury, who stayed until the end of 1976. Michael Cross was to be the school's last British Rector. Towards the end of the school year of 1976 the Government of India cancelled his permit to reside in the Darjeeling district, and with great sadness Cross tendered his resignation. The only inference to be drawn from the Governments's action must be that the changing political climate in India dictated that St Paul's, now a school with an exclusively Asian student population, should be headed by an Indian Rector – a natural and understandable evolution. Cross, therefore, was succeeded by Mr Hari Dang BSc (Hons) (Delhi), MA (Agra), who had previously taught at the famous Doon School at Dehra Dun, and in 1970 became Principal of The Air Force Central School, New Delhi. Today St Paul's is under the Rectorship of Mr J A Gardner, MA (Agra), TCC (Allahabad), an Anglo -Indian and former Senior Master at Mount Hermon School, who succeeded Mr Hari Dang in 1984.

---

* On Mr Gardner's return to Mount Hermon as Principal in 1991, Mr David Howard, MA, BEd, ATCL, former Principal of St Thomas's School, Kidderpore, became Rector of St Paul's.

Auckland House School, Simla

7

Auckland House

One of India's oldest and most famous girls' boarding schools is Auckland House which is still flourishing in the India of today. The following details of its early history may to some extent be taken as representative of the successes and setbacks experienced in similar establishments. The education of girls in India, as of their sisters at Home, always lagged behind that of the boys from the Victorian era to well into the 20th century, but the schools which survived did so because of the dedication of their Principals and staff, often with very little assistance from the establishment of the day.

The idea of starting a select school for girls of European parentage in the Punjab originated with the Rev J B d'Aquila in 1864. He was warmly supported by a group of ladies in Dalhousie who held a 'Fancy Fair' to start the financial ball rolling. A large amount of money was also collected in subscriptions which led to the formation of a committee at Lahore. Simla was chosen as the most suitable place for the new Punjab Girls' School as it was then called, and the Governors of Bishop Cotton's Boys' School agreed to undertake the management of the new school. At their first meeting on the 26th November 1865 it was decided to negotiate with a Mrs Mackinnon with a view to making the private school she was running the nucleus for the new school. She readily agreed and the school opened in 1866 with 32 pupils on its rolls at Holly Lodge, a rented house on Jakku. Two years later the Governors bought the Auckland House estate, one time residence of Lord Auckland, Governor-General of India from 1836 to 1842. After various structural alterations and additions the new school was ready for occupation in November 1869. The Hon. Emily Eden, Lord Auckland's elder sister, gives us a glimpse of Auckland House as it was in earlier days from the letters she wrote to her sister at Home, later published as *Up the Country*. The lumbering gubernatorial party arrives in Simla in April 1838 during Lord Auckland's two-and-a-half year tour up country in the heat and dust of the plains. Miss Eden is jubilant:

'Well, it really is worth all the trouble – such a beautiful place – and our house, that everybody has been abusing, only wanting all the good furniture and carpets we have brought, to be quite perfection. Views only too lovely; deep valleys on the drawing-room side to the west, and the snowy range on the dining-room side... now I come back to the air again I remember all about it. It is a cool sort of stuff, refreshing, sweet, and apparently pleasant to the lungs... red rhododendron trees in bloom in every direction, and beautiful walks like English shrubberies cut on all sides of the hills... it is quite perfection, and altogether the Himalayas are sweet pretty little hills'.

The school's first Head, Mrs Mackinnon, was a forceful lady who 'conducted the school as if it were her own private property' with little regard for the wishes of the BCS Governors. They, however, did not concern themselves over much with the running of their 'sister school' and even the Head Master, officially the Secretary, was unable to give as much time as he should to his responsibilities. A Government Report of 1873 reveals that apart from the Head Mistress, there were five other teachers of varying degrees of competence, but that nonetheless 'the success of the Punjab Girls' School has been undoubted.' There were then 46 girls at the school and the inevitable table showing the social position of the girls' parents is painstakingly listed:

'Civilians 2, Military men 5, Clerks 14, Post Masters 1, Police 1, PWD 3, Teachers 8, Widows 10 and Orphans 2.' The accommodation was all taken up and 'the class of girls is just that which such a school is designed to assist.'

The education imparted at that time was said to be of a useful rather than an ornamental character with $6^{1}/_{2}$ hours daily study – 5 hours a week devoted to English, 3 hours a week to French, 4 hours to drawing and 6 hours a week to muslic. The Circle Inspector's entry in the September 1872 log book declares that he was very well satisfied with the results of his examination of all classes. He found the girls very proficient in Geography and History, with all classes reading well and writing very correctly from dictation. The upper classes were found wanting in Arithmetic and unable to solve questions not in their books. He concludes that the school had suffered from frequent changes in 'governesses' (a situation not uncommon in many such schools of period.)

Mrs Mackinnon went Home on leave in 1872 and resigned while she was there, and by 1876 numbers were down to only 39 pupils. Mrs Toussaint became acting Head Mistress in 1873 and she was followed by Miss Berry 1874-1882, Miss Cooper 1883-1885, Miss Perry 1886 and Miss Slaughter, LLA of St Andrew's 1887-1889. At this point in its history the school almost collapsed, a situation blamed upon the opening up of a Union Church Day School at very low fees and the reviving of the Christ Church Girls' School in Simla. Far from there being a dearth of hill schools in the closing years of the 19th century, it seems that there were too many schools competing for too few pupils. Another excuse given for the failure of Auckland House, as the school was called from 1875, was that its fees were too low and that no boy scholars were admitted above Standard II.

Apart from the excuses proffered for its failure, the school had also encroached upon an endowment it received through a gift of Rs10,000 from a Mr Bromehead between 1870 and 1880, the whole of which was spent in paying off its liabilities.

Contrary to popular belief, the main Church of England girls' schools established in Northern India in the 1860s and after, were not recipients of the Bishop Cotton Memorial Endowment Fund which went exclusively to the Mussoorie School (Maddocks), St Paul's (Darjeeling) and BCS (Simla). However, it is true that the Church of England set up endowments of its own, with Caineville House (Mussoorie) endowed in this way through public subscription in 1864 when it first opened – (alas, this endowment, too, was not invested properly and was dissipated by the turn of the century). But other well-known Church of England girls' schools such as St Denys (Murree) and St Michael's Diocesan School (Darjeeling) do not appear to have been endowed via the efforts of the established Church. As we have seen, Auckland House did receive an endowment through the munificence of Mr Bromehead, but this, too, was soon used up. All these schools and others like them had to rely solely on pupils' fees, with the assistance of occasional Government grants-in-aid, often inadequate, topped up by loans and handouts from Diocesan funds, SPCK grants and, not least, their own fund-raising activities.

It was therefore decided by the Governors to close Auckland House on the 30th November 1889 and to apply to Government to let the house to the highest bidder in order to pay its debts. But help was at hand and the Bishop of Lahore raised enough to keep the school afloat for another year, with each member of the governing body agreeing to share in any loss. Miss Pratt became Head Mistress in March 1890 and undertook to run the school at her own risk and on her own capital. Auckland House thus became her own property and the good lady even managed to liquidate the debts owed to the Lahore Diocesan Board of Education. The Governors, who had taken very little interest in the actual running of the school resuscitated themselves and started to sit up and take notice, but Miss Pratt's tenancy continued and she was allowed to carry on as before – probably much to their relief.

Her staff consisted of three trained teachers from Home, three partially educated at Home, two educated in India, one trained music mistress and two housekeepers. Teachers' salaries sound pitifully low and according to Miss Pratt, 'a salary of Rs 60-Rs 80, plus board and lodging, is quite sufficient for the best of the Indian educated mistresses available.' The Burra Memsahib was in receipt of Rs 200/- per month with others out from Home getting Rs100-Rs150/-.

In her answers to the 1904 Government Committee reporting on the state of European boarding schools in the hills of Northern India, Miss Pratt describes the curriculum of the school as that prescribed in the Code for European schools, with drawing taught throughout the school and twelve girls receiving special lessons in drawing and painting at extra fees. Whereas there were no extra subjects taught at boys' schools involving the payment of supplementary fees, many girls' schools increased their incomes by charging extra for music, art and languages.

Every ten years or so, the Government would prescribe new Codes of Education for European schools, with Principals altering the curriculum laid down according to their own whims and preferences, or depending upon the quality of the staff available. At girls' schools such as 'Aucky', a typical list of subjects taught at the turn of the century was Arithmetic, English, History (English and Indian), Algebra, Euclid, French or Latin, Geography, Domestic Economy, Needlework, Class Singing, with Drawing and Piano as extras. In 1904 it was noted with some asperity that 'none of the girls' schools teaches Urdu, the prejudice against which appears to be ineradicable'. Indian history, too, was bypassed in many schools – the usual typical reaction of the British towards Indian culture.

We are not vouchsafed a glimpse into Miss Pratt's opinions on the teaching of the vernacular or Indian history to her young 'gels', but she must be admired for her strength and determination to keep the school alive and kicking on a financial shoe-string. This indefatigable lady was succeeded in 1905 by Miss Strong, late of Cheltenham Ladies' College, and she managed to persuade several other Cheltenham mistresses to come with her to Auckland House. It was at this stage in its history that the school became known as 'The Cheltenham College of India', a proud boast that lasted at the school well into the 20th century.

From 1908 until as late as 1952 Auckland House's Head Mistresses and assistant mistresses came from the High Anglican St Hilda's Society of Grey Ladies (some based at Lahore), in common with St Denys in Murree (now Pakistan). Deaconess Sybil Turing was Head until 1916, with her Assistant Head, Miss Mary Pearce, MA of Girton College, Cambridge, succeeding her in 1917. A high proportion of the teaching staff were university graduates from Home with the school's curriculum by now totally geared to that of an English girls' public school.

Maude Kerr (Mrs Mannes-Abbott), who was at Auckland House from 1912 to 1919 from the age of 11 to 18, considers that she had a splendid education at 'Aucky' and recalls that there was a great insistence upon all students sitting for exams 'however hopeless'. The majority of her fellow students were English, Irish and Scots, as were the staff, with some of the Kindergarten day scholars from Swiss, Italian and French families. She remembers only one Indian Christian girl then, quiet and studious. As the years went on more and more Indian students went to 'Aucky' and the other hill boarding schools.

During Mrs Abbott's time French was the second language and no Indian language or history was taught. The girls learnt plain sewing and embroidery, but their cookery classes were suspended during the First World War, when bandage rolling and other war work took their place. Two hours on Saturday mornings were spent in mending their clothes and darning their black woollen stockings. (This ghastly hosiery was a feature in all girls' boarding schools in India's hill stations.) There were some remarkable teachers at the school, in particular Miss Gertrude Toussaint, a brilliant pianist who held the Gold Medal of the Leipzig Conservatoire of Music, who was Head of the Music Department. 'She was soloist in various piano concertos in the Viceroy's orchestra, which used to give concerts at the Gaiety Theatre at which we girls attended.' (As an aside, Lilian Stradwick, née Birch, who was a teacher at Auckland House, in the early 1940s recalls a rumour linking one of Miss Toussaint's sisters with Rudyard Kipling, who was reputed to have proposed to her – a gossipy item of which his latest biographer, Angus Wilson, in *The Strange Ride of Rudyard Kipling* seemed unaware, or chose to ignore!) Another unforgettable member of staff was Miss Pearce, who became Principal in 1917, and was renowned for her work with props and wardrobe for the school plays. Miss Pearce was also the initiator of the AHS reunions in London which still take place every year.

School meals were basically English – 'mostly stodge, stews, mince and fish, with porridge and tea for breakfast, bread and butter (scraped on!) spread with black treacle for supper.' The girls could fill up on puddings like spotted dick, suet rolypoly with very little jam, milk puddings and stewed fruit – no fresh fruit. 'The staff had delicious food.'

Apart from organised games such as tennis, netball and badminton, with PT in the gym, pupils could also sign up for ballet lessons from Mrs Coutts of the famous banking family. There were no chores for the girls to do apart from bed-making – everything else was done by the Indian servants, with whom the girls had absolutely no contact. This lack of contact seems to have been a feature in girls' schools run by orders of the High Anglican church in the early days. At St Denys, too, in Murree, it was forbidden for the girls to talk to the servants. Perhaps the motive was a good one with the school authorities bent on nipping in the bud any mini-memsahib behaviour by their young charges towards Indians. But in many other schools, such as my own, warm relationships were struck between pupils and beloved ayahs or bearers, with school magazines always paying tribute to their loyalty and good service.

[This insistence at St Denys that the girls should not address the servants directly sometimes worked in the girls' favour, as Doris Windsor recalls. When they were put into silence one suppertime, a strange humming noise could be heard, which the teacher in charge assumed was one of the girls. She charged the Head Girl to investigate and was somewhat non-plussed when the Head Girl revealed that it was the bearer humming while he was serving the tea, adding in tones dripping with honeyed innocence, that she had been unable to tell him to stop as such a course was forbidden! (Girls: 1, authority: 0)]

In Mrs Abbott's time at Auckland House Sundays followed the usual pattern, with morning and evening services at Simla's Christ Church -

'very splendid, with the Viceroy, Commander-in-Chief and other important people in the congregation. All Simla schools went to a Garden Party at Viceregal Lodge once a year; this was very thrilling, we wore white silk or muslin dresses and had to curtsey to the Vicerine and Viceroy.'

'Aucky' girls had another annual treat when they all piled into rickshaws and went to spend the day at the beautiful house and gardens of Sir Alfred MacKenzie at Mashobra, where they were fed strawberries and cream.

Olga Berridge née Fenin was a pupil at AHS from 1926 to 1930 and, having taken her teacher training at the St Denys TTC in Murree, returned to the school as a teacher from 1937 to 1939. A White Russian born in Tashkent, where her father was Military Governor of the Pamirs, the family left Russia after the Revolution for Malakand in the North-West Frontier Province in 1919. She, too remembers an ordered existence at Auckland House, with occasional treats such as sketching parties with the art mistress and long walks and rambles. School grub had taken a turn for the better by then, and was the province of the Housekeeper, Mrs Hyde, known to the school and three or more generations of Simla residents as 'Granny'. On Sunday mornings Keventer's sausages were served for breakfast, and the Keventer girls were also pupils of the school. For Easter Sunday and the end of the year party the schoolgirls feasted on chicken curry and ice-cream,

'made in a bucket with ice dug out of the ice pit on Jakko. Mondays and Thursdays we had porridge and boiled eggs for breakfast; Thursdays and Fridays fish cakes; Wednesdays and Saturdays lentils with a potato cake or a chapatti... Lunches were usually brown or white stews, sometimes pies. Saturdays was cold meat and salad'.

What we ate during our nine months away from home seems to have made an indelible impression on most of us, although I can't claim such detailed recall of the MHS fare as can those students at AHS of some 70 and 60 years ago!

By the late Thirties and into the Forties, the curriculum at the school at last included the study of Indian history and geography, as well as Hindi, as Jean Binge née Cock remembers. As for the grub,

'School food was adequate! But the tuck box usually played a large part in making teas more interesting. Breakfast was unusual, to say the least, consisting sometimes of mince-on-toast, or lentils, besides porridge and bread and marmalade. The scrambled egg was horrible [known as rumble-tumble to many old India hands], as was liver, and blancmange was known as "elephant's toothpaste".' Extra-curricular activities included the Girl Guides and St John Ambulance meetings, with dancing classes still popular. Asked to point the main differences between going to school in the India of those years and a similar school in England, Jean Cock puts the presence of servants high on her list, 'with whom the girls formed great attachments... [especially] the Head Bearer and the Ayahs and the Cook!' (The no contact embargo must have been lifted by then). 'There was a laundryman [dhobi] living in the servants' quarters, and porters [jhampanis] brought hot water in covered pails up flights of wooden stairs to the washrooms.'

As a day scholar there during the same period, Janet Chapman née Edwards was spared any unpleasant liver or quaint breakfasts:

'I used to take sandwiches for lunch or had a hot meal brought in a tiffin carrier by a servant and ate it in a room reserved for day scholars. At mid-morning break boarders often asked me (and other day girls) to exchange one of my sandwiches for a slice of rather unappetising buttered bread which I would quietly dispose of. The boarders occasionally complained about their food... Delia Mitchell née Morgan told me she lived on the cook's fudge which was very good, and that she often called into the kitchen to buy some on her way back from the dhobi, who washed and ironed on the premises. Incidentally, many of the servants had been at AHS for years, starting as youngsters, and it was therefore heartbreaking for all when, at the time of Independence, they had to be evacuated.'

A quaint custom which would certainly point the difference between 'Aucky' and a school at Home was passed on to Janet by one of her boarder friends, Ruth Rich née Hardinge, who remembered that on the last day of school men used to come round selling mistletoe and narcissi. 'If the girls couldn't afford to buy, they'd barter their tennis shoes, which the men insisted shouldn't have holes.'

Janet's last year at AHS was a memorable one – 1947, the year in which India gained her Independedence and the State of Pakistan was born:

'Ten days after Independence, Simla's peace was shattered by murders, lootings and rifle shots echoing across the valley. We were unable to go to school for several days because of the curfew, but once things had quietened down and the curfew was lifted for an hour or more, my father took a friend and myself to school to pick up the text books we needed for revision as we were about to sit exams prior to taking our JC later on that year. On our way home we met an Indian officer who told us that more murders had just been committed. He had a pistol and escorted us all safely home after seeing some very grisly sights on the way. This was the year when Europeans and Anglo-Indians were talking about 'going Home', but after the troubles started, many Europeans brought their departure dates forward and convoys of them left Simla, leaving the schools somewhat depleted of staff and pupils... When the time came for the children to leave for the long winter holidays, and because there was still some panic in the air, it was arranged for all the schools in Simla to travel to Delhi under army escort.'

Life in Simla would never be the same again, and Janet's memories of her idyllic childhood as a day girl at AHS give us glimpses of the little hill station which are worth recording here:

'I did my prep as soon as I got home, had tea, practised my piano pieces, washed and changed and either went to my twice-weekly music lessons or for a walk with my parents before dinner, a habit most people in Simla enjoyed. Being such a small place we often met friends and acquaintances and, as was the custom in India, we dropped in on people or they did on us. We shopped in the bazaar or on the Mall, dropping in for a chat with Madame Clare who had a dress shop by that name, or for a comic or book at Mr & Mrs De Beau's bookshop, where I was known as "Pahari bundar" (Pahari monkey). (Their daughter was a boarder at AHS). As a special treat I was taken to Wengers or Davico's for tea or to Keventer's for a drink of the cold, creamy milk which came from their dairy at Tara Devi. Then back home for dinner, about 7 pm, after which I read, played cards or listened to the BBC World Service or music from Hilversum, before bed.'

Old girls from AHS can drop many a famous name when reminiscing about their old school: Una Slim, daughter of the Field Marshal was at the school in the 1940s, as was the actress Frances Bennett (Felicity Barrington in those days); and Molly Kaye (M M Kaye, author of *The Far Pavilions*) spent some time at the school as a small girl.

To bring the story of 'Aucky' up to date, the current Principal Mrs Rita Wilson, has kindly sent me the following details:-

'There are 1,025 pupils in the school, out of which 100 girls are from overseas (Thailand, the Philippines, Zambia, Nigeria, England, France and Norway); AHS is financially self-supporting and receives no financial aid from Government or any other agency. The school is Christian-based and an institution of the Church of North India, with the curriculum entirely geared to the Indian school leaving examinations conducted by the Council for Indian School Certificate Examinations, New Delhi.'

Their 1989 school magazine 'Auktimus' reveals a school proud of its history, its pupils receiving an all-round education based on a firm Christian foundation, with a happy blend of what might be called 'European' and Indian culture. This mixture manifests itself in the many holidays the girls receive to celebrate festivals in the Christian as well as the Hindu calendars.

The House system is still very strong, with Lefroy, Durrant, Matthew and French competing in games and athletics, debates, drama, elocution and dance. 1989 saw the introduction of computer classes from Class IV upwards with Computer Science as a compulsory subject. Parents are queuing up to enrol their daughters at AHS, so much so that a new wing is to be constructed – not surprisingly, with a student roll of over 1,000 girls.

Auckland House has had 19 Principals since its foundation in 1866, and these are given below:

Mrs Mackinnon	1866-1871
Mrs Toussaint	1871-1874
Miss Berry	1874-1886
Miss Perry	1886-1887
Miss Slaughter	1887-1889
Miss E Pratt	1890-1904
Miss Strong	1904-1908
Miss Sybil Turing	1908-1915
Miss Pearce	1915-1936
Miss Imri	1936-1939
Miss K Budden	1939-1944
Miss G Wassell	1944-1946
Miss DE Quinn	1946-1952
Miss JF Wylie	1952-1954
Miss Mildred Twiss	1954-1958
Miss AF Atkins	1958-1966
Mrs DS Hakim	1966-1982
Mrs JC Netram	1982-1986
Mrs Rita Wilson	1986 continuing

* As Auckland House enters its 124th year of existence, those Victorian ladies of the 'Fancy Fair' committee and the pioneering 'Grey Ladies' who worked so tirelessly to establish their school in the days of the

* 130th in 1996

British Raj, would be proud to learn that 'Aucky' had become one of the premier girls' schools in independent India.

Old AHS girls still meet at their annual reunions in London, and in common with many old students from schools under the British Raj, several of them have visited the scenes of their Indian childhood over the years. One was Ann Macdonald née Bullock, a pupil in the mid 1940s, who visited Simla in April 1990 and notes in an account she wrote in the annual newsletter that she was delighted to find the school in such excellent hands. She noticed many changes since her day, but was surprised to find that the girls still wear 'the same old uniform'. She continues,

' ... there has been a radical change in the PT classes which are now run by two ex-RSMs. The pupils get additional exercise by swinging, as we did, by their knees from the balconies above the cement playground three stories below. The monkeys are as always much in evidence and frighten the girls, especially when food is visible in someone's hand. Some things never change!'

Auckland House School, Simla
From a turn of the century postcard

8

Pupils and Pedagogues

As we have seen, European education in India started fitfully, gained momentum and, in the years running up to the Second World War and eventual Indian Independence in 1947, was firmly established, so much so that the practice of sending children Home to be educated came to be not considered by some parents as a prerequisite to their offsprings' well-being. In addition the majority of students were Anglo-Indian or Domiciled Europeans whose parents preferred their children to remain in India with them.

We must now examine the calibre of the staff of the old-established schools in whom some British parents placed so little confidence. From their inception in the latter half of the 19th century, the schools' governing bodies insisted that Principals and a proportion of the assistant teachers should be university graduates recruited from Britain. And, as has already been noted, Roman Catholic schools had a constant supply of well-qualified teachers trained by their orders in Europe and the British Isles, with many Roman Catholic orders later founding colleges for the training of country born teachers in India.

The Government in those early days did little in the field of teacher training. They were more concerned with the education of Indians through the medium of the English language. Such official neglect led to a policy of self-help by a few of the foremost European schools, who instituted a 'pupil-teacher' training scheme for school-leavers amongst the Anglo-Indian and Domiciled European community. These small beginnings formed the basis of teacher training departments attached to the schools themselves.

With the dawning of the 20th century, the Government itself woke up to the need for teacher training colleges, but did little to implant any worth while schemes. In 1901 they established a teacher training course at Victoria Boys' School, Kurseong, but this was closed after a year and was replaced by Dow Hill Teacher Training College for women in 1903 until 1939 when it, too, closed down. But young country born men and women were turning to teaching in greater numbers, particularly women, with the result that many more TTCs were established as offshoots of the schools themselves, to which the Government gave grants-in-aid. All were based on the contemporary thinking on education in the West, and trained teachers to primary, middle and high school levels.

The following list, which cannot be exhaustive, gives the names of the main colleges:

1. Chelmsford Teacher Training College for Men, established at the Lawrence School, Ghora Gali, Murree (now in Pakistan). (Originally at the Lawrence School in Sanawar, Simla, Chelmsford College was transferred to Murree in 1924.)
2. St Bede's College for Women, Convent of Jesus & Mary, Simla.
3. Dow Hill Training College for Women, Kurseong.
4. St Xavier's College Teacher Training Department for Men, Calcutta.
5. Loreto Convent Teacher Training College for Women, Calcutta.
6. All Saints Teacher Training College for Women, Naini Tal.
7. Doveton Training College for Women, Madras.
8. St Mary's Training College for Men and Women Poona.
9. Isabella Thoburn training College for Women, Lucknow.

As far as graduates were concerned, many teachers trained in India could read for their degrees in one of the universities established by the British for Indian students, with English as the medium of instruction. This fact is often ignored by elitists among the British living in India in the 20th century. India's famous universities were staffed by eminent men and women out from Home, as well as highly-qualified Indians. Several of the larger European schools in the hills and on the plains had college departments for students wishing to go on to higher education, some of whom went to take their degrees at an Indian university. Others prepared boys for preliminary exams leading to careers in the Provincial Services, in departments such as engineering, opium, survey, telegraph and the Indian Medical Department, but this kind of further education did not take a real hold until into the 20th century.

Jesus and Mary Convent, Simla; (known as 'Chelsea')

The many teachers who trained at a TTC in India found themselves welcomed with open arms on their return to Britain after 1947, their qualifications considered adequate for the professional standards demanded at Home. And the few graduates holding degrees from an Indian university easily found their niche in education, with some of them continuing with extra-mural courses at a British university or Teacher Training College. Alison Coombs, born and brought up in India, whose father was in the Indian Forestry Service, took her Higher School Certificate (Cambridge) at All Saints, Naini Tal, as well as a three year teacher training course there. All Saints, previously called the Diocesan Girls' School, was run by sisters of the Community of Christ's Holy Family, its Mother House at St Leonards-on-Sea. She obtained her BA in English Literature, History and Latin as an external student from Agra University in 1929. Later, she took a post graduate course for her diploma in Education at Reading University, and taught at St Deny's School, Murree, in 1934, and St Michael's School, Darjeeling, from 1935 to 1947, when the school closed down.

Daphne Clifford (née Speechly) was also born, brought up and educated in India. Her father was a Chief Superintendent of Posts & Telegraphs and for five years Deputy Post Master General, Burma. After her schooling at Christ Church Girls High School, Jubbulpore, she attended an Inter-Science course at St James's College, Calcutta, where the Principal at that time was the Rev T H Cashmore, and the English lecturer the Rt Reverend Bishop Herbert Pakenham-Walsh, DD, DLitt, Principal of Bishop's College, Calcutta. After further study at the Scottish Churches College in Calcutta, she obtained her BSc from Calcutta University in 1932, aged 19. 'In England I would just be entering University'. Her fellow students were Indian, and in her class there were only two women, both Bengali Hindus, among a class of over 100 men.

> 'There were a few English and Scottish professors, but in the main and certainly on the Science side there were Indian lecturers and demonstrators, except for a young Scotsman named Somerville who appeared in my last year to take Physical Chemistry.'

The Principal in her day was Dr Urquhart DD, an ex-Chancellor of Calcutta University. As a graduate, Daphne Speechly was able to gain her Bachelor of Teaching Degree from the Loreto College in Calcutta, with the Licentiate of Teaching Diploma available to non-graduates. The eternal student, she also obtained her BA at Loreto, and went on to become Senior Maths Mistress at the Lawrence Memorial Military School at Lovedale, Ootacamund, in the early Thirties, later teaching Maths and other subjects for a brief period at a school in Mussoorie. Daphne Speechly left India for England in 1936.

Another typical example of an aspiring young teacher making good on the strength of the teaching he had received in India is Gordon Laurence, who taught at my old school, Mount Hermon, during World War Two. He obtained his Bachelor of Teaching degree at St Xavier's TTC in Calcutta, and taught Maths and General Science at Mount Hermon. He went on to become Head Master (Senior master) at the Wynberg Allen School in Mussorie for a time, where he taught Physics, Chemistry and – to the lower forms – Hindi. Gordon Laurence came to England in 1961 and taught Maths and Science at Dartford West Secondary School, eventually becoming Head of the Science Department from 1963 to 1981, when he retired.

'I enjoyed my work at Dartford, an old established school with good discipline. Maybe the boys were not as hardworking as the children in India, but I got on very well with them ... they did very well in their 'O' levels.'

These few case histories can be duplicated many times over, and serve as examples of the higher education available in British and post-Independent India in the 20th century.

L C (Kim) Taylor, was a very young master at St Paul's School during World War Two, where he taught from 1940-1942 and 1944-1946. As were so many schoolboys and girls at the start of the war, Kim Taylor was shipped out from his English public school to India to re-join his parents. He had just turned 17 and was still too young for his army call-up. Leslie Goddard, the school's Rector, interviewed the young man in Calcutta in the cold weather vacation, and recognised that he had something to offer the school. Taylor remembers being slightly bemused by the fact that he was teaching boys a good deal older than he was, in a VIth Form with strapping young Indians, Afghans, Malays and Burmese of 19 and 20. After three frustrating weeks of getting nowhere with students, he took the Rector's advice and, during a particularly noisy lesson, picked out the largest of the superannuated toughs stuck in 'Shell', and punished him, guilty or not. This went against his liberal grain, but had the desired effect!

Kim Taylor found St Paul's very isolated.

'For nine months of the year you were miles from anywhere on top of a mountain .... it was a complaint about English public schools in general that they tend to be sealed off behind a kind of Chinese wall, and this was true in the nth degree – and had to be so – for schools like St Paul's. It was a kind of fort, culturally, in an alien country.'

He felt that St Paul's and other schools like it in India were 'out of time' a situation brought about by their isolation, whereas public schools in

England then, and particularly now, are susceptible to changing fashions and opinions.

'Any changes in the world outside were not, as in such schools in Britain, reflected through the boys and their parents coming into the school, but rather through its staff alone. This timelessness made the school much more self-confident. The Rector and his staff had a clear sense of mission, which was to train an elite in India, and to instil what we would call the Victorian virtues: a sense of duty, 'noblesse oblige', high ideals and so on, in to the young men of India's rising middle class. This was, of course, a strangely abstract view to a race concerned more with putting families first.'

Staff of St Paul's meet in the main quadrangle, 1942

Despite his surprise at finding himself in such a time warp, Kim Taylor felt that St Paul's and other schools like it were doing a very necessary job in the light of those days. He found the staff of a high standard, with 'some very bright people' teaching there, thanks to L J Goddard's ability to gather such people around him.'During the war especially, a number of people among the international intelligentsia displaced from their own countries were thrown up on the shores of India.' [Conversely, L J Goddard also remembered meeting some of 'the worst crooks in South East Asia' at his interviews with potential staff in Calcutta!]

The new young master found that the staff were expected to work very hard, with strict supervision expected from them during prep periods, registers of prep set and rigorously checked. 'Staff in England would have regarded all this as unbelievably Victorian.' With memories of his own school still vivid, he was also struck by the extraordinary range of nationalities among the boys, as he was by the paucity of cultural clubs and societies at St Paul's at the time. His youthful enthusiasm prompted him to set about filling some of the gaps with the production of plays and concerts not previously such a feature of school life, and the re-introduction of cross-country runs, paper chases and expeditions into the surrounding mountains.

Old boys of the Forties remember 'Kim' with affection. My brother was never quite certain whether he was a boy or a master! L C Taylor left India after his second stint as a master at St Paul's and, after taking his degree at Oxford, continued his school mastering career at Repton. He was then appointed very young as Headmaster of his alma mater, Sevenoaks, becoming well-known and influential in educational circles from the succession of innovations introduced there during his period of office, 1954 – 1968.

Much of what has been said about the Victorian nature of some of the schools, especially the single sex schools, is probably true. The memories of a high proportion of ex-students – even those at school in India in the 1940s – paint a picture of truly Victorian regimes, with punishments meted out for the pettiest transgressions, and rigid insistence on academic prowess. In the light of the hardening of attitudes towards sloppy teaching and indiscipline in some British schools today, it could be concluded that those neo-Victorian teachers had got things right. They were nothing if not thorough – their pupils were at school to learn, and forgot this at their peril. As for their pupils' isolation from a greater variety of extra-curricular activities such as the ones taking place in schools at Home, many would claim that their own out-of-school pursuits amply compensated and if pupils and teachers were cut off from the latest trends in art, literature, music and drama – and not all of them were, in fact – then they made their own pleasurable voyages of discovery in later life.

A breath of fresh air did, however, filter through a chink in the 'Victorian' curtain during the years of World War Two. Unfortunately, this was very rarefied and did not permeate the atmosphere of the old-established schools. I am referring to the introduction in India of what became known as the 'war schools'. With the arrival of hundreds of British children as 'evacuees' in India, some parents, mainly from ICS, Army and business families, felt the need to set up special schools for their young. As a result they took advice from eminent British officials such as the Directors of Public Instruction in India's Provincial Governments for the formation of such schools. The gentlemen in question seem not to have pointed them in the direction of the schools already available, and readily gave their whole-hearted assistance towards these exciting new projects. None of the schools, however, was funded by Government and relied on private fund-raising and tutorial fees to keep afloat.

No doubt because of the parents' intention that the schools should exist only for the duration of the war, the DPIs saw no irony in their lending their professional assistance to the setting up of yet more schools in areas already saturated with hill boarding schools; schools, moreover, which could have done with an injection of new blood in the form of pupils and teachers from Britain.

The three foremost 'war schools' were Sheikh Bagh in Kashmir, the Hallett War School in Naini Tal and the New School ('Harrow-on-the-Hooghly') in Calcutta, which, after its first few terms, moved up to Darjeeling as a boarding school.

Sheikh Bagh was the brain-child of Eric Tyndale-Biscoe, who would have none of the prejudice against the acceptance of Indians or Anglo-Indians as pupils, although, in the event, Anglo-Indians did not apply and there were few Indian boys. The reminiscences of Sheikh Bagh old boys leave an impression of a mini-Gordonstoun, with many recalling their schooldays with affection and admiration, sentiments in which their Headmaster largely figured. The school was a Prep School, taking a few girls, but mainly preparing boys for their entry into British public schools, with a strong bias towards outdoor activities and a Christian outlook.

The Hallett War School in Naini was established for children whose absence from Britain, it was claimed, would deny them the opportunity of a continuous and exclusively British-orientated curriculum. At the risk of offending many old students and ex-teachers at the old-established schools, I received the following answer from an old 'Hallettian' to my question regarding the Hallett School's raison d'être:

'At the existing European schools in India, Latin and French were hardly taught at all, History and Geography very differently......'

The Bishop of Lucknow and Mr Powell-Price, DPI in the United Provinces, played a large part in the initial formation of the school, with Mr William Christie of the ICS in Lucknow (later Sir William Christie and Chief Commissioner of Delhi) also prominent in guiding its progress during the four years of its existence, 1941-1944. The school was fortunate to have as its principal the Rev Robert Llewelyn, a senior Wrangler and Anglican priest connected with the Cowley Fathers. A former Chaplain at Westminster School, London, Robert Llewelyn was approached to take the helm of the Hallett School whilst on a sabbatical with the SPG Brotherhood in Kanpur at the outbreak of the war. The school was named after Sir Maurice and Lady Hallett, the Governor of the UP and his wife, who both served on the governing body during its lifetime. Once the school was running, the average number on the student roll per annum was 150, with boys and girls in equal proportion.

Robert Llewelyn recalls that apart from the feeling amongst parents that Anglo-Indian schools would not be able to provide the right emphasis to French, Latin and History, the question of diet weighed heavily with some of them. 'It was thought that some children would not be able to adjust easily to the different dietary habits of the Anglo-Indian school ...' Thus were those poor Hallett children denied the delights of 'aloo chops' and 'kofta curry', to say nothing of 'sooji' porridge and pumpkin in its various disguises!

Cynthia Langdon-Davies recalls that the staff were all certificated and (except for games and PT) degree-holders.

'There were three who were not British: an Indian science teacher, Mr Joshi, a gentle and courteous prince of Kumaon, much loved by the children and the only teacher who was never ragged; a Russian art master, and a Swiss PT mistress, Miss Rutteshauser, a Belsen wardress-type dragoness who was taken away by the police one day in the middle of PT and locked up for the rest of the war. This was a fantasy come true .'

The 'war schools' all drew their teaching staff from the wives of Government officials, army officers and businessmen serving in India, together with a few Indian or Anglo-Indian teachers. What a bonus those wives must have experienced in finding occupations for which they were trained as readily available to them, saving them from what might have been a boring existence as a memsahib during their war time sojourn in India. And how lucky the 'war schools' were to find them. Thus, the question of staffing the schools was not the problem it might have been, but the Principals had to contend with the difficulties of finding the right premises and transforming them into a school worthy of the name. Robert Llewelyn remembers some of the hazards he had to face.

'The school stood about 900 feet above the nearest road so that everything from a sack of flour to a piano had to come up on the back of man or beast. Apart from stocking up with furniture and equipment, there was also so much that needed to be done to the dilapidated buildings, both in building up and pulling down, for they had in some cases been pronounced unsafe owing to the shifting hill side. A constructional disaster which remains in my mind was the girls' lavatories, where you had to stand on the seat to close the door, but I believe we got the doors refitted to open outwards before the term began. The first day was, not surprisingly, pandemonium, for no one knew anyone else. I recall one boy asking me what sort of fellow the headmaster was – I was 31 and perhaps looked younger – and that I showed a senior girl to her cubicle only to discover that she was one of the mothers.'

The buildings taken over by the Hallett School were formerly the premises of a well-known school established by the American Methodist Episcopal Missionary Society in the closing years of the 19th century. This was the Philander Smith College, largely attended by the children of missionaries, with similar schools founded in Mussoorie through the liberality of a Mrs Philander Smith in memory

Sherwood College, Naini Tal

College Prefects – 1942

Governor's wife opens Fête and Fair – Lady Hallett is escorted by the College Principal (Rev A.E.Binns)

Fête and Fair, Founder's Day

College Staff, 1940

of her husband. My researches do not reveal how long these institutions lasted into the 20th century, but the buildings of the Philander Smith College in Naini appear to have had a chequered career. When retracing his steps to the scenes of his childhood in 1979, John Wall, an old 'Hallettian', discovered that his old school buildings formed part of the Birla Vidya Mandir, an Indian school named after the Indian industrialist, Birla. He translated the Hindi legend inscribed over its portals as 'The Centre for the Pursuit of Wisdom' – no doubt with a wry smile. His sister, Cynthia Langdon-Davies retains happy memories of her years there, aged 14 to 17.

'I think everyone who was at Hallett really loved it. Those who went back to school in England afterwards felt very much on a par. Our exam results somehow were amazingly good; we all seemed to get through with Matric exemption....'

The Hallett School children also took the Cambridge Senior School Certificate, as so many children in the old-established hill schools did.

The Hallett's youthful Headmaster, Robert Llewelyn, went on to become Principal of the famous Sherwood College for Boys in Naini Tal, and served there from 1951 to 1966. The school was founded in 1869 by Bishop Milman as Naini Tal Diocesan School, changing its name to Sherwood in 1937, named after the estate on which it had been accommodated in the 1880s before a covetous Government 'commandeered' the school and its grounds in 1895 in order that a new Government House might be built. After being shunted about from pillar to post in temporary accommodation for the next couple of years, Sherwood College survived the vicissitudes of the Government's autocratic take-over bid by eventually establishing itself on some land on a spur of Ayarpatta Hill in 1897 where it has flourished ever since, a shining example of a very *pukkah* boys' boarding school in Northern India. Robert Llewelyn became Principal at a very difficult time in the school's history: British families were leaving India in droves after Indian Independence, and numbers on the school roll had dropped drastically. The new Principal was undeterred. By 1957 he had brought the number of pupils up to 370. His apprenticeship as Principal of the Hallett War School, which he had had to fashion from nothing, had proved a good training ground. Llewelyn was not the only memorable

Principal in the long Sherwoodian roll call. His penultimate predecessor had been the great Alwyn E. Binns (1932-1947) who, to quote Colvyn Haye (Old Sherwoodian late 1930s/early 1940s) 'really put Sherwood College on the map'.

'Having filed into morning chapel, the new boy had his first glimpse of the fearsome Binns in billowing clerical robes as he swept in from the chapel vestry. This was the legendary man who made Sherwood what it was, an Anglican school which produced muscular Christians in the manner of Arnold's Rugby, with corporate life centring on Chapel worship, academic excellence and compulsory games.'

On the 1st June 1973 Mr D R A Mountford, an old student of the Lawrence School, Sanawar, and subsequently on the staff of St Paul's School, Darjeeling, assumed the Headship and is still at Sherwood today. The modern Sherwood has girls on its roll of pupils, and computer studies have been introduced. Mr Mountford's closing words in his brief history, 'The Sherwood Experience', in the Souvenir publication celebrating 'Sherwood: 1869-1992', sums up the ideals of his own and other such schools in Independent India and Pakistan:

One constantly repeated criticism nowadays of schools such as Sherwood is that they foster an elitist society of privileged youth. To these critics one can but dedicate this Souvenir in the hope that they will be inspired by the noble traditions and ideals which are cultivated here. If indeed the result is an elitist snob, then such schools have surely failed in their endeavour and the whole effort covering over a century of labour has been nothing but illusion and self-deception. Can this be true? The Sherwood experience would suggest otherwise.

To return to the 1940s, the other 'war school', The New School, had as its principal, Harold Loukes, the eminent Quaker educationalist, who until 1940 had been lecturer of English at Delhi University. As a Conscientious Objector, Harold Loukes felt that he ought to be doing something 'that the war threw up' and accepted the post of Head of the New School. Again it was a DPI, Mr Walter Jenkins, who threw himself into the task of getting the school started as a result of requests from parents who intended to bring their children out to India. The new head, like Eric Tyndale-Biscoe at Sheikh Bagh, felt strongly that he could not associate himself with any hint of racism and insisted that the school be described as open to all children who might have been educated in England.

'This would have let Jawahar Lal Nehru in if we'd had him, but in the event Indians and Anglo-Indians didn't actually apply. What got around was that this was a school for English children, so that is how it worked.'

When asked to liken the New School to a school in England, Mr Loukes thought that Bedales would be the nearest equivalent, or any typical Quaker School. It, too, was fortunate in finding highly-qualified staff, many of whom were wives of Government officials, army officers or businessmen, with some war widows, and all recruited in India. Mr Maurice Draper, late of La Martinière College in Calcutta, who held his BSc (London) with Honours in Chemistry, taught the school Chemistry, and Physics to O, (then School Certificate) level, also teaching Maths. His wife held a BA degree and Teaching Diploma, and taught History and Geography. The Drapers enjoyed their time at the New School during 1943 and 1944, and Maurice Draper pronounced the school

'a complete success, the spirit and atmosphere and the approach to work serious ... the pleasant conditions [were] due largely to Harold Loukes, but to some extent to the wartime urgencies (making the best of it and pulling together etc.)....... the difficulties were mainly to maintain qualified staff over the four year period, and to keep a high standard in the boarding arrangements (house staff, servants, catering.)'

Cecily Draper jokingly recalls the large number of servants needed, with the proportion of pupils to servants said to be 169 to 170!

Margaret Martyn, wife of an ICS officer, taught at the school both while it was in Calcutta and Darjeeling. An MA with History Honours and a Teaching Diploma from Manchester, she vividly remembers the problems teachers faced while the school was still in Calcutta, with the fans whirring overhead in classrooms divided by screens 'so that History vied with Maths or French for attention.'

As well as studying for the Cambridge Overseas School Certificate, the New School offered its pupils preparation for the Higher School Certificate in the VI form. Children were taken at the school from four and a half to eighteen. The school premises were made up of four rented houses, with Eden Falls, just below St Paul's School, forming the school's main building. Its proximity to St Paul's led to the New School's 'borrowing' equipment and space from that school when required and they also received help from Victoria Boy's School at Kurseong, as Maurice Draper, the New School's Science Master recalls.

During its short life, the New School even published a school magazine, with articles from students demonstrating orginality and imagination with much picturesque use of language. One contains a spoof account of 'St Agatha's Co-educational Seminary' of Worplestead, Hants, with its prospectus referring to the strictly co-ducational constitution of the school, and boys allowed a fifteen-minute talk with the girls every day, 'under the personal supervision of the Headmaster'! The author of the prospectus refers to the inspiring leadership of Dr L J Mainwaring (Loukes), the Headmaster, and quotes the tribute paid by the missionary Bishop of Chota Pegpur while visiting the school: 'Meeting staff has made me feel a better man. I realise how much worse I might have been' ... Harold Loukes entered into the spirit of things and wrote a play entitled 'Corpse in the Common Room' performed by the St Agatha's staff, and directed by the author, with the scene 'laid throughout in the Staff Common Room of St Agatha's.' At the risk of embarrassing him, I note that the BBC's former Delhi correspondent, Mark Tully, figures in the school's magazine of May 1942, which published his story 'Once upon a Time' when he was in Transition Form aged six and a half with further offerings from him aged seven and seven years eight months in 1943, after which I understand the embryo broadcaster went Home to continue his education.

On the drama front, the New School presented some adventurous productions, with 'Quality Street' at St Xavier's College Theatre in Park Street, Calcutta, 'The Blue Bird' at the Gymkhana Club, Darjeeling, followed by 'Trelawney of the Wells' at the same venue. 'Trelawney' had the distinction of receiving a critique in 'The Statesman' newspaper, with the play's proceeds donated to the War Fund. Inter-house plays, too, were ambitious with 'The Ascent of

F6' put on in 1944, all a far cry from our Gilbert and Sullivan offerings. But I do remember being involved in a modern version of 'Hamlet' at MHS, playing the part of Hamlet's secretary!

The New School was indeed an exotic bloom to us boarders at a traditional school in Darjeeling, but now that I have learnt more about it through my researches, I realise that it must have been great fun to be there and, like other 'war schools' was a resounding success. The last verse of an unsigned poem entitled 'Will you remember?' in the final edition of the school magazine of December 1944 recaptures the golden days of those Hughli Harrovians and their contemporaries at the other schools, as it must for earlier students down the years:

'Will you miss – flowers swaying beneath the weight of Sikkim bees?
Will you hear – temple-bells rejoicing in the night?
Will you smell – the ingratiating incense of stately pine-trees?
Will you see – the swooping glide of red-feathered kite?
Will you remember – your close friends and memories for old times' sake?
Now your heart is gladdened in leaving. In despondence will it ache
For past times of brighter youth? Or have you no feeling?
In years distant – will you remember..... Darjeeling?'

Yes, oh, yes, must be our heartfelt reply!

'Harrow-on -the -Hooghly: The New School, Calcutta and Darjeeling, 1940-1944' by John Lethbridge, published 1994, is available from The Old Bakery, Thames Street, Charlbury, Oxon OX7 3QQ.

Part II

"Oft in the stilly night
Ere slumber's chains have bound me
Fond memories bring the light
Of other days around me"

Thomas Moore

9

Going Up

By the time I went to Mount Hermon School, in the 1940s, getting there was relatively easy. We left Calcutta's Sealdah Station on the East Bengal Railway's 'big train' at night, bound for Siliguri in the foothills of the Himalayas the next morning. After breakfast in the station 'restaurant' we boarded the 'toy train' of the narrow gauge Darjeeling Himalayan Railway and puffed up the winding hills to Darjeeling, arriving in the carly afternoon. Then it was a bus ride down to school in the valley below the imposing edifice of St Joseph's College at North Point. Our tin trunks and hold-alls (bedding rolls) arrived later, but by what mode of transport my memory simply cannot dredge up after 50 or so years! Others have better recall, as you will see.

The journey up to school was not such delirious fun as the one we made down on 'Going Home Day' nine months later, but it was invariably enlivened by the more adventurous spirits leaping off the toy train as it looped the loop at various points along the winding track, to jump on again as it snaked back.

Our 20th century journeys were a far cry from those made by children going up to school in pre-railway days. Emily Eden refers to a journey made by three little children from the plains to Mussoorie as long ago as 1838. (From this it is apparent that there must have been some schools established there even before 'Maddocks' – probably private institutions.) Miss Eden kept a journal describing a two-and-a-half year tour of what were then called the Upper Provinces made by her brother, Lord Auckland, and his entourage when he was Governor-General of India. She and her sister, Fanny, were his 'consorts' and Emily's journal, written between 1837 and March 1840, was eventually published as *Up the Country* in 1866.

In an entry dated 25th February 1838 while the enormous, cumbersome, splendid gubernatorial party was encamped at Panipat near Delhi, Emily notes that Mr T (the District Agent) told her that a palanquin had been brought to his house containing the three children: a little girl of nine years old and two smaller brothers. They were going to Mussoorie, had been travelling three days, and had about a week's more journey. The children travelled in the uncomfortable 'dhoolies' of the day, a kind of palanquin. When one set of bearers got tired usually after eight miles, they were replaced by others, and these children were finally dumped at Mr T's house as the bearers felt that their charges were too tired to go any further. And so they must have been with the shaking up they received in the dhoolies by day and their nights spent in remote 'dak' bungalows (government rest houses for travellers used as staging posts for the relaying of mail). Their parents would have had to write a series of letters to the various postmasters involved along their children's route, booking the accommodation and provisions needed. They had no redress where damage, loss or discomfort were concerned as the Government had expressly announced that 'neither Government nor any officers are responsible for the misfortunes and disappointments which are inseparable from dak travelling'.

Miss Eden was appalled at such cavalier treatment of the young and noted:

> 'Mr T had them washed and dressed, and fed them and kept them for half a day, when he was obliged to send them away for fear they should lose their dak. He said they were very shy, and would hardly speak, but he made out their names and gave them notes to other magistrates, and some months afterwards he saw them at school at Mussoorie; but it is an odd way of sending children to school.'

Forty years later as we have seen from the memoirs of Edmund Cox, other children going unwillingly to school were the scholars of St Paul's School for Boys in Darjeeling, some of whom, in 1877, would have taken up to a fortnight to get from Calcutta to the hill station. There was no 'toy train' in those days – the DHR was not ready to go into service until 1880, and even then it didn't run all the way to Darjeeling. So those early Paulites would have had to make their way from a broad gauge railhead in the foothills (the line to Siliguri uncompleted until 1878) by dhoolie, pony, tonga or bullock cart. And to make the bullocks get a move on, they would have lit a fire under them, a practice still in use in the 20th century, as many an old 'koi hai' will remember.

We little knew as we lay miserably between the sheets and blankets of our bedding roll (those indispensable Swiss roll bundles carried by all travellers on Indian journeys) in the 1940s, that our own trips up to school were positively luxurious compared to those of the sad little children of Miss Eden's journal, and Mr Cox's unkempt charges. We could only see nine long months stretching ahead far from home and family.

Had we known of Lord Dalhousie's role in making our journey to school so easy, we would probably have cursed him roundly. For it was during his tenure as Governor-General in the 1850s that the railways were established in India, transforming the lives of its native citizens and colonial rulers alike. In a Minute he wrote as Governor-General, he noted that 'the commercial and social advantages which India would derive from their establishment are, I truly believe, beyond all present calculation.' The East India Company, still the paramount power in administering the vast sub-continent during Dalhousie's period from 1848-1856, agreed to the setting up of two short experimental lines to be run by newly-formed private companies called the East Indian Railway and the Great Indian Peninsula Railway. On the 16th April 1853 the GIPR ran a train of fourteen carriages carrying 400 guests along the 21 mile track between Bombay and Thana and by February 1855 the EIR had trains operating along a line from Calcutta to Raniganj coalfield.

The mutiny in 1857 disrupted further progress but with the arrival of peace in 1858, railway lines began to criss-cross the whole of India. The East India Company disappeared and the Governor-General became the Queen's Viceroy, answerable to a British cabinet minister. The railways became the responsibility of Government who permitted private companies to run them; superhuman feats of engineering were performed by English engineers, Anglo-Indian supervisors and Indian workers; bridges spanned rushing torrents; tunnels were blasted through mountainsides; acres of forests were felled to provide sleepers for the railway tracks. By the turn of the century railway workshops were established employing thousands of men to make the hundreds of components needed. The early locomotives and rolling stock came from Europe, later used as models to be copied in Indian workshops.

But there was a problem. Despite Dalhousie's recommendation that the width of the railway should be standard throughout India, this never came about, and trains ran on tracks of four different gauges. Lord Lytton, who was Viceroy 30 years after Dalhousie, had a passion for the metric system which resulted in the metre gauge (3ft.$3^3/_8$in.) being used as well as the broad gauge (5ft.6in.), with two narrow gauges of 2ft.6in. and 2ft.0in. However, even Dalhousie could not have expected the mountain railway systems to run on broad gauge tracks – there was not enough room for such a luxury along those twisting mountain tracks.

Apart from the idiosyncracies of the gauges, every railway company had its own particular uniform, and there was intense loyalty amongst employees for their own 'firm'. A job on the railways became the prerogative of thousands of Anglo-Indian men and it is to their everlasting credit that the Indian railway system became such a success.

What evocative names they had, those proud companies: The Bombay and Baroda, the Great Eastern, the Bengal-Nagpur, the Punjab and Delhi, the East Bengal, the Madras, the Sind, the GIPR and the EIR. The latter's headquarters was at Jamalpur, a model of paternalism with its well-planned housing built around the works, with streets called Victoria Road, Prince's Road, King's Road and Steam Street, with the added advantages of a swimming pool, a library, and a night school for apprentices and a Masonic Lodge. There was also that prerequisite for Anglo-Indian social life, the Institute lovingly known as 'the Inster', where the railway community played Housie Housie (Bingo), went to dances and played tennis. In common with other companies, the EIR had its own militia, the EIR Volunteers, complete with band, where membership was in most cases a condition of service with the company. The EIR also established its own boarding school, Oak Grove, in the healthy climate of Jharipani below Mussoorie for the children of its employees.

P.L. (Les) Paul was a pupil at Oak Grove aged 11 in 1942 until the age of 17 when he left at the end of 1948, and vividly remembers the train journeys to and from school:

'Because the school was primarily for the children of the East Indian Railway, an Oak Grove Special train was *de rigeur*. The entire journey took two days and started at Howrah Station and terminated at Dehra Dun, picking up pupils from the North Western and other subsidiary railways at places like Saharanpur. The entire train was devoted to Oak Grove pupils and had a cloth banner of the school badge tied to the front of the locomotive. Among the ordinary railway staff, coolies, bearers etc., this Oak Grove Special became known as the Saithan Ghari (devil train) because of the mayhem we pupils used to cause on all the stations on the journeys both to and from school. Since our parents were all senior officers of the railway, this became an accepted occurrence for which we were never reprimanded.'

After a one and a half hour bus ride from Dehra Dun up a winding road to Jharipani, during which nearly all the 'little devils' were sick, there was a further few miles to walk or - for the littlest devils - to be carried in 'dandies'. As usual the school boxes were carried up the steep slopes by the Bhutanese porters with straps around their foreheads, the veins in their necks and foreheads practically bursting.

The train loads of children leaving India's principal railway stations on the plains en route for school in the hills were referred to by the various teachers in charge of transporting them as 'batches', like so many scones!

A little eight year old in the Calcutta batch en route for St Joseph's College, Darjeeling, was Basil La Bouchardière. He had all his schooling at this highly-acclaimed school, established in 1888 by those excellent educationists, the Jesuits, and has vivid memories of his traumatic removal to his alma mater in March 1922. His father was a surgeon in the Indian Army at the British Military Hospital in Barrackpore, 17 miles north of Calcutta, whence the young Basil was put on a train to Sealdah with other little boys in his 'batch' in charge of a Jesuit priest.

'The heartache of leaving home for the first time was relieved by the feel of three crisp Rs 1/- notes in my pocket, in those days

4s.6d, untold wealth to an eight year old. In those days the train left Sealdah station at about 3 pm, arriving at Santahar, 100 miles further on, at 8 pm, when we changed trains from the broad gauge to the metre gauge. After a halt of one hour for dinner, then followed the night run to Siliguri, when we were to transfer to the 'toy train' – our affectionate name for the Darjeeling Himalayan Railway. Siliguri was the stop for "chota hazri" [breakfast] which consisted of hot, buttered toast and tea – scrumptious. It was then 7,000 feet up to Ghoom, doing loops, double loops and zig-zags, an incredible feat of railway engineering through the Terai forest, from tropical to temperate, to emerge briefly into the cold mists of a spring afternoon amid the green, tea-clad slopes around Darjeeling.'

The young Spadgies (the nickname for the boys at St Joseph's) had to be fed and watered again before reaching Darjeeling, this time for lunch in the Kurseong refreshment rooms. The 'batch' organisers must have needed Quartermastering experience on the many journeys they organised all over India's plains and hills. The Kurseong stop was marred by the loss of the young schoolboy's precious rupee notes:

'When we emerged from the refreshment room we were swamped by a swarm of Bhutia and Tibetan "locusts" offering incredible bargains in the shape of diaries, note books, pens, pencils, key-rings, penknives, leather wallets and heaven knows-what-else to tempt schoolboy fingers itching to spend. We were usually fleeced paying ten times more than we should have.'

He remembers Darjeeling station as a horrible, ramshackle place.

'We always walked to North Point from the station ... about two miles along the "cart" road from Darjeeling to Lebong: motor cars appeared much later in about 1928. We each carried an attaché case containing toilet things. Our trunks and bedding-rolls were brought in a long procession of bullock carts from the railway station to the school, to be unloaded and carried indoors by the school servants.'

Over a decade later, another young scholar en route for her boarding school in the foothills of the Himalayas was Winsome Fink (Mrs Denise Coelho). She was to spend the seven years from 1934 to 1940 at Dow Hill School for Girls, a school set up by Government, primarily

Bird's Eye View of St Joseph's College, North Point, Darjeeling circa 1938

Aerial View of Dow Hill School, Kurseong (Taken from a jet 'plane by Wing Commander Mickie Blake an 'Old Boy' of Victoria Boys' School, Kurseong)

for the children of its employees but accepting children from other families resident in India, at Kurseong, a hill station below Darjeeling, 4,864 feet above sea level. Dow Hill, and its 'brother' school, Victoria School for Boys, came into existence in 1897, the year of Queen Victoria's Diamond Jubilee, the boys' school named to commemorate the royal event. The schools still exist today, and have a flourishing old students' association, with ex-scholars from all over the world attending the annual reunions. Recalling the start of the school journey at Sealdah Station, Denise Coelho wrote in her memoir of Dow Hill schooldays, *Orchids & Algebra* –

'Unless you've had personal experience of a major Indian railway station, it's almost impossible to imagine the chaos which prevails and somehow sorts itself out before the train departs.... one picked one's way gingerly between prone and shrouded bodies asleep despite all the din and racket around, with babies wailing, women squabbling and metal pots clanging ... we eventually arrived at the luggage weighing enclosure where an ancient and much-taxed Avery platform scale worked overtime weighing the heavy tin trunks and bedding rolls. Once on the platform we searched on the lists tied to the carriage door handles. If we were separated from our friends we either appealed to the teacher on duty or took the law into our own hands by swapping our places with other girls ... swift action had to be taken or the enjoyment of the train journey could be ruined.

We arrived at Siliguri in the early hours of the morning. Drawn up against the platform was the 'toy' train .... we ran across and bagged our compartments. This time it was a free-for-all with no name tags on the handles of the sliding doors. Then off we trooped to Sorabji's, the station caterers, for a set breakfast of cereal, thick slices of bread and butter, hard-boiled eggs and tea.

We left Siliguri just after 8 am and the train travelled for some distance on the level main Siliguri road. Often small boys ran alongside the train begging baksheesh or performing agile feats of jumping on and off the running boards, showing off to us ... soon the flat land disappeared and the little train began to climb up...when progress was slow and the train hugged the mountainside, we used to lean out and gather handfuls of interesting ferns, stagmoss and little wild violets and primulas. But we avoided a plant called marram grass which could rip your hands to pieces.'

After their four and a half hour journey on the 'toy train', the school party arrived at Kurseong:

' ... we grabbed coats and cases and scrambled across the railway tracks on the main cart road to reach the road leading up the hill towards Dow Hill. Here there was a roadside stable for the hill ponies which were patiently tethered for hire, and also a line of 'dandies' with their coolies. When I first became a boarder I always travelled up the hill in a dandy, sometimes with a teacher... the ride was quite an adventure... often it swayed alarmingly as we negotiated the steeper slopes or hairpin bends. When I was older I was allowed to ride up on a hill pony, "Darjeeling Tats" we called them...'

The journey in the 'toy train' has left an indelible impression in the minds of thousands of school children who went to boarding schools in India's hill stations, as Denise Coelho – with her total recall – has so admirably demonstrated. In the year that she left Dow Hill, my brother, Geoffrey Innes, was en route for St Paul's School for Boys in Darjeeling, and soon after leaving school in England was moved to write a similar nostalgic account of his journey on the DHR with rather more boyish enthusiasm on the technical details of the train and the commercial aspects of the tea plantations through which it chuffed.

Cynthia Langdon-Davies recalls her journey to the Hallet War school at Naini Tal:

'My brother and I travelled from Lucknow, one of the shortest journeys (overnight plus three or four hours). Other children came from Kabul, Kathmandu, Calcutta, Kashmir. For nearly everyone the journey meant getting to Lucknow, usually by train, then on by overnight train to the railhead at Kathgodam, then a crazy bus ride on a switch-back mountain road with the mountain face on one side with a sheer drop of several thousand feet on the other. Survivors of this bus ride got to lake level at Naini-Tal (6,000 feet) where all motor transport ended. We then hired hill ponies for the last lap up to the school itself which was at 8,000 feet. Somehow our luggage arrived on the backs of coolies.'

As we have seen, during the last war several other such schools were established in the hills for the children of expatriates and one of the most famous was Sheikh Bagh Preparatory School in Srinigar, founded and run by Eric Tyndale-Biscoe from 1940 to 1946. His father, Cecil Tyndale-Biscoe, the well-known CMS missionary, was closely connected with the CMS School for Indian boys in Kashmir, eventually becoming its Head.

Sheikh Bagh's sister school was the Garden School, founded by Miss Mary Grove and lasting from 1935 to 1947. This was a nursery and preparatory school for children aged from three to ten, many of whom went on to Sheikh Bagh. One of the Garden School's first pupils was Gerald Studdert-Kennedy aged four, who later 'graduated' to Sheikh Bagh for his prep school stint before returning to England for the remainder of his education. Of his journey to school, he recollects -

'At first my father was chaplain of 'Pindi' [1941 – 42] and it was just a question of the bus run with one night on the way, over the mountains. Then he was chaplain of Simla, so there was a further train trip, with another night on the way, and the final run up the foothills on the mountain diesel. Marvellous journeys. Some responsible adult always around, obviously, 'tho I remember one stretch along the main line with six of us horsing around in a compartment, a great block of ice on the floor, first bananas and then soap flying experimentally towards the electric fan. I still carry the scar of a neat cut from the fan that nearly severed the artery on my right wrist. But all Indian journeys must be unforgettable. One got sick on the bus and very tired but all the physical impressions are very vivid.'

Way down south in the Nilgiri Hills, other children were fighting off nausea on their journeys to Octacamund and Coonoor. One such was Peter Butler, a schoolboy at Breek's Memorial School in Ooty from 1942 to 1945, aged 13 to 17. Depending where his architect father was based, the travelling sometimes took as long as three days by train, car and bus.

'I still live one journey when I was feeling very ill, with my brother, who had measles although we didn't know it at the time.

It was hot, unbearably sticky, with dull, uninteresting food, the train sometimes speeding, sometimes crawling at a walking pace. Of course, one musn't forget the bed-roll complete with blankets, sheets and pillow, all black at the end of the journey along with the owner.... and the monkeys at remote stations diving through the window and pinching the food ... the various types of window sashes, mosquito nets, louvres, glass (black with soot) .... the dry, flat countryside, the ant-hills, the bustling stations, even the remote ones. And of course, the bus to Ooty, bulging with hangers-on riding on the roof, the dust from passing vehicles choking us, the ride fit to make the strongest sick, but one dared not be – conditions were bad enough already.'

Breek's had the distinction of numbering the late Sir Basil Spence, the architect, on its roll of pupils. The school exists today, with pupils drawn mostly from Indian families.

Convent schoolgirl Jane Erskine remembers that her journeys to the Presentation Convent, Kodaikanal, in the 1950s were magical.

'I adored the trains: three different types of window shutter to choose from – slats, wire gauze and one other I can't remember, was it glass or something solid ... ? The monkeys at Kodai Road station who would pinch your belongings if you weren't careful ... stops along the way at familiar places for bananas or coconut water. Girls came from all over India and Ceylon in 'batches' accompanied by a mistress, usually a nun – Bombay batch, Calcutta batch, Coimbatore batch, Ceylon batch. The Ceylon batch were the only ones who came by air in the early days – all the others by train. Latterly parents were given the choice of air or train, the former being more expensive, of course.

Kenneth Kendall, the broadcaster, went up to school in the Nilgiris from the age of eight to ten. His father was a metallurgist working in Marikuppam, Mysore, and the young Kendall took the long train journey from Mysore, leaving at night, changing to the mountain railway the next morning and arriving at Coonoor in the afternoon. His destination was Hebron School, Coonoor – unlike some British parents, his own were loath to send a little seven year old to England and plumped for Hebron for their son's pre-prep education. The school was founded in 1899 by evangelical missionaries as a girls' school, taking boys up to the age of ten. Kendall made many such journeys between plains and hills in the years 1933-35 as Hebron had English-style terms, and its pupils were not away from their parents for nine long months at a stretch.

Today Hebron flourishes as a co-educational school, is housed at Ootacamund and is still run by evangelical missionaries, mainly from New Zealand and Australia. Its student body comprises over fifty per cent from European (the catch-all term for 'white' in India) missionary families, with other children of expatriates working in India, as well as those from Indian Christian families. The school provides 'O' and 'A' level courses as well as preparation for entry into British public schools and other schools overseas, with the school year divided into three terms, the longest holiday being over two months between mid-November and end-January. A Hebron prospectus includes a paragaph on travel -

> 'The Nilgiris are easily accessible by road, rail and air. Children travel to Hebron from all parts of India, and also from Nepal, Bangladesh, Pakistan, Singapore and East Africa. Where possible group travel is arranged, and the school gives assistance in making homeward travel bookings.'

I wonder if they call the school parties 'batches'? Compared with the almost total Indianisation of many of the erstwhile alma maters of generations of hill-school kids, Hebron is indeed unique.

By the 1950s, air travel completely transformed the transporting of the school batches to their various hill schools. The Hudson children, Rosemary (Mrs Fletcher), Andrew and John, whose father was a missionary lecturer at the Baptist Theological College at Serampore, West Bengal, went to my old school, Mount Hermon, from 1960 to 1964. As John, the eldest, recalls –

> 'We went by air to Ambari or Bagdogra, depending on whether you travelled posh Indian Airways or cheap Air Carrying Corporation..... then a Land Rover up the hill which always took 1 hour 50 minutes uphill and 2 hours 10 minutes downhill – work that out!'

The luxury of air travel was denied to Peggy Hoskins (Mrs Coldwells) daughter of a Bengal Civil Servant, en route for Loreto Convent in Shillong, Assam, on her school journeys in the late thirties. But she had another element to contend with. Having left Sealdah Station at midday, she and her batch would arrive at Parbuteepore early next morning and cross the mighty Brahmaputra river by boat (on which they were served a breakfast of bacon and eggs), finishing their journey by country bus with wooden slatted seats on a perilous ride up the Ghat which allowed for one-way traffic only.

From the time they were established in the mid and late 19th century, most hill schools took day scholars as well as boarders. We called them 'dayskis' at MHS and envied them greatly. The young Rex Dyer was a day scholar at Bishop Cotton's School for Boys in Simla during the 1870s. He was to become Brigadier-General Dyer whose exploits in the Amritsar massacre of 1919 have earned him a place in the annals of Indo-British history. One day, he was sent to bring his sisters from school, and according to his biographer, Ian Colvin, was returning when 'he came full face upon a hyena, which stood motionless in the narrow hill path barring his way. Rex, remembering what he had been told about animals fearing the human eye, advanced slowly, staring steadily at the horrid jowl, turned as he passed the animal, and still staring, walked backwards until he was out of sight.' Later, he accidentally brought down a monkey, having missed the bird he was aiming at in the Simla forests and was so distressed at the pathetic spectacle of the dying creature, its fur bespattered with blood, that he gave up shooting animals.

The unfortunate monkey might have been an ancestor of the bandar log (Hindi: monkeys) scampering through the Simla forests when Janet Edwards Chapman was a girl. She was a day scholar at Auckland House School for Girls in Simla from 1937 to 1947, when her father worked for the Posts & Telegraph Department.

'Strange, the things one remembers, like the big chestnut tree on the ridge we had to pass on the way to school, which always had monkeys hanging from its branches or sitting beneath, and we would try to walk nonchalantly past, hoping they wouldn't nip at our legs. Until we grew older, either my father or mother took me to and from school or, on rare occasions, an ayah or a cook/ bearer, We walked everywhere, whether raining or snowing. It took about 20 minutes to school and in one dreadful downpour I shared a rick-shaw with another girl, but that was probably the only time I travelled in such style. Some girls rode ponies, but I only did so as a pastime – until I fell off!'

A little day scholar at Dow Hill School when she was 12 years old in 1919 also remembers her sometimes scary walks to school in Kurseong, where her father was a postmaster under the Raj. This was Linda Coombes (Mrs Archer) who walked three miles through the woods to school followed by her chowkidar.

'He would carry my books and frighten me with stories of bears in the winter. When the winter line settled in I had to stop going through the woods and take the longer way by winding road. At one point I would let the chowkidar catch up with me as I passed, with bated breath, a naked fakir, ash-covered and sitting in the lotus position in a small dark cave. I became familiar with such scenes from my childhood but nevertheless was always afraid... In Madras I was taken by rickshaw to my school and occupied the journey by catching up with my home work.'

Today the school batches fly in comparative comfort to the foothills of the magnificent ranges of India and Pakistan, but the remainder of their twisting upward journey still has to be completed in motorised transport of one kind or another.

Who knows – one day aeroplanes – maybe even helicopters – will transport them on the final lap to school? Then it will be their turn to regale successive generations with their own 'plane tales from the hills'.

10

Living There

I'm sure those early American Methodist missionaries who founded my old alma mater, Mount Hermon, originally named Queen's Hill School for Girls, would not have considered it a public school in the English sense of the word. They were totally without pretensions as to the provision of a socially pukkah school for the middle class and were primarily motivated to provide a secondary (High School) education for the 'children of missionaries and other English speaking people in the land' (India). The school that was to become Mount Hermon was founded in 1895 under the auspices of the Methodist Episcopalian Church of America. Its founder and first Principal was Miss Emma Knowles, a missionary sent out to India with the Women's Foreign Missionary Society in 1881. Emma Knowles played a major role in establishing the Wellesley Girls High School in Naini Tal and having worked at the Calcutta Girls' School she realised the need for a similar school to be set up in Darjeeling's favourable climate. Her plan gained the approval of the Church authorities in the United States as well as in India, but no financial aid was forthcoming from either quarter. It was only by borrowing and by paying rent out of her missionary salary that she was able to open her school in 1895 in a rented house called 'Arcadia' in the heart of the town, with just 13 pupils on the rolls. Disaster struck in 1899 with the great landslip of that year, killing ten pupils. In 1900 the school re-opened in two rented houses named 'Queen's Hill' and 'The Repose', which were later purchased with a third house, 'Woodville', on ground leased from the Maharaja of Burdwan. These premises were above the railway station, and the school officially became 'Queen's Hill School for Girls'. A new wing was added in 1902 with financial aid from the Women's Foreign Missionary Society and building grants from the Government of India.

Emma Knowles worked tirelessly for her school until 1915, and retired from active missionary service a few years later. Her greatest hope was to see her school established in a permanent building 'before her call should come'. She died in 1924 aged 84, but she got her wish when Miss Carolyn Stahl, who became Principal in 1918, was able to write and tell her of the purchase of the Mount Hermon Estate in 1920. A slump in the tea industry led to the sale of the large estate belonging to the Lebong Tea Company, an ill wind which blew some good for the Methodist missionaries looking for a site for the school. The site was bought for a bargain price of Rs 50,000/- by Bishop Frederick Fisher of the Thoburn Methodist Church in Calcutta. Fred Fisher was the moving spirit behind the purchase of the site and the building of the new school. Later he was to instigate the purchase of Fernhill in 1927, which was to become the senior boys' living accommodation – again at a bargain price, a mere Rs 35,000/-. Cottages sprang up on the new estate and the school itself was officially opened in 1926, still called Queen's Hill and by then taking many more boys. In 1930 the school was re-named Mount Hermon School, incorporating the original Queen's Hill School for Girls and Bishop Fisher's School for Boys, eventually becoming the fully integrated co-educational boarding school that I knew in the 1940s.

The story goes that the school received its name during a prayer meeting of some of the missionaries, the Bishop and Miss Stahl seated around Miss Stahl's fireplace. 'When they rose from their knees after praying, the name 'Mount Hermon' came to them...' This is a snow-capped mountain 9,232ft high on the Syrian Lebanese border, 25 miles west south west of Damascus, and I am struck by the fact that other non-conformist missionaries also named their school after a biblical place – the Hebron School down in Coonoor, later to move to Ootacamund. (Hebron lies in the biblical valley of Eshcol and is reputed to be one of the world's oldest towns and the burial place of Abraham, Isaac and Jacob.)

Since the school was founded in 1895, for nearly 60 years it was run by the methodist Episcopal Church of America through its Calcutta Schools Society, the Management Committee comprising members of other non-conformist churches and missionary societies under the chairmanship of the Calcutta Methodist Bishop. In the early 1950s a new 'united' committee took over, with co-operating missions from the Australian, New Zealand and British Baptist societies, as well as British Methodists, the Presbyterian Church of Wales and the Church of Scotland. The religious ethos of the school remained evangelical, as it does today, but the largely American influence came to an end with the appointment in 1954 of the Reverend D G Stewart, an Australian Baptist, as Principal. David Stewart was Principal for ten years and was then succeeded by Graeme Murray, a New Zealand Baptist, who held the post for 15 years. In 1979, the Reverend John Johnston, an Australian Baptist and the school's Senior Master, became Principal, retiring in 1989 after 30 years' service on the school staff.

Today Mount Hermon has an Indian Principal, Dr Arun Nehemiah MSc, PhD, an Anglo-Indian Vice-Principal, Mr A L Edgar, MA, MEd, and a largely Indian staff coping with nearly 700 pupils.* There is also a flourishing Teacher Training College on the Estate, until recently the responsibility of Mrs Valerie Johnston. Many of its trainees are Anglo-Indian. The College was established in 1972 when the Undergraduate Men's Training College at St Thomas's School at Kidderpore, Calcutta, was transferred to the management of the newly-formed Mount Hermon College of Education Society by Government order and with the co-operation of the Governing body of St Thomas's School. The Mount Hermon TTC is recognised by the Government of Bengal's Education Department and students are awarded their trained Teacher's Certificate for Anglo-Indian Schools after a two year course. The College accepts both men and women students with hostel accommodation provided.

When I arrived at MHS, the Principal was an American Methodist and the school catered for a large proportion of American Missionary children, as well as boys and girls from a wide range of nationalities and backgrounds, a situation which did us all no end of good. Needless to say, the Americans were not as hung up about class as were many of their British counterparts in the field of European education in India, steeped in the public school ethos of

---

* Dr Nehemiah and Mr Edgar were in post for less than a year. Mr Jefferson Gardner was Principal from 1991-1993 followed by Mr JR Emmanuel. The current Principal (1995) is Mr Gilbert Samuel, MSc, MA, MEd, PG Dip, CSc.

producing 'leaders of men'. Educational standards were nonetheless high, following the European Code of Education laid down by Government, and adhering to the pattern of exams at 13/14 (Junior Cambridge certificate) and 16/17 (Senior Cambridge school leaving certificate). Many American ex-students today voice their pride at having been part of an educational programme which produced High School graduates in the Cambridge system, and some remember their shock on returning to the US for further education when students did not stand in a teacher's presence, or when answering questions in the classroom! All in all, we Brits benefited from the co-educational American atmosphere and the Americans from the 'Manners Makyth Man' ethos of the British public school system.

My induction into the school was singular, to say the least. Having arrived in India in May, two months after the official school 'batch' went up to Darjeeling, my brother and I were taken up to our respective schools by my mother. I was devastated when she left Darjeeling to return to Calcutta, and even staged a runaway attempt. A friendly teacher was taking a taxi into town and I persuaded her to give me a lift as 'I had a pass', I lied. So trusting was this Good Samaritan that she didn't even ask to see the exeat. I then made my way to the Gymkhana Club which I knew an honorary auntie of mine used to frequent, and told her that I hated school and wanted to go back to my Mummy in Calcutta. Very sensibly (and cruelly to my ten year old mind) she returned me to school.

The most unnerving thing about my introduction to MHS was the fact that I had been placed several classes below my scholastic abilities. Being a skinny, undersized little shrimp, the school authorities could not believe that I was the age my mother said I was, and put me in the Babies' Dormitory and Standard II with the eight or nine year olds. This seems hard to believe, and it is possible that the Principal may eventually have applied to Somerset House as I recently came across a 'short' birth certificate amongst papers passed on to me by my mother confirming that I was indeed 10 going on 11. This vital document was countersigned by Mr Dewey, the then Principal. I see from an old school prospectus that new pupils were required to produce their birth certificates and transfer certificates from their previous schools on being accepted by Mount Hermon. My law-abiding mother would certainly have sent my birth certificate; the transfer certificate may not have been available as I am not sure that English schools followed this excellent practice. (Every European school in India provided a transfer certificate containing details of a pupil's academic standing when he or she left the school to go elsewhere in India – a common occurrence in a land where fathers were constantly being posted all over the sub-continent by their companies, the Civil Service, the Army, etc.)

In any event, the damage had been done, and my first few weeks at MHS were most unhappy ones. I slept with the 'little kids', some as young as four or five, was bathed by an ayah, an ignominious ritual far beneath me at my great age, and sat in class going over the elementary stuff I had learned years ago. The result was that I rose like a rocket from Standard II to Standard V and gained the false reputation that I was a brilliant egghead. I was eventually safely installed in the middle dormitory and took up permanent residence in Standard V with my peers for the rest of the school year. (In those days Mount Hermon in common with many other English-medium schools, used the old-fashioned 'Standard' instead of 'Form'. Today they refer to 'Classes'). It had taken me some time to settle into my rightful niche, with homesickness and friendlessness vying with each other to make me truly miserable. Hence my abortive bid for freedom via my aunt.

With the passing of the years I became a seasoned boarding-school-wallah and, I realise with hindsight, none the worse for my encounter. However, I still harbour the conviction that to send a little seven year-old to boarding school, particularly for nine long months as was our fate in the hill stations of India, and even for the shorter terms in British boarding schools, is to deprive both child and parents of the sharing of family life essential to both. It could be said that this was done for the best reasons in India (although some British children did stick it out on the plains and went to the excellent schools available in the larger cities) but as far as Britain is concerned I feel that any child below the age of 13 should not have to bear the terrible alienation that such a step involves. As it was, in the kindergarten classes at MHS some of the little mites were as young as three and four years. However, at nearly 11, I should have counted myself lucky that I'd been spared the experience for so long.

Riffling through old photographs, I note that some of us looked a rag-tag and bob-tail lot, except on Sundays when we were spruced up for Chapel in our best uniforms, blazers and sometimes hats – but we were mentally and physically adventurous, the world our oyster. At this point I feel moved to drop a name. It is Tom Stoppard, the eminent playwright. Unfortunately he doesn't feature in any of my photographs as he came to the school after I had left at the end of the 1943 academic year. His mother, a widow with two young sons, had married a British officer in India, and the young Tom (seven or eight years old at the time) was sent to Mount Hermon with his older brother. Not surprisingly Mr Stoppard remembers little of his time there, only that the Headmaster was Mr Boyle. He says,

> 'I have a great longing to re-visit the place, not because it meant very much to me when I was there but I have a curiosity about how much of the experience might be recalled by a visit. I left in 1945 or early '46.'

* If Tom Stoppard does succeed in making his pilgrimage to Darjeeling, who knows? His next play could be set at a boarding school in the foothills of the Himalayas during the period of the British Raj. A happy thought.

There was no such thing as boredom at school, or rather, that was what was intended. Our day was mapped out meticulously from the moment we got up. Servants performed the main cleaning chores, as one would expect in a country like India, but we were responsible for our own bed-making and dormitory tidying. We may have been little mini-memsahibs and sahibs during our three month holiday with our parents on the plains, but our boarding school far, far away from home cut us down to the right size. In addition to our five to six hours daily in the classroom, we had to attend morning and evening study (prep): a couple of hours at each end of the day with a teacher prowling around the room to ensure that we completed our assignments. No wonder our academic prowess was well up to scratch with our noses to the grindstone.

---

* Tom Stoppard did go back to Darjeeling and wrote a nostalgic piece, 'Going Back' in the Independent magazine of 23.3.91.

Night-time study was excused to those who wore 'gogs' and had produced the necessary letter from parents stating that the eye specialist had proscribed reading under electric light. I was one of those lucky ones, but this didn't stop me from reading in bed.

My spectacles may have become a trifle rose-coloured, but looking back I am struck by the fact that at Mount Hermon opportunities were presented to all – anyone could achieve anything from wizardry on the sportsfield to whizzkiddery in the academic field or artistry on a musical instrument. My friend, Doris White née Hunt remembers not an eyebrow being raised at her passion for Maths, and no insistence that as a female she should be encouraged in other directions. Dr Gustav Kars, the senior Maths teacher, became her mentor and helped to lay the foundations of her eventual career as one of the few women Quantity Surveyors in the England of the early Fifties.

Gustav Kars was a 27 year old Austrian refugee who, with his parents, had 'found sanctuary' on the Mount Hermon Estate. I don't know if they would have used such a grand phrase, but all we knew as children was that the Kars family had to report periodically to the British authorities, in common with many so called enemy aliens who were in India during World War Two. Mount Hermon was lucky to find such a teacher in those hard times. As well as teaching Maths to the senior and middle school, Dr Kars was also an accomplished musician.

'Gusty' played his part in encouraging me to apply myself diligently to my piano studies, with many references to the famous Royal Academy of Music in London, to which he said I might obtain a place if I worked very hard. As in so many European schools in India, music played an important part in our lives, with well-qualified teachers presenting their pupils for examinations by visiting professors from England for Associated Board and Trinity College exams in various instruments, mainly piano. My ego received a distinct boost on receiving a highly marked distinction in my Transitional exam, with the honour of being 'first in Bengal'. My early grounding at MHS, where I was taught by the redoubtable Mrs Murgatroyd, stood me in good stead later in England when studying for my LRAM teaching diploma, not as 'Gusty' had predicted at the Academy itself, but as an external student

* The name of Gustav Kars is frequently mentioned by ex-students at our periodic old school reunions, and in the early Seventies while watching a television programme on the Leeds Piano Competition I was privileged to hear a riveting performance from the young contestant who carried off one of the prizes, a certain Jean-Paul Kars. Enquiries elicited the information that he was the only son of Gustav Kars, our beloved musical mathematician of all those years ago. Dr Kars and his wife were then living in Paris, but we have since lost track of him. If any reader of these pages has news of him, I hope he or she will get in touch with me. He was just one of the remarkable MHS teachers I shall always remember.

'Gusty' (Gustav Kars, Maths teacher,
music lover and mentor to Mount
Hermonites of the early 1940s)

---

* His name comes up again in John Lethbridge's recent book on his old school in Darjeeling, 'Harrow-on-the-Hooghly' - the New School in Calcutta and Darjeeling 1940-1944. 'Gusty' went on to teach at the New School after his stint at Mount Hermon.

Mount Hermon School, Darjeeling, Main Building, right wing

Fern Hill Boys' Hostel

Mount Hermon senior girls read their letters from home – 1942

147

11

Religion

Memories of the musical activities at MHS which included regular 'sacred concerts' turn my thoughts to our religious instruction. Religion played a large part in our lives, with much evangelistic fervour from our missionary teachers as well as visiting preachers. I was particularly struck by a sermon extolling the faith that can move mountains. Well, wasn't there a whole range of beautiful Himalayan mountains right outside the dormitory window? I got down to a really good pray one night, asking the Lord to shift one of the peaks and next morning was disappointed to note that my prayer must have been by-passed by more pressing calls to the Almighty. This temporary hiccup didn't deter me from joining some of my more devout companions in a visit to a lady missionary's room for a heart-to-heart evangelistic chat. She asked us to cross the bridge and be saved. We readily complied. This was just before supper and we ignored the bell ringing for us to get into line and march into the dining room. We emerged from her room tearful, cheerful and uplifted. What did it matter if we were late for supper? We had been SAVED. The teacher on supper duty was unimpressed.

I'm sure I learnt more about the Bible at MHS than I would ever have done at Home. Our Scripture lessons were pretty thorough and we could have become expert couriers for groups wishing to retrace the steps of the Apostles. When meeting my old scripture teacher Ezra Hershberger after a gap of over 40 years, a charming American gentleman who is also a talented artist and contributed much to the success of the school's Art Department, he recalled intercepting a note passed from me to one of my chums during one of his lessons. 'Wish he'd go on a missionary journey, ' it read, and to his credit we didn't get punished.

The Mount Hermon equivalent of Sunday School was 'Christian Endeavour'. One could become a member of the Junior or Senior CE groups which met every Sunday at the Community House, a log cabin on the estate, for hymn singing, prayers and a gospel message from visiting missionaries. The hymns were melodic and lively. General Booth, the founder of the Salvation Army, is reputed to have asked, 'Why should the Devil have all the best tunes?' à propos the jolly hymns sung by his devoted army, but I think the Methodists must have beaten him to it with their tuneful choruses from the Methodist Hymnal. We just loved belting out 'Come to the Church in the Wildwood,' 'In My Heart there rings a Melody' and 'I went to the Garden Alone.' The latter had words which could be applied to situations both sacred and, had our teachers known it, profane. Girls went misty-eyed or giggled as they sang, 'Oh He walks with me and He talks with me / And He tells me I'm not alone / And the joy we share as we tarry there / None other has ever known.'

Such irreverence apart, to be a Christian Endeavour member was to pledge service to the community, with offerings taken on Sunday going towards the upkeep of the school for Nepali children on the Mount Hermon Estate. And the actual running of the 'chapters' of the CE was carried out by the young members themselves, with staff in a supervisory role only.

There was religious tolerance at MHS and Church of England children were allowed to go into Darjeeling for instruction from the Vicar of St Andrews in preparation for their confirmation. These visits were an excellent excuse to get out of school and into the fleshpots of Darjeeling. Our route back to school often took in the ABC Chinese restaurant for a quick fix of Chinese chow.

In spite of my apparent flippancy regarding the religious aspect of my schooldays, some good must have rubbed off to form the foundations of a faith, albeit shaky at times, which has sustained me in later life.

The memories of most past students reveal a mixed bag of tolerance and intolerance towards their fellows of other faiths, with what seems to have been a greater degree of tolerance practised by most Roman Catholic orders towards the children of other denominations in their charge – this, despite Anglican protestations in some quarters that young Church of England souls were in danger of ensnarement by Rome. Indeed, women in particular insist that religious tolerance in Catholic girls' schools was of a high order. Richard Cooksey, a schoolboy at Goethal's Memorial School, Kurseong, in the Thirties, would disagree. 'Religious subjects played a big part in the curriculum and nothing was done for the religion of any other denominations. In fact, every attempt was made to convert them to the Roman Catholic faith.'

Jane Erskine remembers that Presentation Convent, Kodaikanal, was multi-religious and run by Catholic nuns with Hindus, Muslims, Jews, Anglicans and Catholics all living happily together and respecting each other's beliefs. Her older sister Janet says, 'It was not until I left PCK that I realised there was such a thing as religious, colour or racial prejudice in the outside world...' Jane continues:

'Catholics went to Mass every day as far as I can remember, early in the morning, and anyone else who wanted to could also attend but there was study for those who didn't – no lounging in bed. Everyone attended Mass on Sunday, joining in the singing and also in the various Catholic processions and festivities during the year. Being basically an Irish order, the feast of St Patrick on 17th March was a school holiday and a great celebration. The seniors started off the day by serenading the nuns early in the morning outside their windows. Breakfast always seemed extra special. There was a long walk, and then a big party in the evening, usually fancy dress.'

But, whatever the religion, most schools were obsessed with chapel and church attendance – a feature of school life imported from Home (Britain, America, France, Belgium or Portugal) – with Sundays being holy days in the true sense of the word.

Dow Hill, an Anglican school, allowed Catholic children to attend Mass in their own little chapel in the school grounds. A young mistress at the school was responsible for the religious care of the Catholic girls, who had their own weekday prayers in a separate classroom, joining the rest of the school at Assembly for the secular portion of the meeting. Denise Coelho remembers Miss Lumsden, the young Catholic shepherdess, guarding her flock zealously, ever alert to the dangers of possible 'contamination': 'When the Nativity

Play was about to be performed in the Anglican Chapel, a couple of our Catholic friends wanted very much to see it.' Their request to do so was answered with an emphatic 'No' from Miss Lumsden. 'After this I think she watched them very closely in case they had any tendencies to become lapsed or to go over to "the opposition"'. Denise and other Senior Anglican girls gatecrashed when a couple of Catholic priests from the Seminary came to visit the Catholic girls. 'Starved as we were of the company of males, even priests were a welcome diversion... these two were not only young but one in particular, Father Hussey, an American, was extremely handsome.' The girls sat adoringly at his feet and Denise still has the Ordination Card she managed to get from him. Also among her school friends were a number of Orthodox Jewish girls who shared some of their Passover food with her, 'which I found rather dull and uninteresting...'

Dow Hill girls and Victoria School boys worshipped at the little Anglican chapel at the bottom of the slope near the top 'flat' at the boys' school, and one of the compensations for sitting through the Sunday services was the opportunities for exchanging glances with each other across the aisle. If a girl was a Prefect on Lower School duty she had to escort the little ones to Sunday School, 'so it was a case of forever to-ing and fro-ing along the road to Victoria with little free time on that day.' Good Fridays were particularly holy, with no diversions on the playground or the fetching of library books, a request for which earned the stern rebuke 'to go and sit down quietly somewhere and think about the day.'

Dorothy Smart née Greenwood and her sister arrived at 'the Dio', St Michael's Diocesan School for Girls, Darjeeling, in 1925, aged seven and a half and six and a half, where they stayed for the next six years. She remembers the religion there as High Church of England. 'My sister and I were excused the Church and Chapel routine at first as our parents were other denominations and had brought us up accordingly, and therefore we had not been christened. However this was soon put to rights. A Scottish Presbyterian friend of mine was asked by one of the teachers one day why she wasn't in Chapel. Her reply was, "Please Miss I'm a little heathen"'.

In Jean Cock's day at Auckland House in the 1940s all denominations were expected to attend the Anglican church and chapel services as a matter of course, and they did – 'Hindus and Muslims as well'. This was a rule at many of the boarding schools, both boys' and girls', although in later years, as we have seen, in some schools, notably St Paul's and BCS, chapel services embraced a kind of universal faith by weaving stories from Eastern religions into an all-purpose ecumenical tapestry. With typical Eastern pragmatism Indian parents seem to have exercised a religious tolerance of their own, no doubt deciding that the education their children were receiving in these bastions of muscular Christianity outweighed any potential harm by the imposition.

While at the Doveton High School for Girls in Madras aged 15 to 17 in the 1920s, Linda Archer née Coombes remembers the current Headmistress as far removed from some of the teachers in her former schools, who propounded a somewhat black and white interpretation of the Bible. Miss Sampson MA (Tripos), introduced the senior girls to half-hourly lessons on Ethics... 'based, of course, on the social and moral mores of the day with the bias towards Church of England thinking.' Having asked a girl to give her interpretation of Hell, Linda recalls the Head's shocked reaction on receiving the answer that it was a place of torment in flames for those who did wrong.

> 'She closed her eyes and said with great vehemence, "It is most certainly not – it is a state of mind and not a place" [adding] that erring people suffered deeply for not being on God's side, for breaking his rules and for not being the whole person that He had created us to be.'

Thirty years later, up at Hebron School in Coonoor, such enlightenment was not vouchsafed to Alison Beresford:

> 'There was so much evangelising that I would have said that the religion at Hebron was Plymouth Brethren... We had so much teaching about the scriptures that Satan to me was a real person who lived under the ground. Once when I was digging in the playground I intended to dig quite a deep hole just to see what

there was down there... I might get down to Hell... I must have struck a stone or something but to this day I can visualise my horror, thinking it was Satan's finger nail pointing at me, and that was the end of my digging I can assure you.'

It was a general consensus of opinion amongst little Hebronites that red should be their favourite colour, 'Jesus's blood, the best colour in the world.' Black, synonymous with Satan's blood, was to be avoided.

'I remember that every Saturday after breakfast we turned our chairs round to face forward and were made in turn to recite a verse of our own choosing from a chapter of the Bible previously allotted to us during the week.'

At the end of term those who could recite not only their own verse but chapter and verse of everything learnt during the term would receive a Bible as a prize, 'for which the senior girls competed fiercely.'

Sallyann Proctor (née Smythe), at Hebron from 1944 to 1947, aged 7 to 10, remembers her constant anxiety during breakfast as she waited for the dreaded recitation of her own text. (One can't help observing that such anxiety must have had a deleterious effect on the poor little children's digestion and probably set the pattern for later adult dyspepsia.) She, too, recalls that religion seemed to dominate the pupils' lives at Hebron. 'I remember if there were quarrels among friends, the worst thing you could say was, "God doesn't love you"!' But, like Alison, she is at pains to add that nonetheless she was very happy there.

'It was a bit of a hell-fire evangelical school but I have fond memories of it, playing tennis and going for lovely walks to Tiger Hill and Lamb's Rock, picking and eating wild guavas and the lantana flowers everywhere, playing in the tea gardens and the streams running through them – also the "special days" when the tables were beautifully decorated with coloured rice etc.'

Alison was wrong about the Plymouth Brethren. An ex-Principal of the school, J C Ingleby, claims that the religious ethos of Hebron today can best be described in an extract from the Headmistress's report of 1967:

'What are we at Hebron aiming at? What kind of people does the world need? We are convinced that it needs men and women who are disciplined and equipped mentally, physically, morally and spiritually to serve God and man in this generation. To this aim we are committed, and to do this nothing less that God's power day by day is sufficient. We depend on Him.'

Such sentiments could apply to the majority of Christian schools in the Indian sub-continent under the British Raj and after. It was – and is – only their methodology which differ(ed). Truly a case of 'In my Father's house are many mansions.'

Primrose Cooper, MA (Oxon) Head Mistress of Bishop Westcott's Girls' School at Namkum, Ranchi, from 1968-1971, had to come to terms with the teaching of Christianity in a school where 75 per cent of the pupils were Hindus. She tried to find links between Christian and Hindu festivals and used the symbolism of light for the similarity between the Hindu Diwali, when lamps are lit in honour of the Hindu god Rama, and All Saints, with which Christian festival it conveniently coincided.

Uneasy about ending prayers with 'through Jesus Christ our Lord', this enlightened Head substituted this with 'for your Name's sake' feeling that thus the name of God would be special to each person. 'They could take that prayer to themselves, addressed as it was to the God whose name was known to them.'

She was amused and pleased at the letters she received from Indian parents in reply to her own telling them that there was to be a 'Quiet Day' at the school, and asking their permission for their daughters to attend. Said one, 'It will be very good for Jyoti to be quiet for a day' and another, 'Yes, she may attend the Peace Day.' So enthusiastic were the Hindu girls about their 'Quiet Day' that they asked for another to be arranged before Father Matheson, the priest in charge, went back to Calcutta. They were amazed and delighted to learn that Father Matheson knew their own scriptures, and Primrose Cooper will never forget the little Bengali girl who said, "You know, Miss, he says you can pray in any position," 'and when I asked why this was so important she replied that he said that you can pray lying on your stomach if you like, and that their pandits didn't tell them this as there is a special position for prayer. The penny had dropped for her in a big way. She was free – worship wasn't just a matter of assuming particular positions.'

She was also struck by a Hindu saying to her, 'You know you Christians think that Jesus belongs just to you and we want to make it quite clear that as far as we're concerned he belongs to the whole world.'

During her time at Ranchi, Primrose visited the Rama Krishna Mission just outside the town. Rama Krishna is a reform branch of the Hindu religion which started in the 1870s under the influence, strangely enough, of the zeal of British missionaries of that time. The man who had really started it was Ram Mohun Roy in Calcutta and he was so impressed by the zeal of some of the Christian institutions who cared for and educated orphan children, that he said, 'We must look for our own spiritual roots, it's all in the Vedas but we must find it again.' They have, and the first time she went to the Ranchi branch of the Rama Krishna Mission with the Natarajans (parents of two of her pupils) to meet Swamiji, their personal Guru, she observed 'there he was on the verandah in peach-coloured robes and the thing that tickled me was that also on the verandah was a peach telephone – truly a "two-tone" Guru!'

With a sense of humour always just beneath the surface, Primrose recalls a meeting with the father of two of her pupils. This parent was bent on obtaining the Head's permission for his girls to be let off from school to attend a family festival.

'He was a spiritualist: you always questioned which spirit he was in – you didn't dare light a match by him! He told me that the Goddess Kali appeared before him in a dream last night, "and she said that my two children must be with me for the family festival." We both understood that honour was at stake, and I told him the children were not allowed to stay away for three days but that they could have an extra half day. Anyway his honour and mine had been satisfied and he said, "The Goddess Kali bless you, Miss Cooper." As she's the Goddess of destruction I shrank back when I heard this! I was quite glad when these children came back after the festival bearing a huge pink iced cake which was "thanks from the Goddess Kali!"'

Primrose Cooper remembers the school's final assembly at Christmas with particular pleasure, with Mr Nandy, the Bengali dancing master playing a prominent part in teaching the girls to dance to the Christian carols.

'He loved "Ding dong merrily on high" and "We will rock you" and had a whole line of girls carrying palm branches and moving to the music. In a sort of pang of Western conscience, after I'd told him how beautiful the dance had been, I said, "How do you feel about asking your class to dance in this way when most of the girls are Hindus?" He laughed and said, "Miss Cooper, for me dance is worship and I love the Lord Jesus with all my heart and I am pure Hindu."'

A deeply committed Christian herself, Primrose Cooper was always concerned that bridges should be built at the school to enable all faiths to cross over and exchange knowledge of each other's beliefs. She came to admire the 'pin-drop silence' present at religious services, particularly those celebrating special festivals in the Church calendar.

'The girls could listen for hours. There was none of this seven-minute sermon stuff for them. They could concentrate for at least half-an-hour at a time on what they felt merited their proper attention.'

As a teacher at another Anglican girls' school in Naini Tal before becoming Principal at Bishop Westcott's, she was impressed by the 'natural, built-in reverence' of her Hindu and Muslim charges when she was taking prayers in chapel, in stark contrast to the Christian girls, then mostly from Anglo-Indian families, 'who were larking about in the back row, pushing hymn books along the pews and generally misbehaving themselves.'

Bishop Westcott Girls' School celebrated its 50th Jubilee in 1971, Primrose Cooper's last year as Principal. Founded in 1921 by the Metropolitan Bishop Foss Westcott, a name famous in the annals of European education in India, the administration and academic supervision were originally in the hands of the Clewer Sisters. In 1924 the Sisters of the Anglican Order of the Community of St Denys, Warminster, took over, and an early Principal's Report reveals that by 1926 'there were approximately 70 girls at the school – English, Scottish, Irish, Jewish and Italian, including a few small Indian children (not in saris), who came as day-pupils to learn English.' No doubt there was a large complement of Anglo-Indian girls, for whom the school was initially founded. The school is flourishing today with upwards of 900 pupils on its rolls, mostly

Indian, and continues to be based on a firm Christian foundation. There is also, of course, a Bishop Westcott Boys' School at Namkum, just as there are Bishop Cotton single sex schools for both boys and girls in some of India's important cities and hill stations.

The Chapel at St Paul's School, Darjeeling

Photographer: L.C.'Kim' Taylor

St Paul's Choirboys outside the Chapel

12

Discipline and Punishment

Discipline at MHS was strict and on the whole, fair, with most punishments fitting their crimes. As has been said, respect towards teachers was called for and adhered to as a matter of course. Certain privileges were denied when rules were broken, like the cancelling of exeats, and heinous crimes were paid for by corporal punishment. I was never whacked and seem to have been in blissful ignorance as to any dramas which involved corporal punishment. I have since learnt otherwise from both my fellow alumni and those before my time. A student of the 1920s remembers a boy being caught stealing, with the lady Principal of the day deputing one of the servants to give him the cane in front of the whole school. (The servants usually came from the happy-go-lucky, jolly, smiling Nepalese and Bhutia people. What such a task did to his psyche one cannot imagine. His world must have become topsy-turvy if he gave any thought to a situation where he, a member of the 'subject' class, had to mete out punishment to a young 'sahib'!) Another from my time remembers a classmate being thrashed by the Principal, resulting in the offender being sent hurtling into a nearby 'almirah' (wardrobe). I would have been prepared to swear that our sweet, gentle Principal in the early 1940s had never swished the cane against anyone. However, enquiries have elicited the information that even he was called upon to steel himself into administering corporal punishment to erring boys from time to time.

The girls' punishments seem to have been more ad hoc. One of my companions still harbours resentment against a woman missionary teacher who swished her round the legs as she was climbing through the window of her locked classroom after school hours. The offender considered the punishment particularly unfair since she was breaking-in in order to retrieve some forgotten text books needed for revision for the next morning's test! Whereas I was not the recipient of any bodily chastisement, I can remember writing out lines and having to learn poetry. And when I and two of my fellow 'myopics' stole downstairs from the dormitory to the classrooms during night study and hurled an empty tin down the corridor, the contents of which we had recently consumed (frankfurters as I remember), there was certainly trouble in store. Despite all their efforts, the school authorities had not taken into account the boredom suffered by those excused night study and this was our response. Retribution was the last thing in our minds as we heard the satisfying clatter and pictured the heads of our diligent companions jerking up in astonishment from their prep.

But retribution came. The next night at supper, the teacher on duty, the popular, but disciplinarian Dr Gustav Kars, who had been on night study duty when the crime took place, called for silence and held up our tin. He invited the culprits to stand and we were bidden to a meeting with him after supper. We shuffled off to our appointment and sentence was duly passed. Passes to Darjeeling were stopped and he made us feel like worms. We wriggled away and laid low for a long time, the peace of night study periods never shattered by us again.

To Denise Coelho, Dow Hill School in the 1930s seemed to be chock full of rules and regulations. Even looking directly at an accusing teacher was frowned upon, and speaking up for oneself when taken to task was a crime.

'In our day it was definitely a case of speak only when spoken to, and never answer back. If one wanted to get off lightly it was best to speak in an apologetic and submissive manner.'

[If a teacher failed to bring a girl to heel her last resort was to send the offender to stand under the clock outside the staff common room, in full view of the Principal's office.]

'Young girls would turn and stare pointedly ... older girls would sidle up and ask questions ... teachers came and went, asked questions and made mental reservations about a girl's character. Our biggest fear was that the Principal might come by and ask why we were there ... Sometimes we found ourselves "forgotten" and left standing for periods much longer than our behaviour warranted ... the sensitive girls learned a salutary lesson, the case-hardened ones brazened it out with little alteration in their ways.'

The age old problem of bed-wetting was given short shrift at Dow Hill, and, in common with so many other boarding schools of the period (barring St Paul's under L J Goddard), culprits were draped in the offending sheets and placed in a prominent position for all to see. 'That this method of correction did not cure the problem seemed unimportant.'

Another Dow Hill boarder from 1919 to 1926 was Win Ballantyne née Milwright who recalls the worst punishments as the cancellation of outings and home visits at week-ends, including the withholding of a treasured parcel from home, usually for crimes of the pettiest kind. Even losing her umbrella took away one of Win's treats, but such a crime was serious during the torrential rains of the monsoon period.

The pattern of chastisement in girls' schools from the early years of the 20th century up to Indian Independence in 1947 seems to be similar, with black marks, confiscations, detentions and withholding of privileges all playing a regular role in boarding school life. Imposed silence, too, was a favourite punishment, and as a pupil at the Anglican St Denys in Murree, Doris Windsor née Perkins recalls such an incident as a pupil there from 1918 to 1921:

'I remember spending at least two days sitting in silence (the whole school) waiting for someone to own up to the theft of one of the girls' Easter Eggs. Everyone was bored without lessons so some of the prefects did some detective work and, by following a trail of grains of sugar, discovered the culprit – a student teacher! She had been "above reproach" and had not been required to sit in silence and own up!'

St Michael's Diocesan Girls' School (the 'Dio') in Darjeeling appears to have been more enlightened in matters of discipline and punishment by inculcating a sense of responsibility with a strong Prefect and House system. As a boarder there in the 1930s, Dorothy Smart née Greenwood remembers that

'we lived by the House system and this could be very serious for an individual through the displeasure of other members of the House. I was in "Janu" and the other three were "Kinchin", Everest" and "Pandim", all Himalayan mountains. Each House had a Head Prefect and was divided between about four "families", each one having a family prefect. We sat with our families for meals, and slept in the same dormitory with each prefect disciplining the family. You can imagine how unpopular one would be if one let the side down with "bad marks" – also one's school work affected the House – so you did your best to get good marks for lessons.'

St Michael's ('Dio') girls, Darjeeling, 1920s.
Their outsize boaters were later cut down!
(From original photo formerly owned by the late Elsie Ann Nissen,
née Nailer,teacher centre in hat.)

There were, of course, Houses and Prefects in many of the other girls' schools in India, whose Heads were merely following a system that had worked well at Home.

At Caineville House School, Mussoorie, in 1936, girls were given black marks if they failed to wear their topees in summer when crossing the quadrangle, as Barbara Haye (née Jahans) remembers only too well.

'Each girl had her own pigeon-hole for her sola topee and the pigeon-hole shelving flanked the main entrance leading into the school hall - in fact the sola topee display was a visitor's first view of the school! The 'house system' was firmly rooted in the school and the houses in 1936 were Wales (later Windsor), York, Gloucester and Kent - named after the sons of George V and Queen Mary.'

The 'Sir Roger de Coverly' dancers – Caineville House School, Mussoorie, 1939 (So very, very English!)

Later on as a pupil at Wellesley Girls High School in Naini Tal in the early 1940s she found the house system working equally well 'for who wanted to lose marks for Browning, Cavell, Keller and Nightingale?' As for sterner disciplinary measures, she recalls only one occasion on which she and other seniors were gated from attending a Sherwood College function, and this was because of their persistent late arrival at Saturday morning singing classes.

'How it hurt not being able to see our boy-friends! The boys, of course, used to ogle us and write us billet doux until one day four of us were summoned to the office because a letter had arrived through the post from a group of four boys to four of us girls. We thought our last days had arrived - but no, our American

Principal, Miss Kennard, merely read the letter to us, told us that our parents would disapprove of our replying, and then dismissed us. We could hardly believe our ears! However, letters continued to pass from hand to hand and it was all such innocent fun. By 1943, my Senior Cambridge year, we had lost interest in school boys, for many of those we knew were in the forces fighting for King and country in World War II.'

Barbara Jahans became a teacher after training at St Bede's College, Simla, and returned to England after the war. In 1950 she married 'Old Sherwoodian' Douglas Haye after his demob from the RAF. Wellesley School did not survive after Indian Independence in 1947. The American Methodist missionaries who ran it returned to the US, the school was closed and the property sold to the Government of India. A sad end to the school whose motto was 'Nothing is Worthwhile Without Work.'

The writing of lines and memorising of poetry were other favourite punishments. Kathleen Court née Hickman was at Mount Hermon from 1913 to 1920 and recalls having been kept in very frequently with mistakes having to be written out three times each.

'I once had to write out "the verb to be takes the same case after it as before it" and so I am not likely to say "it was her" for example!'

Kathleen once had to sleep in the Head's room after some particularly bad behaviour and also remembers having to lie on her back on the floor for half-an-hour at a time to correct her round shoulders, something she considered as a punishment but no doubt meted out by the American missionary Headmistress with the very best intentions, an unwitting disciple of the Alexander technique.

As a boarder at the Catholic Loreto Convent, Darjeeling, in the early 1920s Diana Leslie née Harris suffered her share of lines, confiscations and detentions, but was puzzled and angry at two strange incidents she experienced at the hands of the nuns.

'One confiscated a toy black cat of mine and never returned it. It stood on her dressing table. Another nun said, "Come in here, I want to speak to you,"and sat down on the bench in the bathroom beside me, leapt up and ran out, locking the door behind her! I had no idea then or thereafter what it was all about. I was furious at her behaviour and turned on both bath-taps as far as they would go to waste as much water as possible, and then looked out of the barred window and pretended to be a damsel in distress!'

One wonders what further chastisement awaited her for wasting water, an ever precious commodity in the Darjeeling of those days, and even more so today.

Peggy Coldwells was also at a Loreto Convent in Shillong in the late 1930s and while she was spared any eccentric behaviour from the nuns in charge of her, she recollects strict discipline and punishments much the same as those meted out at Dow Hill. Rule breakers had to sit under the clock outside the nuns' cells and admit their misdemeanours to all who enquired why they were there – retribution through humiliation. Also, 'we were denied jam and other tuck at meals, although this was supplied privately by parents sending up tuck parcels.'

Enid Tod née Crick went to school at the Nazareth Convent (Franciscan Order) in Ooty during the years of the First World War and she and her schoolmates felt the worst punishment was to be hauled up before the Mother Superior.

'If we transgressed several times, no matter for what reason, we knew that we would go before the Mother Superior. This occasioned sheer terror, silent prayers for forgiveness and a feeling of being practically an outcast. And yet all it involved if I remember rightly was a stern, if kindly, ticking off and the direst threat was that one's parents would be informed of one's behaviour. This always had the desired effect. Nuns instilled a great desire to conform, not to be singled out, not to have a bad report, not to incur displeasure. In short, they made us somewhat timid characters and I have remained one to this day.'

Jane Turner (née Erskine) celebrated her third birthday at the end of the war at the Presentation Convent, Kodaikanal, S. India, where she spent 6 months in the charge of her nanny. Later, at the age of 7 she was sent to St Mary's Convent, Kotagiri, South India, in the late 1940s aged around 7 or 8. Although she loved school and was not unhappy, one day she decided to run away.

'Something must have upset me, so I hid in a culvert after play when the other children went back inside, climbed a hill behind the school, crossed the Maidan and went to the Club where I thought my mother might be. When I found she wasn't there I went on to the house of one of her friends, Daisy Kaye (mother of M M Kaye, author of *The Far Pavilions* and other books on India), altogether about 3 miles. Daisy immediately put me in the car and drove me down to our tea estate (about 6 or 7 miles) where my parents were having a dinner party. My equally horrified mother immediately put me in *her* car and drove me straight back to the Convent as she knew they would be frantic – there were no telephones so no way of telling them I was found! Far from being punished, I was welcomed back with open arms by one of the nuns, Sister Finian, about 4' nothing tall, who gave me a slab of real Cadbury's milk chocolate – the biggest treat anyone could have!'

Down in Coonoor at Hebron School as 'recently' as 1950-55, Alison Beresford née Brewis recalls punishments which seemed positively archaic and at times sadistic.

'I remember that as soon as we woke up in the morning we had to kneel down and say our prayers and if we'd wet our beds those prayers were the worst I ever remember saying! On one occasion I was told by the Matron that I had to get up and wash my sheets and as I was only just turned five it threw me completely, I'd no idea what to do ... a friend of mine in similar circumstances was shut in the laundry basket as a result of what she'd done in the bed.'

Alison also remembers with horror the punishment given by the same Matron to her younger sister for a minor misdemeanour when the little tot had a peg fixed to her tongue, her hands tied behind her back and was made to stand in a recess behind a curtain and left all alone.

'I was due to go for a walk with her to Pooh Corner, a place quite well-known to Hebronites of that time, and when I noticed that my sister wasn't there I nipped into the Nest (little ones' dormitory) to see why she was late and I could hear this whimpering. So I threw back the curtains and saw her. I hadn't got the courage to take her out and bring her with me but I took the peg off her tongue and undid her hands.'

Alison still insists that 'we had a reasonably happy time and soon settled down', and it must be acknowledged that the staff carrying out such arcane discipline were in the minority and that the Principals of their schools could have had little idea of what was going on. There are always eccentrics in the teaching and caring professions in any part of the world who have a low tolerance threshold and are patently unsuited to such work. Alison Beresford also remembers that the slipper was used frequently:.

'We used to have rubber-soled slippers with a peep-toe and they were very, very pliable. Gosh, it was painful, always on the bottom. "Bend over your bed" – WHACK – and it was two or three a day usually.' Naughtiness at mealtimes merited a sojourn at the 'Piggy Table' 'which was a little table covered with newspaper in full view of everyone in the dining-room. The bigger girls had to wear sandwich boards proclaiming their sin, but as nobody in the Nest could read, we never knew what they'd done wrong...'

Another five year old, Daphne Clifford née Speechly was sent to a convent boarding school in Bombay with her siblings at the end of World War I for a short time, and she too, came up against the cruel kind of punishment being meted out at Hebron in the early 1950s, but this time at the hands of the nuns.

'Here, the favourite punishment, mostly for talking during ablutions, was to have the tongue tied with a string to keep it hanging out of the mouth while standing behind the teacher's or nun's chair in the playground ... if you put your tongue back in your mouth to swallow and were caught you would incur an additional period of punishment, and if you dribbled on to your dress you were equally unpopular!'

The origin of the words 'tongue-tied' is now hideously clear ...

Later, as a seven to 14 year old, Daphne went to the famous Church of England school, Christ Church Girls' High School at Jubbulpore, an important military station in those days. This was the sister school to the equally well-known Christ Church Boys' School and both schools were renowned for their brilliant Heads in the Twenties and Thirties. The names of Alice Levi and the

Reverend G C Rogers are revered by thousands of old students and anyone connected with 'Anglo-Indian' education. A pupil in Miss Levi's time, Daphne Clifford recalls a fairly strict regime, with much 'by-hearting' from Shakespeare as well as 'lines' as punishments for petty rule-breaking. Games and recreation, too, were denied culprits who were late, talked in silent periods, read library books during prep and, most heinous of crimes, smuggled letters out to boys via day girls.

Punishments for illicit contact with the opposite sex is a constant feature in the reminiscences of old students attending single sex schools, and the staffs of boarding schools in India continued their vigilance and punishment in this direction even when it seemed a more liberal stance was being taken at the schools on which they modelled their own in Britain. Daphne Clifford remembers being unfairly accused of going out to meet a boy-friend 'behind the fence' and being suitably punished, when she was late for 'fall-in' and was not believed when she truthfully explained that she had had to go to the loo: 'It took me ages to get over my bitterness at the ugliness and unfairness of the accusation.'

Masters at Breeks Memorial School in Ooty during the 1940s were keeping an equally vigilant watch on their charges' sexual proclivitities, as Peter Butler remembers.

'Discipline was firm and fair, fairly strict for boys up to Grade 7 (4th year) and very firm where girls and boys meeting was concerned. It was a religious school, the HM a Plymouth Brother, so generally the thinking was narrow. Punishments consisted of gatings, lines and the cane, including the cancellation of games or privileges. The misdemeanours were talking in prep, after lights out, being absent without leave or out of bounds, cheek, anything, and certainly if found being too friendly with a girl. Expulsion occurred once or twice and I came pretty close!'

John Erskine, another ex-Breeks boy who was there as a day scholar from 1943 to 1946, remembers lines, being hit by teachers for minor offences and beaten by the Head for serious ones. He made a sentimental journey back to the school in 1993 and says, 'I don't think it has had a coat of paint since I left. It looked exact the same in the old building, though it has grown a lot with many new buildings and is now for fee paying middle class Indians. There are now some 850 pupils whereas in my day we only had 150/200. The Headmaster's study still smells exactly the same and I don't think has been dusted since I left. It was rather sad to see all the old Cups and Trophies still in their display cabinets, but looking very tarnished, un-loved and worse for wear. I bought a school tie, still the same one as when I was there, cost Rs25.00, about 0.50p!'

Corporal punishment was the ultimate and much-used sanction at boys' schools in India. Alan Glynne-Howell, a pupil at Bishop's High School for Boys in Poona from 1920 to 1928 still recalls the canings he received at this famous school, founded by Bishop Harding, the second Bishop of Bombay, in 1864. He grew to love and revere his English and Latin teacher, Ralph Doran Aikin, 'the single greatest influence in my life', and received the last caning he had at school from his 'Guru'. Incredibly, this was for obtaining 72% in the Senior School Latin test.

'This was, I believe, the highest mark in Standards VII, VIII, and IX (I was in Standard VII, aged 15) and all did the same test. I felt wounded and betrayed. But then in the annual examination I got 86%. I never forgot his rehabilitating comment: "That is more nearly what I expect from you!" '

Another brush with authority, this time for a prank involving the destruction of a drinking water cistern which poured its contents on to the unsuspecting HM's wife who was doling out provisions in the store room below, led him to the Head's study for retribution.

'When I was ushered into the dreaded presence I was surprised and quite disarmed at the sight of the smiling aristocrat behind his magisterial desk... He lighted one of his Havana cigars and addressed me through a cloud of fragrance. "Now, deah boy, would you care to examine the pattern of this excellent carpet?" and he indicated the spot. Unsuspecting and in my boyish naivety, I actually stooped down by the chair. Four stinging swipes from that practised cricketing and golfing arm reduced me to a state of catalepsy. When I was able to stand again, a letter addressed to my father was thrust into my hands.'

Alan Glynne-Howell went on to become a school master himself after a distinguished academic career at three of India's foremost universities,

Lahore, Bombay and Benares. Although philosophical about the punishments meted out to him and his fellows in India's public schools during the British Raj, deeming them as a means towards self-discipline, he harbours a lingering doubt:

'But now, have we advanced or regressed from that era when patterns of the British Public Schools were sedulously imposed in educating young Anglo-India? (I use the term in its widest social aspect.) As an old school master who was so closely concerned with the fashions and standards of old Imperial India, and who has experienced too the enlightenment of the present days, like the knight bereft, in Tennyson's Idylls, I stand defeated quite – "revolving many memories", and the end is sadness.'

Zbyszek Plocki, a young Polish 'refugee', was brought to India by his mother when Stalin changed sides in World War II and was obliged to free the people he had originally imprisoned in Russia at the beginning of the war. His mother was administrator of a Home set up in Panchgani for Polish children ill with TB and her little 7 year-old son became a boarder at St Peter's Boys' School from 1943 to 1947. He now looks back in wonder at his sudden transplantation into a typically English boys' school 'founded in 1902 to provide education to the European, Anglo-Indian and Christian communities according to the principles of the Anglican Church' as a recent prospectus records. He, too, associates the odour of cigarette smoke with his memories of the canings he received in the Head's study and recalls that discipline in the school was 'fairly brutal' with transgressors caned for any and everything and expulsion as the ultimate sanction.

There was no sparing the rod in Richard Cooksey's day as a pupil at Goethal's Memorial School at Kurseong, which he attended from 1932 to 1937 aged 12 to 16.

'Corporal punishment was the order of the day and was liberally handed out on little or no pretext. Punishment was meted out for class work and any misdemeanours. This was the outstanding characteristic of the Irish schools. (Goethal's was run by Irish Christian Brothers.) They knocked the education into their pupils. The Head Master used a cane but the rest of the staff used the strap, two pieces of leather about an inch wide and a foot long roughly sewn together, many with a piece of lead inserted. The strap was used mainly on the palms and caused severe pain.'

Patrick O'Meara also remembers 'the wretched strap on the hands, mostly for the purpose of keeping one up with study programmes' at St Mary's (RC) High School, Mount Abu, the hill station in Rajasthan, where he was a boarder from 1941 – 1946. Again, this was a school run by the Irish Christian Brothers. It had originally opened in 1887 as Abu Railway School for the mainly British children of the employees of the then famous BB&CI (Bombay, Baroda and Central India) railway company, and in 1924 was taken over by the Society for the Propagation of the Gospel until 1929 when the number of children had dwindled to a mere handful of boarders and a few day scholars. The school was then given to the Catholic Bishop of Ajmer who in turn gave it to the Christian Brothers, in whose hands it has remained ever since. The young Patrick O'Meara also suffered caning for breaking bounds and other misdemeanours:

'We would short the electrical power supply so that we would not have to do night studies (we were called the "telegraph boys" or "electricians".) We were also caned for swimming in the school water-supply tanks (when our description changed to "the tank corps"). These canings happened regularly, but all too often when the Brothers were in a "bad mood" or felt sadistic. If ever "The Deserted Village" had truer lines in the section on the village schoolmaster, here they were: *Full well the boding tremblers learned to trace the day's disasters in his morning face/Full well they laughed with counterfeited glee at all his jokes, for many a joke had he.*'

But the glee of Patrick and his schoolmates was far from counterfeit when they managed to get their own back on a particularly sadistic master:

'One of the funniest things I remember was when one of the chaps in our class pretended to be eating chocolate during lessons. The master captured the chocs which were then the relatively unknown "Brooklax" laxatives and, as was the common practice with "captured" booty, he wolfed down the whole packet himself. He took us for games on our pitch that evening. The pitch was about half a mile away from the "bogs" which were therefore inaccessible *"in emergencia"* ...

Poor old Brother Barry, to my knowledge he NEVER captured anything again!'

At the St Francis de Sales Boys School in Nagpur, miscreants were caned nearly every day, sometimes whole classes at a time whether guilty or innocent, in the years running up to World War Two. An ex-student had reason to give thanks for this toughening-up process when he was able to withstand the floggings he received as a Japanese prisoner of war. His fellows in the battalion broke down, and he alone refused to divulge military secrets in spite of the terrible punishment he received, in his opinion all thanks to his boyhood beatings at the hands of the Goan priests. Years later, he showed his scarred back to a hushed school assembly. They roared with laughter when he said 'it had all been kids' stuff after years at SFS.'

Basil La Bouchardière, too, remembers the wielding of the strap as a favourite instrument of punishment at the famous St Joseph's College, Darjeeling, in the 1920s. But in his opinion the Jesuits were always meticulously fair in deciding when to use it. Once a crime had been committed the miscreant had to report to Fr Prefect (of Discipline), to whom he gave details of his offence, and 'six of the best were duly administered on your sit-upon' with a leather covered strip of whalebone. He also recalls alternatives to the strap with the stopping of privileges for less heinous crimes, and expulsion reserved for bad language, gross misbehaviour and stealing.

'In 1926 at the time of the General Strike in Britain, the senior boys of fourteen and over went on strike. Two lay masters and four boys were expelled * "ek-dum". That put paid to that. I was twelve years old and terrified. Why go on strike? In retrospect school was good. Our physical and mental abilities developed and grew in a healthy and happy climate. Jesuits are educationists!'

Smoking figured as a flogging offence at Victoria Boys' School in Kurseong and as a junior there in 1914, Les Boalth recalls boys being flogged by the Head in front of the whole school. The culprits were usually senior school boys and their painful and humiliating chastisement 'deterred the little fellows like myself from trying to ape the adults.'

---

* Hindi: immediately

James Staines was a boarder at St George's College, Mussoorie, from 1917 to 1924, aged nine to sixteen. More familiarly known as Manor House, and established by the Irish Brothers of the Order of St Patrick in the 1850s, St George's gave boys an excellent education, with thrashings top of the disciplinary hit parade. In his absorbing account of his life in India, *Country Born*, Staines remembers that some Brothers were more humane than others, and recalls his many brushes with authority.

One in particular reveals the strain imposed upon the Head Master of the day by the high spirits of his charges. After a boyish prank in the classroom went awry and the 'cave' system broke down, the HM burst through the door. Trying to break up a conker fight in full flood, he grabbed the nearest conker and tried to smash it to smithereens on the desk, 'but he missed and caught his knee a crack. He then went beserk, laying about him with his cane, not caring on whom it landed or where.' The unfortunate man realised that he had over-reacted and immediately tried to make amends:

'He rummaged in his pocket, produced a five-rupee note, slammed it on his desk and was gone .... He was ashamed of his outburst and feared it might have unpleasant consequences for him if the matter were reported in the right quarter. But the bribe worked. The prospect of five rupees worth of "puri-tack" (Indian tuck) from Barlowganj bazaar made it easy to overcome any discomfort we might have suffered. He had behaved badly, but so had we.'

Up in the Lawrence Military School at Mount Abu in the early Thirties aged seven to twelve, Frank Hippman received his share of caning and the writing of lines

'for every little thing. I had the cane for literally blotting my copy book, and for knocking down mangoes and eating them. I knew of boys being caned for not eating the food, and girls caned for getting lost while on an organised walk. Three of us were once locked in a spare room for an afternoon while the rest of the school went out to watch a cricket match because we'd lost our cap badges, i.e. someone had thought it a bit of fun to pinch them.'

Another 'Lawrencian', actually a 'Sanawarian' at the famous Lawrence School in Simla's Sanawar hills, was Donald (Jock) Howie, who started his schooling at the school crèche in 1922 aged two and half, ending up as Head Boy when he left aged eighteen and a half in 1937. 'Corporal punishment was very much in vogue for boys, with detentions also imposed on Wednesday half-holiday afternoons. The girls' punishments consisted mainly of detentions.'

On leaving Sanawar Jock Howie went on to spend a year at BCS, Simla, where he prepared for his Inter-Arts exam in their College Department in order to gain a place at the Chelmsford Teacher Training College in Ghora Gali (Murree). The rest of his life was devoted to school mastering and he retired from teaching at a school in Taunton in the 1980s.

An older schoolmate of Jock Howie's, Harry Brisley, was at the school from 1923 to 1927 and he remembers an intensely military discipline pervading the school. He vividly recalls that

'we were controlled by bugle calls as well as bells. We were woken by the "Reveille" at 6 am, called to meals and to parade by the "Assembly" and ordered to bed by the "First Post" and the "Last Post." "Lights Out" was the last call at 9.30 pm.'

As we have seen, corporal punishment was the order of the day at Sanawar, and Harry Brisley remembers a perpetual feud between boys and staff, 'especially the military staff who were responsible for discipline.' During the cricket season at net practice, boys would get their own back

'if the CSM had been bloody-minded during parade that morning... He was left-handed and the bowler would bowl him a rising leg break on his leg stump which would invariably hit him on his right hip above his pads. He would know at once that the hit was intended and grabbing the spent ball in anger he would chase the bowler and fling the ball at him with all his might... The bowler, knowing what would happen, had already disappeared around the corner of the barrack in record time!'

The age old bugbear of fraternisation between the sexes was rife, too, at Sanawar.

'It was a caning offence just to look across the church aisle at the girls! Discipline was terribly enforced, so much so that I had come to think of the CSM as a sadist. He was literally hated by all the boys.'

At BCS, Bangalore, where Cecil Wilkins was a boarder from 1925 to 1933 aged nine to eighteen. He recalls

'mostly caning on the buttocks... The number of strokes varied from two to six and were for cheating at lessons, smoking, absenting oneself from games, stealing, bullying, bed wetting, low exam results, breaking Boarding House Rules and persistent use of bad language.'

In the late 1920s a boy who ran away from school

'was caught and caned before the whole school prior to being expelled. [... I realise how lightly I got off at Mount Hermon ...] The caning was inflicted by the janitor, a retired army sergeant, and the number of strokes this time was eight or ten.'

Boys late for meals were made to stand in the corner, chatterers during study periods had to stand on their chairs, and those who overstayed their exeats were gated.

Down at the Lawrence School at Lovedale in the Nilgiri Hills in South India, Ted Coulby was a pupil from 1924 to 1933, aged seven to seventeen. While he was at Lovedale, classroom misdemeanours merited the usual lines and detentions, with defaulters outside the classroom paying for their crimes with extra drill, window-cleaning and floor and wash-room cleaning. Inevitably, more heinous crimes were punishable by caning across the hands or on the clothed bottom.

Nearly 40 years later, when John Hudson was at my old alma mater, Mount Hermon, from 1960 to 1962, aged thirteen to sixteen, all this physical stuff seems light years away, as it does compared to my own almost 'cushy' school days in the 1940s. By the time John was at the school, it was being administered by Australian Baptists.

'Caning was very occasionally used but there were few problems – I think because the prefects who administered almost all discipline were elected by the students of the upper school and held almost universal respect because they clearly were not the creatures of the Head. I can't remember punishments as a serious problem; I think there was a system of black marks after which people lost privileges but it hardly impinged on me. I was a goody-goody.'

Prefects of the Lawrence School, Lovedale, 1944

Senior Girls at the Lawrence School, Lovedale, competing for the Netball Trophy, 1935; with the Headmaster, Rev R.W.Simpson.

To Eric Tyndale-Biscoe, founder and Principal of Sheikh Bagh Prep School for boys – and some girls – in Kashmir during the last war, discipline had to be inculcated from the word go. His famous father, Cecil Tyndale-Biscoe, later Canon, had transformed the CMS school for Kashmiri youths into a bastion of muscular Christianity, an incredible feat as the average Kashmiri youth was a Brahmin who viewed his fellow man as far beneath contempt, and to whom the Christian concept of brotherly love and assistance must have been totally alien. Eric Tyndale-Biscoe founded his own school not for his father's Kashmiri youths, although some Kashmiri boys did go to Sheikh Bagh, but for British expatriate children whose parents were in India during the war.

He wrote to these parents about his intention to start up the school in 1940 and was amazed and gratified to receive many enthusiastic replies. He records his high hopes for the school's future in his own book, *The Story of Sheikh Bagh:*

> 'So our chance had come. We should now be able to try out on British boys the methods of education that had been so successfully employed on Kashmiri boys for fifty years ... We intended to keep a very close association with the Mission School and hoped that by bringing British and Indian boys into contact we might help to overcome some of the prejudices that cause dislikes and animosities. From the start we were determined that there should be no discrimination about the boys we took. If Indian parents wished their boys to come to our school, we should welcome them. We knew that both British and Indian boys would be benefited by this association.'

Some years ago when I was in correspondence with Mr Tyndale-Biscoe, I asked whether his student roll included any Anglo-Indian boys. While he himself put no embargo on the entry of Anglo-Indians, none in fact applied. He cited a case where a Colonel of a British Regiment applied for his son to enter the school with the proviso that 'no Indian or Anglo-Indian boy shall be admitted to your school.' He regretfully replied that he could not comply with this proviso and would therefore not send an application form, whereupon the Colonel wired back for the form to be sent immediately! The story had a happy ending. The boy, later a Colonel in the army himself, went to Sheikh Bagh. Eric Tyndale-Biscoe confided that he often wondered whether the boy's father was putting him to the test. He was of the opinion that such prejudice was probably due to the age old fear of parents that their children would speak with a 'chi-chi' accent, and back in 1980 found this same prejudice about accents operating in New Zealand, where he was living, with some British immigrants horrified at their children speaking in New Zealand or 'Oz' accents.

To return to the early days of the school – Sheikh Bagh adopted the Mission School's crest and motto, 'In all things be men' and Tyndale-Biscoe was to follow this dictum to the letter. Athletics would play a great part in the curriculum with the object of developing boys physically and

> 'to train them to have a corporate spirit; to help them overcome timidity and to learn endurance... Our aim was to help every boy, and especially those who were not natural athletes. A boy may have no ball sense, and be a complete duffer at team games, but there is no reason why he may not be quite good on the water..... a stiff climb, or a long expedition on foot or cycle... It was to be a Christian school in the full meaning of that word, and as far as we were fitted to fulfil that object. Boys leaving us, we hoped, would have realised that Christianity is a glorious and happy, a difficult and dangerous life.... school was to be the preparation for life.'

Sheikh Bagh opened with 41 boys and five girls on October 23rd 1940 with carpenters, masons and blacksmiths interrupting lessons with their noise. But the founder was quite unprepared for the high spirits of his new charges. 'We never considered the possibility that boys could have become so wild and out of hand within a few months of leaving school in England.' Discipline was required and Tyndale-Biscoe had to choose the right methods of chastisement. He and his wife received a rude shock on the first morning to find a set of garden cushions reduced to feathers and rags scattered all over the lawn, and empty water bottles smashed for target practice. In his chapter 'The Bear Garden' he tells of his decision to tread gently at first, 'and that it would be unwise to try to break them with violence.' In this decision he was opposed by some older staff members,

> 'whose memories of school were that discipline and the cane were synonymous. A year or two later I came across the same mentality, when one of the parents criticised me for not permitting prefects to beat the smaller boys. He took his boy away from us soon afterwards, though whether for this reason or another, I do not know......

[If that parent had manged to conquer his abhorrence of the exisitng European schools in India, his son might well have received the thrashing he deserved at BCS, St Paul's, a Catholic boy's school or a Lawrence school, but, in all fairness, my researches have so far revealed no instance of caning by prefects.]

Later, Tyndale-Biscoe had a jug of water brought to him by a servant at supper time in which crusts of bread, butter and other oddments were floating about. The punishment was for the same jug to be put on the table at breakfast time, when he told the boys that this would constitute their mealtime drinks for the rest of the day. 'But, Sir, someone has spat in it,' left him unmoved.

'Whether the boys drank the concoction or not, I do not know... But the main thing was that we never had a similar case to deal with.'

Sheikh Bagh Preparatory School,:The 'Bear Garden' in December 1940
(From 'The Story of Sheikh Bagh' by E.D.Tyndale-Biscoe)

If a boy was unpunctual for a meal, he would miss the meal and Tyndale-Biscoe records, with no little satisfaction,

'This soon settled the problem... it had a miraculous effect on one boy who had evidently never gone without a meal in his life before.'

In this fashion Mr & Mrs Tyndale-Biscoe struggled on through the first two terms.

'It certainly wasn't the school of our dreams, but it was to be that
or nothing. We were going to win through with our methods, or
not at all.'

And win they did, with the majority of boys remembering their prep
school days at Sheikh Bagh as some of the happiest days of their
childhood, and testifying to this fact at many an old Sheikh Bagh
reunion. Eric Tyndale-Biscoe did ultimately have to resort to the cane
when all else failed, and one old boy remembers feeling 'unpleasantly
heroic but guilty afterwards.'

At Woodstock School, Landour, Mussoorie, from 1935 to 1940,
David Little remembers being whacked on the bottom with a ping
pong bat as his punishment for various misdemeanours, a far cry
from the canings he might have received as a boarder at 'Home.'
Transgressors would have to line up in the boys' hostel and two or
three not very hard whacks were administered in turn. Woodstock,
was founded in 1854 as a Protestant Girls' School and sold to the
Board of Foreign Missions of the Presbyterian Church of America in
1874. It eventually became coeducational, is essentially American in
character and to-day is run along the same lines as Kodaikanal
International School. Several of our American classmates at Mount
Hermon went on to Woodstock to continue their education before
returning home to the States.

One such was Gordon Hostetler, a student from 1948 - 1951. He
recalls demerits for untidy bed-making with three demerits
warranting a gating. Any more than that could result in an
interview with the Principal and possible expulsion. He recalls that
many of the older boys owned pistols and rifles for which he
presumes they had licences. Although the school authorities
appeared fairly tolerant about the school's 'gun culture', they were
jerked into drastic action when one of the boys fired shots through a
window over the the heads of staff. As a result all guns and
ammunition were called in and destroyed by immersing them in
boiling water! But both English David Little and American Gordon
Hostetler were aware of a fairly 'laid-back' attitude from officialdom
on the whole. Gordon was pleased not to have to wear uniform:

'We wore jeans or old army surplus clothes and when we were
given blazers and offered badges, only one person wanted a badge.'

180

David marvels at the trust placed by the teachers in the students:
'In English public schools even leisure activities were always supervised by masters but at Woodstock as long as you signed the book in the hostel and wrote where you were going and how long you would be, you were allowed to go off on your own - on trips to the bazaar (but girls had to be in groups or escorted), walks in the forest, hunting for beetles, sliding down the 'khuds', hunting animals and birds, swimming. I now realise how such an attitude established a sense of self-discipline and trust.'

Janet de Vries, nee Erskine, too, remembers a similar experience at Presentation Convent, Kodaikanal, in the 1940s:
'I was sent to school in England for a year, but was so desperately unhappy I begged to be allowed to return to PCK, which I did. The comparison was terrible: I was used to the freedom and trust of PCK whereas the schools in England seemed to be run on the very opposite principles.'

Jack Howie in the uniform of a Sanawarian boy, 1937

13

Leisure

Out of the classroom we were free to roam around the beautiful Mount Hermon Estate. There were walks and organised picnics to Black Rock, a huge rock down the 'khud' (hillside) leading to the tea gardens below; there was swimming in the 'swimming hole', the pool down at Fernhill where the boys lived. This was not an enjoyable experience in freezing water full of slimy weeds and amphibious creatures. Today there is an excellent modern swimming pool, the envy of other Darjeeling schools,[but water shortage means it is often out of use].

On our rambles we would collect beetles. Most memorable was the 'dung roller', who did just that. Another was the stag beetle with its little antlers which could nip the unwary quite painfully. But a favourite sport was catching 'croakers' (cicadas) as the unsuspecting creatures came to rest on a tree trunk. Poor things. I suppose we must eventually have opened up the match boxes in which they were incarcerated and given them their freedom.

One of the rituals we followed during our leisure time, usually before supper on fine summer evenings, was to walk round and round the main school buildings in twos and threes or in larger gangs. This was usually a segregated activity and the time for a little subtle flirting. We eyed the boys and they eyed us, with explosive guffaws from both sides. Not having had a steady boyfriend myself, this was the nearest I got to calf love. Some steadies walked round together, and were the subject of catcalls mixed with envy.

A highlight in the school year was our trip to Tiger Hill to wait for the sun to rise over Mount Everest. We would be called at around 2 am and trek in the inky darkness to the station, where we took the train to Ghoom. From Ghoom we continued our hike to Tiger Hill. The sun didn't always oblige, that is it certainly came up, but sometimes the mountains were shrouded in mist. But who cared? This was our most exciting outing, not to be missed. It was here that boyfriends and girlfriends could walk hand in hand in the gloaming under the eye of a benevolent teacher. And it was here that I actually walked hand in hand with a Parsee boy, a once only performance for both of us. When morning had broken we would go to the tea stall at Ghoom station and drink hot, sweet tea out of earthen 'chatties' (pots) before boarding the toy train for the return journey to school. Today this is a tourist attraction for visitors to Darjeeling, but it surely can't be as much fun as it was for us all those years ago.

Another event we looked forward to every year was Sale Day, held on the 17th May. We school kids took part in making items for various stalls, ably assisted by 'the Cottagers', the name we gave to the American missionary parents of our classmates who spent a large part of the year in the cottages of the school estate. We gobbled down their butterscotch and lemon meringue pies even faster than the illicit sweets we used to buy from Hafiz's shop up the road from school. And many of us were introduced for the first time to American hot-dogs and 'taffy', that delicious American candy which we, too, learnt how to make, organising our own 'taffy pulls'.

Once a month a 'Social' was held by and for the members of the Junior and Senior 'Christian Endeavour' groups in the Community House. This was all new to me. I'd heard of parties, but 'Socials' were quite beyond my previous experience of high jinks. We danced 'The Grand Old Duke of York', played 'Musical Chairs', 'Winks', 'Tails', 'Queen of Honesty' and 'Bangs', according to a list of games in an old school magazine of the period. 'Bangs' must have been the American version of 'Are you there, Moriarty?' when two people lie on the floor blindfold holding a long folded pad of newspaper each to whack the area where the answering voice came from. 'Winks' I do remember. The girls sat round in a circle with a boy behind each chair, with one boy behind an empty chair. When we got a wink from the spare boy, we'd rush over and sit in his chair before our own partner could stop us by holding us down. Very romantic and rough. At 9 o'clock we'd stuff ourselves with sandwiches, cakes and sweets, washed down with several stiff lime juices, followed by more games. The Music Department supplied the music on one memorable occasion in the shape of the Mount Hermon Jazz Band, and the evening would end with 'Good Night Ladies' and 'Merrily We Roll Along.' Ah me, such innocent fun. We loved every minute.

On the 24th May 1941 an 'Empire Day' concert was staged with songs and scenes from the British Isles and its Empire. I was a Scottish fisher girl in a group imploring the assembled company to 'Buy Our Caller Herring'. The audience was guided through the countries of the British Empire by an American boy in the guise of a Cook's Agent. Girls in sleighs sang 'Jingle Bells' in Canada, with others representing New Zealand in a Maori dance; a lifelike kangaroo stole the scene on a visit to an Australian homestead which included, inevitably, a spirited rendition of 'Waltzing Matilda'; my friend, the nascent Quantity Surveyor, gave a rumbustious recitation of 'Gunga Din' and is still trying to live it down; and so on, all over the Empire on which the sun was about to set, had we in our innocence been aware. The climax depicted Britain at war, with senior students resplendent in service uniforms (where did they come from?) in a march past to a stirring chorus of 'There'll Always Be An England'. 'Rule Britannia', according to a report in the school magazine, was a fitting climax to this patriotic occasion. The teachers and cottagers had worked themselves into the ground to put the show on, and the orchestra had rehearsed until all hours. We, the participants, were on cloud nine. The proceeds from the concert went to the Red Cross.

Things must have been a bit flat for us after the concert was over and there were no after school rehearsals to attend. But there were still plenty of things to do during our leisure hours. The school had its Cubs, Scouts, Bluebird and Guide organisations. There were no Brownies in India, some sensitivity being shown in the use of such a word in an Asian country. So the little girls joined the Bluebirds and flew up to the Guides when they came of age.

Despite the leisure pursuits available 'on campus', in most children's hearts the best possible goal was to have fun away from school. A school prospectus states that 'no pupil is permitted to leave the school premises unless accompanied by a parent or an authorised escort'. But I distinctly remember walks along the Cart Road into Darjeeling with not an adult in sight. As we got older we must have been put on our honour to behave responsibly if allowed out on our own, with one of our number taking the role of the 'authorised escort'. For earlier generations the cinema was taboo, but we were allowed an occasional visit to the 'flicks' to see Laurel &

185

Hardy or George Formby films. Rumour has it that a Methodist missionery teacher from an earlier era actually set foot in a Darjeeling cinema, and somebody 'snitched' on the unfortunate lady, with dire consequences. We were lucky enough to be at the school during the War years, bringing with them a more relaxed attitude.

One of our greatest thrills was to go to tea at Pliva's Restaurant, usually accompanied by a visiting parent or friend. Once I was even taken by a well-loved teacher as a treat (for good behaviour?). There were many such restaurants in India, usually owned and run by Swiss or Italians. (One of the most famous was Firpo's in Calcutta, the happy hunting ground for off-duty officers during the war, and mainly renowned for its night life. The prevailing snobbery of the period dictated that British Other Ranks were debarred from patronising Firpo's.) I would like to think that officialdom relaxed its attitude when serving men were on leave in Darjeeling, but a fading memory cannot recall any khaki-clad figures at Pliva's. The restaurant in our day (now re-named Glennary's) represented the archetypal teashop beloved by visiting parents treating their offspring in any town at Home boasting a nearby boarding school. Only the spinster ladies in their flowered overalls were missing, to be replaced by turbaned bearers in gleaming white coats, who watched over their young customers with the customary indulgence accorded to the 'babalog' (children) by their own bearers and ayahs.

Another way of getting away from school legitimately was by making use of the once a month visits to brothers or sisters at neighbouring schools. This was called 'Sister Sunday', although brothers were also at the receiving end of such visits. My brother would come down to see me, and I would go to see him at St Paul's in far off Jalapahar. We would compare notes about the horrors of school and on one memorable occasion our special twin relationship was demonstrated when we both discovered that we'd been kicked out of our respective gangs in the same week. We derived as much comfort as we could in the circumstances.

When our mother came up for a short break from Calcutta's heat, we were allowed out for the week-end to stay with her at Durley Chine, a refined boarding house run by 'Brooky, a formidable Irishwoman called Mrs Brooks. Then we knew real joy. Mornings were spent skating at the Gymkhana Club or going for rides on the Darjeeling 'tats' (ponies), and school seemed a million miles away, with only that sinking feeling on Sunday evening when it was time to take the taxi back.

There is no doubt that the authorities administering most of the schools in the foothills of India's mountain ranges and its plateaux towns did much to sweeten the pill of their pupils' nine-monthly incarceration at boarding school, particularly in the 20th century. Many encouraged inter-school entertainment, with Dow Hill and Victoria, Auckland House and BCS, attending each other's dances, and the majority gave their charges full rein to roam the forests around the schools. The boys' schools featured regular treks to the lower mountain peaks for their scouts and army cadet corps, with Sheikh Bagh in Kashmir introducing skiing in Gulmarg and boating on the nearby lakes.

Many hill stations experienced very wintry conditions towards the end of the school year, and Auckland House girls were allowed to skate on the frozen tennis courts at Blessington; in the summer months they would go on picnics to Petersfield, Mountain Home and Annandale. On a more sophisticated note, older girls went, chaperoned, to tea dances in the town.

The majority of schools granted month-end exeats for week-ends with visiting parents or day trips to town with a few schools allowing visits to town every Saturday. Win Ballantyne remembers that there was not much to do in Kurseong unless one could visit friends on a tea-garden,

'but we were allowed free rambling in the forest around the school when we were older. The flowers, trees and water courses were always a joy. In 1925 my cousin and I were allowed to ride from school over the Begora range down to the Teesta Valley to stay the week-end with family friends at the Cinchona Plantation at Mungpoo'.

And at Dow Hill the girls were encouraged to don their pretty dresses and put bows in their hair for the inter-school dances with the Victoria boys.

'We foxtrotted and waltzed, did the Lancers and Quadrilles to the music provided by good dance pianists (obliging souls), and looked forward to the refreshments served during the evening.'

This sounds the height of sophistication compared with our socials at Mount Hermon, and the only dancing we did took place illicitly behind the stage curtains in the Assembly Hall when the girls pushed the boys round in a vain effort to teach them to dance. This was during the monsoon when the torrential rain drove us indoors. I never got the chance to dance as I was one of the 'good souls' at the piano, bashing out 'In the Mood' or a 'funky' (jazzed-up) version of 'What a friend we have in Jesus'.

Denise Coelho was not quite so enthusiastic about the Dow Hill dances, and dreaded being 'the target for the less adept dancers among the nervous young Victoria bucks.' She was more interested in the refreshments handed around by the boys, especially samosas, 'those tasty triangles of puff pastry filled with curried potatoes and peas... Anything we were unable to consume in the hall we carried off triumphantly to the dormitory for a feast after lights out.' In her day there was also the occasional visit to Kurseong's 'flea-pit' cinema, 'The Globe', accompanied by a mistress. The girls' unruly behaviour on one occasion when the film broke down several times resulted in the party being marched out of the cinema. 'We never saw the film we'd so looked forward to and instead it was a long and sorry three-mile hike back uphill for all of us.'

Nearly all schools had a ten-day or fortnight's holiday in July and October (the Pujas). A few lucky pupils went down to the plains to stay with their families, but the schools usually organised picnics and other delights for those left behind. Ian Bristow, a boarder at St Joseph's College, North Point, Darjeeling, vividly remembers 'the Ocs' of the early 1940s. 'Even when they fell in September they were still called "the Ocs" except by one small, logically-minded boy who insisted on calling them "the Seps".' The priests and lay staff worked hard to make 'the Ocs' memorable. Huts made of matting were constructed on the hockey pitches of the lower school, each with a hole in the middle of its roof to let out the smoke from the cooking fires.

'The only things we cooked were toffee or fudge. Toffee was made of boiled sugar and poured into greased enamel plates; fudge was made in the same way except that condensed milk replaced the water. Clearly two weeks like this would not only lead to boredom but also ruin the teeth for life, so "field days" as they were called, only took place every other day...'

Alternate days were spent on picnics to well-known places, including a trip to see Mount Everest, 'but it was always hidden.' Some boys took spare shorts with them and swam in the deep 'nullahs' (rain drains 3 feet wide by 3 feet deep) at the roadsides, which had filled with water through blockages, 'only crawl or backstroke, as they were too narrow for breaststroke. The water was always cold and swimming was sheer bravado and never enjoyed.' [These 'nullahs' would overflow in the monsoons, and I am told that a little boy holding his mother's hand was swept away forever when the water burst out from an overflowing drain – and this in the 1950s. Darjeeling seems to suffer even more now with landslides and avalanches brought about by deforestation.]

'The food at the "Spadgies'" picnics was carried by bearers, and the priests always wore their white cassocks on picnic days. The organisation was superb... games were organised... coloured hard-boiled eggs hidden beforehand had to be found... there was swimming in a reservoir... The return home was less well organised, tired legs were allowed their own pace home, but even the youngest had an incentive to get back to school quickly as in the evening there was the "flicks".'

Film shows on the school's own 32 mm sound projector took place every night during 'the Ocs'. Ian Bristow can still quote the names of the 'latest' films he saw: Errol Flynn in 'The Sea Hawk' and 'Dodge City; Tyrone Power in 'Captain Blood'; Freddie Bartholomew and Spencer Tracy in 'Captains Courageous'; Mickey Rooney in 'Boys' Town'. The lights went on after every reel, but the excited filmgoers found this no hardship as it provided an opportunity to prize out their toffee from the enamel plates.

'Spadgie' parents would have been shocked to know of their sons' adventures in the dangerous nullahs, as would so many parents of children at other hill boarding schools. On our many hikes at Mount Hermon, we, too, took risks. Looking back at my younger self, I am horrified to think that we used to drink from any little brooks we came across, repositories of all manner of rubbish chucked there by the Bhutia and Nepalese villagers, no doubt including untreated sewage, to put it politely.

June Wallin née Anderson was a boarder during my time at Mount Hermon, and came to the school from Assam, where her

American parents worked among the primitive Naga people as Baptist missionaries. June was used to an adventurous life in Assam riding pillion through the jungle on her father's Harley Davidson motor-bike. She recalls hiking to the Rangeet river via the tea-gardens below our school before the monsoon broke in 1941. The trip down was fun, sliding through the tea-gardens and getting blisters, because no-one owned "Reeboks" in those days.

'We ate our lunch while dipping our sore and tired feet in the river. Coming back up the mountain was another story because we had used up our drinking water and the heat was intense. We begged oranges off the Nepalis carrying them to market and decided to stop for water at one of the tea-garden estates. The Englishman in charge invited our tired, hot bodies in for tea. What a delight – even a cake from Pliva's. Later when we told Mrs Dewey (the Principal's wife) about it, she said he'd been a recluse for ages, ever since his wife left him and went home to England. He clearly enjoyed our company.'

In the 1920s, MHS boys living down in their Fernhill dormitories 'had no bounds', as one of them, David Francis, recalls,

'provided we were at all meals, prep etc. or at a week-end told the matron (who provided the sandwiches) where we were going and that we would not be back for tea. We often hiked to the Tukvar tea estate to pay a courtesy call on the Manager and discuss our route with him. And he always left orders with his staff to give us a cold drink if ever we called when he was out.'

The Scouts, too, made two trips a year through the foothills and higher, including Sandakphu, Phalut and Gangtok, where the troop covered 100 miles in seven days.

'We swam in water draining from the Kurseong hills down to the plains, in the Rangeet and the bitterly cold Teesta (from the ice of Kinchinjunga) and collected butterflies on our way.'

Today's conservationists would probably be appalled to learn that Fernhill boys once went on an orchid-hunting foray at the behest of their matron. She bribed them with a prize of 'gur' (lumps of raw sugar) according to the quality, quantity and scarcity of the plants found. The boys responded by 'culling' nearly every orchid in the forest areas around Fernhill, even climbing the tallest trees with an ingenious system of pulleys attached to their weighted tin trunks. They then carefully re-planted the orchids outside the dormitory where the Matron hoped they would entwine themselves around a rustic fence.

On a more urbane note, students who attained a certain monthly scholastic standard were allowed to go to the pictures in Darjeeling on a Monday night, which made them swagger with pride as the only schoolboys at the cinema. This kind of concession from Methodist missionary teachers as long ago as the 1920s is impressive, as we 1940s 'Hermonites' were – erroneously – of the opinion that school life before us was much more strait-laced.

As a schoolboy at St Paul's, Darjeeling, 1940/41, Theon Wilkinson, who arrived there from his public school, Radley, remembers a privileged existence during his leisure time. As a senior, aged 16, he was eligible for frequent exeats into town, and his letters home describe many a blow-out at Pliva's for lunch and tea. His father had friends in high places and the young Theon used to drop in to Government House for tennis and tea or squash and lunch. His weekly letters home also included meticulous accounts of the films he'd seen, viz. 'Bachelor Mother' with Ginger Rogers – 'nothing special'; 'The Gang's all here' with Jack Buchanan and Syd Walker, and 'Let George do it' with George Formby in the starring role.

SPS boys, too, did their share of trekking and camping with the school's cadet corps. After one particularly gruelling exercise, Wilkinson assured his parents that although he'd enjoyed it on the whole, 'the trek to camp was hellish, carrying rifles and sliding down khud sides.' The boys slept on the floor of an empty bungalow, paraded all morning, carried out manoeuvres and had a 14 mile march uphill from 3,000 to 7,000 feet, returning to school exhausted.

John Walker makes the sad little comment that at the Lawrence School at Ghora Gali in the 1940s here was not much time for leisure between classes and sport and 'what spare time that was left to us seemed to be taken up mainly by finding ways and means of curing hunger'. The school did, however, run an annual Founder's Day dance, 'well-supervised, and occasionally arranged visits to the cinema in Murree.'

191

(Photographer: L.C. 'Kim' Taylor)
On a trek from St. Paul's, Darjeeling 1941

'Fours' on the lake – St. Joseph's College, Naini Tal

14

Sex, Drugs and Rock 'n' Roll

15

Games

Before coming to the organised games we played, I must dwell for a moment on a weird game called 'Gooli Danda'. This is probably the same as 'Tippy Cat' in England, now no longer popular. 'Gooli Danda' was played by hitting a small bobbin-shaped piece of wood about four inches long with a heftier stick. You placed the bobbin on a raised mound of hard earth, whacked one end of it with the larger stick and when it was in the air gave it an almighty thwack. You gained points according to how far you managed to hit the bobbin. One of the girls in a class above me was a champion 'Gooli Danda' player. Her two long blonde plaits swinging, she could whack that 'gooli' for terrific distances and we all practised hard to reach her exacting standard. She was even better than some of the boys. (Weren't you, Frances Ghey?)

Hill schools in India were as besotted with games as were their counterparts at Home. *Mens sana in corpore sano* and 'Play up! play up! and play the game!' vied with each other in importance, particularly in boys' schools. At Mount Hermon, these manifestations of the public school ethos were not always apparent, but I think the 'healthy mind in a healthy body' bit played its part. This is not to say that we were unsportsmanlike, but that those who weren't particularly keen on games weren't made to feel like lepers.

There was, of course, the house system at MHS In our day the girls' houses were Windsor, Tudor and York and the boys' were Wesley, Fisher and Swan, a happy Anglo-American compromise. Wesley took its name from the great Methodist preacher, Fisher from Bishop Frederick Fisher, the American Methodist Bishop who had played such a major role in the establishment of Mount Hermon School in the 1920s, and Swan was after the American Swan family, notably Charles L Swan. Dr Swan joined the Kindergarten at MHS in 1914, later completing his education at the well-known Philander

Smith School in Naini Tal, with higher education in the States. He returned to Mount Hermon in 1929 and taught there until 1936. His younger brothers, too, were students there in the 1920s and 1930s. Charles Swan is now 85 and as enthusiastic as ever about his MHS connections. An accomplished musician and singer, he will always be remembered for the many 'Going Home Day' songs he composed, particularly for 'Old Walls are Friendly Walls', the song we used to sing at the end of the school year which reduced school-leavers to tears. Today the houses are Fisher, Dewey (after our own beloved Principal, the Reverend Halsey E Dewey, 1938-42, 1945-47 and 1951-53), Knowles after Miss Emma Knowles, Founder and Principal 1895-1915 and Stahl (after Miss Carolyn Stahl, Principal 1918-29), with boys and girls unseparated.

In our day there were house as well as inter-school matches for the girls in hockey, tennis, basketball and badminton, although the basketball remained inter-house as we were the only girls playing this exciting game. The boys, too, had inter-house and inter-school matches in hockey, tennis, cricket and football. They came late to basketball, long after it was an established sport for girls, which seems strange when one considers that basketball has always been a popular sport for men in America. Rugger was out as far as any of the boys' hill schools was concerned. The ground was too hard.

Inter-school rivalry was greater amongst the boys than the girls, MHS boys' teams keenly contesting those from St Paul's and St Joseph's in football particularly. I don't think our boys were all that hot at cricket. But boys' hockey matches were a joy to watch. A few of the teams had Nepalese boys in them, some of whom even played barefoot. Their skill and agility in commanding the ball was legendary, and it all looked very rough to us girls, although our school teams usually put up a good show with visiting teams from other girls' schools.

I have a vivid recollection of a team coming to play us at hockey from the New School, a wartime school established in Darjeeling in 1941 for English children called back from Home. Naturally, we rather resented this cult of exclusivity and were also intimidated by it. So overcome was I to be walking along with a New School young lady that when she accidentally dropped her hockey stick as we were leaving the pitch, I hastily picked it up for her and stammered,

'Oh, I'm so sorry, ' as if I'd dropped it myself. Our team beat them that day, 1-0.

Athletics, too, played an enormous part in our sporting activities. Apart from our own school Sports Day, MHS athletes used to take part in the 'District Sports Day', an annual event in which all the Darjeeling schools competed. Our boys and girls won many track events and it may have been their keen sense of rivalry with the boys within the school which resulted in MHS girls carrying off many of the prizes in competition with single sex schools such as Loreto Convent and St Michael's Diocesan Girls School. An element of tomboyism probably helped.

While watching a TV programme featuring cheer-leaders at an American football game, I thought of my own school days and wondered fleetingly why MHS, an American-run school, had never thought of introducing this rah-rah element at athletic events as a spur to our teams. Perhaps the British element on the staff served as a brake to such excesses! However, I note from an ex-teacher's reminiscences in a special historical edition of the school magazine, that he, an American, had indeed introduced the idea in the 1950s. The Reverend W W Jones served at the school as Vice-Principal from 1973-77, but as a young teacher twenty years before he decided to put his plan into action during a District Sports Day:

'We came to the finals one year, and I made problems for the District Sports Association by preparing the whole school for American-style cheering, complete with drums, horns, tin cans and lids to be beaten, and organized cheers completely distracting the opponents. Unfortunately this hulla also distracted the officials, who had to stop play until I would agree to stop the din.'

This informal attitude towards games and sport was also alive and well at Woodstock School, Mussoorie, at school sports displays. In the late 1940s and early 1950s Gordon Hostetler and his fellows would display their pride in not being regimented by not walking in straight lines. 'We hated "to be all posh"', he recalls. And David Little remembers that ten years earlier the only games he played at Woodstock were basketball, baseball and hockey, with cricket and football conspicuously absent.

Girls' schools had their fair share of games such as hockey, netball (rarely lacrosse), basketball, badminton and tennis, as well as gymnastics and track sport. Some schools were not as well-equipped as others with hockey pitches or tennis courts and had to go to venues away from the school. On reflection, it seems strange that fair play and esprit de corps were never thought as important for girls as they undoubtedly were for boys.

The schoolboy teams of the 'Anglo-Indian' boarding schools in India attained an extremely high standard. From the 1920s to the 1940s, for instance, many old boys – English, Anglo-Indian and Indian – went on to represent their countries in international matches abroad, including the Olympics. Both Anglo-Indian boys as well as girls were excellent hockey players, some of whom starred in international matches. Sports Days, inter-school matches and athletics competitions were highlights in every school's calendar. There was never any lack of teams to play against and learn from, with British Army teams and Planters XIs always willing to turn out for matches, however distant. Boys from the hill boarding schools would travel down to the plains for important matches against well-known schools such as La Martinière and St Xavier's in Calcutta. Theon Wilkinson was in the St Paul's Cricket XI in 1940 when the team went down to play against La Martinière in Calcutta. They travelled down to Siliguri on an ancient, swaying bus 'and five boys were sick', where they transferred to the Bengal Express in an intermediate class compartment with 15 bunks. They all had a bad night 'due to insects after the Divali festival' (myriads attracted by all the lights).

Such visits offered other bonuses: the boys swam in the La Martinière pool after nets practice, shopped at Calcutta's New Market and – you've guessed it – went to the 'flicks'. They rolled into bed in the La Martinière dormitory at 10 pm (which at that time had 60 boarders and 250 day boys) and played the match the next day, rounding off the day's excitement with yet another film at one of Calcutta's plush, air-conditioned cinemas. On Sunday they attended church at St Paul's Cathedral and roamed round the market again (no Sunday closing for those astute traders). Then it was back to the cinema in the the afternoon to see a cowboy film, followed by an evening service at the Cathedral lasting one and a half hours. After supper the SPS team boarded 'the big train' at Sealdah station for their return trip.

The Lawrence schools, too, placed a great emphasis on games. Oliver Brisley, at the LRMS in Sanawar for 10 years in the 1920s and early 1930s says,

> 'Ours was a cricketing school – our Principal was a fanatic – and to be awarded one's Colours for the 1st Eleven was to be one of the Gods.'

The boys of the team were decked out in new Viyella shirts, white flannels and blazers, with a red and white sash to wear around the waist. The blazers were piped in red, and an all white cap completed the ensemble, which was supplied by the school, the pupils paying nothing. For players who produced above average performances, the letter LRMSCC were embroidered (by the girls) on the peak of the cap.

> 'During the season the 1st Eleven played at least two all-day games a week against various touring Indian Club teams, and once a year a combined staff and boys' team played against the Maharaja of Patiala's team at his summer residence at Chail. We had to go by rail to one of the stations on the way to Simla and there we were met by a fleet of Rolls Royces and driven to the top of the mountain to the guest houses. The Maharaja had had the top of the mountain sliced away and made a beautiful cricket ground surrounded by trees, the highest cricket ground in the world. This trip was a great treat for the boys as not only were we treated as Pukkah Sahibs and enjoyed lovely and plentiful food, but we had the opportunity of playing against top class cricketers, some of whom had played or were still playing Test cricket for India.'

The Second World War threw up some opportunities for schoolboys to experience the thrill of pitting their skills against the expertise of older sportsmen in matches against soldiers on leave. Les Paul recalls the arrival of a battalion or two of the famous Chindits who came up to a temporary camp at Jharipani to rest after the Burma Campaign. The Oak Grove School football team were beside themselves with delight when they beat the Chindits hands down, but 'the situation was soon reversed when we challenged them to cricket not knowing that they had one or two county players. They had us fielding all week-end for about three wickets so the score was even in the end!'

Schoolchildren in Panchgani (literally five tables or tablelands), a semi-hill station some 4,300' above sea level in the Western Ghats of the State of Maharashtra, would play their games on Tableland, the largest of the five 'tables' which had been set aside to provide playing fields for the various schools in the area and many exciting cricket, football and hockey matches would take place. Zbyszek Plocki, a boarder at St Peter's School from 1943 to 1947, remembers wonderful evenings on Tableland, which was reached by climbing a hill and going through a cave known as the Devil's Kitchen. But the young schoolboy, precipitated by World War II into an environment totally different from that of his native Poland was far more struck by the beauty of his surroundings than by how many runs were scored or goals kicked. In the monsoon rains Tableland would fill with water and become a huge lake, visible for miles around. During the Festival of Gumpati Ganesh, the elephant god, the local population would fashion mud statues of Ganesh and float them in little illuminated baskets on the lake, a magical scene which the adult Zybszek can still conjure up to remind him of his schooldays in Panchgani.

Sports and games mad were those 'Anglo-Indian' public schools in India, and this obsession can be said to have sprung from the Christian gentlemen who left England to promote the ideology of a healthy mind in a healthy body in Queen Victoria's fast expanding Empire. Just such a one was Bishop J E C Welldon, called to the Bishopric of Calcutta in 1899 'with the express purpose of welding together the British Empire and the Church.' He had been Headmaster of Harrow School from 1881 to 1895 and preached the gospel of empire-building via fair play and esprit de corps to all who would listen. While in India he played a large part in the promotion of the public school ethos into the 'public schools' set up in India's hill stations and larger cities on the plains, just as his eminent predecessor, Bishop Cotton, had done during his short time in India 40 years before him. But Cotton's brilliance in setting up the schools had more to do with his Christian no nonsense approach to education than Welldon's credo of games being the making of manly chaps and empire-builders.

But many headmasters in India emulated Welldon's example. Cricket became the game of games. Most schoolboys enjoyed it for its own sake. Few of them could have realised that the game they loved was actually a stepping stone to their future success in life. Not many of those boy cricketers became empire-builders. In his excellent and witty book, *The Games Ethic and Imperialism*, J A Mangan quotes a poem by Donald Hughes entitled 'The Short Cut', from Leslie Frewin's *The Poetry of Cricket: An Anthology* which admirably sums up, albeit facetiously, the establishment thinking of the period:

THE SHORT CUT

In Queen Victoria's golden day,
Beneath the mild and settled rule,
The grand old game I used to play,
With decent chaps in a public school.

And I soon found out as I played the game,
That you need not score a large amount,
But the shortest cut to the heights of fame
Is to get to know the chaps who count.

In Oxford's fields, I found it true,
For the Captain was my closest friend,
And so I acquired my Cricket Blue,
Though I always batted near the end.

It is good to bowl with an action high
Or to smite the leather hard and far,
But it's better to wear the proper tie
And to keep your end up at the bar.

Leave lesser men to their golf-clubs then
Or to play with racquets and a net.
For this is the game for gentlemen
Till on our race the sun shall set.

The greatest glory of our land
Whose crimson covers half the maps
Is in the field where the wickets stand
And the game is played by DECENT CHAPS.

(Photographer: L.C. 'Kim' Taylor)

Lucy guarding topees while the Paulites play

16

Grub

The thought of food was always uppermost in every mind. We moaned a lot about school grub but it was a question of never mind the quality, feel the width. Breakfast was fairly basic with 'sooji' porridge, which I can only describe as creamed grit, followed by doorsteps of bread and butter. It seems unbelievable now, but if one's parents paid extra, their little darling could have an egg for breakfast! Darjeeling hens were no great layers, and those that did laid very expensive eggs. I seem to remember being the recipient of a minute pullet's egg from time to time, usually the consistency of the inside of a golf-ball, and smelling like a science lab experiment. Another token of a parent's love was the despatch of the occasional food parcel which included the famous IXL tins of jam which the lucky ones could spread on their doorsteps. A peculiarly watery, ginger-coloured tea accompanied the meal, a noxious brew which had nothing in common with the renowned Darjeeling teas we were to savour in adulthood.

Our main meals of lunch and supper followed the pattern of stews whose provenance was not immediately apparent, curry and rice, chops etc., with vegetables. We seemed to eat quantities of sweet potatoes – perhaps they were cheap and in good supply. An MHS colleague tells the story of the school dog hovering under one of the boys' tables for scraps, only to turn away in disgust after an exploratory lick at some gooey spinach, upon which the boy offering the delicacy was caught by the teacher on duty and made to consume it, dog lick and all!

My favourite dishes were 'aloo' chops and 'kofta' curry. The chops were actually a kind of rissole made of mashed potato and mince, and we called the curry 'ball curry' on account of the little ping-pong balls of curried mince it resembled. 'Dahl' (lentils) was also served regularly and I loved it. Today lentils and rice are considered very healthy whole-foods, so we must have thrived on it. The bearers would rush about the dining room carrying plates skilfully balanced along their arms almost into their armpits. We were also allowed second helpings and signalled our needs with cries of 'Walrus (the old mustachioed bearer's nickname), extra, extra!' If we were still empty after the meal, we would make potato sandwiches to take out with us, and trade pudding for bread. Bread was in constant demand and during sung grace ('Be present at our table Lord') the air was alive with hisses of 'Bags I your bread' before anyone else could get in first. A friend of mine who had spent some of his schooldays at St Joseph's Catholic school up the hill from us tells me he's hard put to stop himself whispering 'Bags I your bread' as he eyes the rolls on his companions' plates when attending a private dinner or public function. Thousands of hill boarding school children will know just what he means. Our diets were supplemented with the delicious fruit we used to buy from itinerant fruit sellers – oranges, pomelos, custard apples, passion fruit, mangoes, guavas, plantains, to name a few. I can still see a child sitting in the playground eating an orange in slow motion surrounded by envious friends begging for the tiniest piece: 'Come on Mun, gimme a flake...'

Another treat to take our minds off what we considered a starvation diet was the ritual of sucking at a tin of condensed milk, either purchased from Hafiz or amongst tuck parcel goodies. You punched two holes in the tin, lay on your white-counterpaned bed and sucked the gooey nectar out of the tin. The very thought now makes me want to 'frow-up', but we were never sick.

We also bought Indian sweets and curry puffs * (Indian restaurants have metamorphosed them into samosas today but they'll always be curry puffs to me) from itinerant box-wallahs, gradually building up our immunity to the tummy bugs so prevalent in India but to which we rarely succumbed.

Curry puffs notwithstanding, our school diet must have been the right one for growing children as we stayed generally healthy apart from the usual childish epidemics of measles, ordinary and German, chicken pox, mumps, etc., which every school in the world has to

---

* Purists have pointed out that curry puffs and samosas are two different things.

cope with. At the first sign of the dreaded spots, swollen glands or other telltale symptoms, we were packed off to the Isolation Hospital above the quad where we stuck things out until we were better. The fact that we were supposed to be in quarantine didn't stop our friends from flinging up food parcels (sometimes the inevitable slices of bread) or fruit to us from the quad below to be fielded by us from our vantage point on the path in front of the hospital. I suppose it was all right as long as we didn't send any germ-laden empties back.

In those days diphtheria was still a pretty deadly disease and it hit the school every so many years. I can remember lining up with the whole school to have our throats swabbed. The Civil Surgeon of Darjeeling had decreed that there was a carrier in our midst. The poor girl was eventually identified and the necessary medical steps taken, but there was inevitably a kind of stigma attached to her after that.

We also had to have our injections against cholera and typhoid – I don't remember any precautions taken against malaria – and the after effects, as so many jet travellers of today will confirm, were sometimes very nasty.

Even in the comparatively enlightened 1940s, the custom of purging for whatever complaint persisted and we were dosed with castor oil or the dreaded 'mag. sulph.' for the slightest reason.

I see from an old prospectus that dental inspections were made annually, but I can't remember opening wide, or even going to the dentist. A dentist in Darjeeling was certainly visited by some of my friends as their horror stories readily testified, but perhaps I was one of the lucky ones. Not according to my current dentist. He makes rude remarks every six months at the overcrowding of my bottom teeth, adding that it could all have been sorted out when I was 10 or 11. Perhaps the school dentist was only looking for holes or rotten teeth – overcrowding was probably not considered a threat in those days.

The girls who had reached puberty had to cope with their periods, something which I, apparently physically retarded, didn't have to face until I was well into my teens at home in England. The poor things had to bring homemade sanitary towels up to school, which were placed in special bags for the 'mehtarani' (female sweeper) to bash the living daylights out of. At least the girls were spared the task of washing their soiled linen themselves. 'Kotex' was an exciting and daring word we saw in magazine adverts, and would probably have bunged up the loos anyway. There was a distinct coyness about the whole menstrual business, and I remember long conversations in the dormitory as to whether one should sit down in the bath when one had 'it' with some declaring that even washing one's hair was very dangerous! I counted myself lucky that I wasn't yet an 'old girl'.

Feeding active, hungry 'kids' at hill schools must have presented the catering staff with many problems. Not only did they have to buy the raw materials, but they had to ensure their transformation into edible meals. Indian cooks have always been noted for their ingenuity, which was probably taxed to the full when catering for large numbers in limited kitchen space with few labour-saving devices. There were, of course, many willing hands in the shape of the numerous other servants available – cook boys, 'jhampanis', etc.

A few schools stuck to typically British menus with, as we have seen from the memories of AHS girls, good, filling stodge making regular appearances. Others attempted a mixture of East and West with varying degrees of success. Some schools could supplement the diet with fruit from their own orchards, with others serving butter made in their own dairies, or meat from their own farm stock, but this was rare.

Colvyn Haye remembers English food at Sherwood College, Naini Tal, 'and by that I mean nauseating stews, pallid roasts, bangers and mash, Welsh rarebits, mince with mashed potatoes, treacle and toast, occasional meat and vegetable pies, and sickening sago and 'soojee' puddings with lumps in them.'

He also recalls delicious curries, dahl and rice on high days and holy days, much appreciated by him but looked down upon by a xenophobic comrade. The latter's 'Must we really eat this Indian muck?' resulted in the table prefect's perfect put-down that if he really couldn't face it, the boy next to him should have his plate.

Colvyn Haye's brother, Douglas, also a boarder at Sherwood from 1938 to 1942 recalls his luck as a music student in receiving a surprise supplement to the school fare.

'Boys studying piano and theory of music under the direction of their brilliant and revered music master, George Thompson ('Than' pronounced 'Tharn' to the boys), had been finding it somewhat difficult to wake early enough to present themselves at the Music Block for piano practice at 6 a.m. The problem was solved by the inducement of a mug of sweet, steaming cocoa and biscuits served in the Music Block by Than's faithful bearer only for those arriving on time - a bit of extra grub that not only got us out of bed, but which made music practice a much sought after experience ...'

Many schools followed the practice of serving 'chota hazri' (little breakfast) very early, between 6.30 and 7.30 am, followed by 'burra hazri' (large ditto) at 10.30 or 11 am. 'Chota' was usually frugal – just tea with bread and 'scrape'. The later breakfast was a strange feast, which could include a cereal followed by a hot dish such as fish or meat loaf, even curry and rice, the curries made from meat, vegetables, eggs or fish. Byron MacNabb, an American at St Joseph's Darjeeling, from 1919 to 1926, remembers this dietary pattern 'with an afternoon meal of a meat, potato and vegetable course plus a second course of curry, with fruit for desert.' Down at Breeks in Ooty in the early 1940s, Peter Butler was offered a small hen's egg or a large duck's egg at Sunday breakfasts, and remembers 'bubble and squeak' being served with monotonous regularity.

From her wartime schooldays at the Nazareth Convent in Ootacamund, Pamela Rye (née Humphreys) remembers 'raji' porridge which tasted like chocolate sand. (A near relative of the creamed grit 'sooji' served at Mount Hermon?)

Lunches were served around noon if there had been only one breakfast, and as late as 2-3 pm for those who'd consumed a 'burra hazri.' Again, lunch was a fairly substantial meal.

Jane Erskine found the school grub perfectly edible at both her 'little' school, St Mary's, Kotagiri, and the Presentation Convent in Kodaikanal where she was a pupil from 1951 to 1955 and again in 1960/61. 'I look back on everything as being delicious,' she says. 'Certain dishes were memorable – lots of curry and pepper water which I've never had anywhere again. I don't remember hating anything.' She seems to have been spared the unspeakable 'sooji' or 'raji' porridge, the stews of doubtful provenance and the inedible puds.

Tea at most schools usually took place any time between 3 and 5 pm, consisting of bread and butter with the inevitable black treacle, or IXL and homemade jam from parents' tuck parcels. The last meal of the day was supper around 6 pm, substantial or fairly light according to the balance of previous meals, and this could include soup or dahl and rice. St Michael's schoolgirls in Darjeeling used to sing, 'There is a happy school far, far away, where they have dahl and rice three times a day.'

Zbyszek Plocki was struck by what he now calls the very formal 'nuttiness' of evening meals in the 1940s at St Peter's Boys' School in Panchgani. Boys had to be properly dressed including ties and jackets, and every table had a figure of authority at its head (prefect, Matron or member of staff). He remembers the food as being of a high standard, and in the background was a softly playing radio, usually American jazz or swing music. Mail was distributed at lunchtime and if the envelopes contained money, this was taken away and equivalent chits were given out for the purchase of tuck from the box-wallah who was allowed into the school compound. This removal of hard cash was to prevent boys from sneaking into Panchgani town to spend it. Town was out of bounds because of the danger of catching the plague. Rats were very prevalent in the area and the authorities came to the school on more than one occasion in order to rid it of rats! The boys did not mind having their money converted into chits with the box-wallah as, apart from the usual favourite sweetmeats and imported chocolates, he used to sell American sea rations comprising 2 or 3 cigarettes, chewing gum, the ubiquitous Spam, Herschey chocolate bars, cheese, condensed milk and instant coffee.

Kenneth Kendall, at Hebron in the early 1930s as a pre-prep schoolboy, still recalls that curry was a special treat, 'and we had to eat it in the proper way, with our fingers off plantain leaves.' Twenty years later, Alison Beresford, too, loved the mulligatawny and rice they had on Sundays, and recalls another so-called treat, 'Malabar pudding'.

'But it wasn't very nice – cold tapioca (inevitably called "frogs' eggs") stuck together like a blancmange with thick brown molasses over the top. Our real favourite was a big stodge pudding called "Caleb's Hat", named after one of the bearers.'

On their way to the dining room the hungry boarders would pass a large tub of greens soaking in water rippling with drowning beasties, and if they looked up at one of the dining room walls, they could ponder at the message it bore: 'And be ye thankful.' Edward Dance, a contemporary of Kenneth Kendall's, found the school fare 'all right' except for the Thursday menu when there was a 'brown pudding' (a forerunner to 'Caleb's Hat?'), a kind of boiled suet pudding. 'I remember spending a whole lunch time sitting in front of it, without submitting and eating it.'

In some schools, sweet potatoes were regularly used instead of the normal variety, and pumpkin appeared in various guises, dressed up as a sweet or forming the basis of a curry. This ubiquitous gourd seems to have been universally loathed.

John Walker at the Lawrence School, Ghora Gali, in the 1940s remembers horrible stews consisting of 'jhits' (tough, gristly, fatty meat) served with spuds and 'deceivers' "turnips, which we were deceived into thinking were spuds until the first bite."

At BCS, Bangalore, Cecil Wilkins found the food good, wholesome and generally tasty. He disliked vermicelli, used in many schools in soups or as a breakfast cereal, 'because it looked like worms.' But he loved the yellow coconut rice and curry served on alternate Sundays, and the crisp jam tart for supper on Tuesdays. (I marvel again at such total recall as to the exact day on which certain meals were served, even at a distance of 65 years!)

Oliver Brisley, a Sanawarian of 60 years ago, found the food pretty awful. 'We never saw an egg and "ghee" (Indian cooking fat) was substituted for butter.' Ted Coulby, at the Lawrence School at Lovedale, Ooty, remembers the diet as basic, repetitive, inadequate and frequently unpalatable. Favourites were puddings and tarts, and most loathed was the weekly meal of curry and rice.

'All of us knew what a good curry should taste like. School cooks, although Indian, made curry without ever frying the spice ingredients! The result was a weak curry powder-flavoured soup in which floated pieces of the toughest beef that you've ever experienced.'

One never knew what one would find floating about in a curry. At Woodstock, Gordon Hostetler remembers coming across the jawbone of a goat, and one particularly memorable year there were weevils in the macaroni as well as in the dreaded 'sooji' porridge. (Indignant Woodstock readers must remember that this was almost 50 years ago in a bad year on the food front and that to-day, no doubt, the catering arrangements at Woodstock are vastly improved.) Those intrepid Woodstock lads would supplement their diet by hunting for the pot, and Gordon Hostetler recalls them shooting barking deer and various birds. On one memorable occasion an English member of the gang shot a panther and the school *kansamah* (cook) was pressed into service to cook one of its legs for the budding Huckleberry Finns – an unusual dietary supplement to the usual school fare!

At Mount Hermon in the early 1940s there was a riot in the dining room to demonstrate the boarders' dissatisfaction at the 'grub'. This was quelled but I don't remember if there was any significant improvement in the menus. A student of twenty years later deems the food as the worst he has ever known: often badly cooked and rarely appetising, with menus based on Indian meals. As in my day, however, teas and breakfasts were of the British variety (minus the bacon and eggs, of course!) and Adam Taylor, a young teacher who did a six month stint at MHS in the early 1970s, found the food 'ghastly'. He put this down to the fact that the diet was based upon the budgets of the poorest students and that for egalitarian reasons the staff had decided to eat the same food as the pupils, with the result that all fared equally badly. However, when he was ill he was very well fed in the school sanitorium.

Just as we did at MHS, Dow Hill schoolgirls would use food to barter for favours sought and offered. They, too loved 'aloo' chops and not many would part with theirs. But 'bathroom scrubbers', the sweet pumpkin fritters served as dessert, were forced down by many an unfortunate debtor as payment for favours received. Hill school boarders were as adept as children the world over in labelling hated dishes with the most disgusting names and I shall never feel the same again about baked custard, a really rather palatable little 'pud'. 'Pus and Scabs' was the name those Dow Hillians gave it!

On a more cheerful note, a student at Sheikh Bagh in the 1940s declares that he would willingly settle for the 'grub' he ate there on a regular basis, including the chicken curry every Sunday, for the rest of his life. Eric Tyndale-Biscoe would have been pleased to hear this, especially as he had a terrible time obtaining supplies in wartime

Kashmir. Bread was short so, nothing daunted, he had two bake ovens built, and the school was able to provide boarders with home-baked bread. Tinned food had disappeared from the shops and parents were asked to send up as much as possible with their sons when they returned at the start of the school year in February.

Tyndale-Biscoe also decided to keep rabbits, 'but pi-dogs broke in and killed two of them, giving rise to the famous remark by one of the boys, "the rabbits'll be dead by the time we eat them."' Later an electric fence was erected to ward off the depredations of mongooses, dogs and jackals.

Students at the older-established schools were unable to award any seals of approval such as that given to Sheikh Bagh by its grateful pupil, but they were cajoled into submission by the various treats doled out on Sundays and on special feast days. There would be cake, sweets and jam for tea, and some cooks could make very good fudge and toffee. At Loreto Convent in Darjeeling, Diana Leslie's favourite saint was St Francis: every girl would receive two mangoes on his feast day. (Mangoes were often re-cycled by little girls in many of the hill schools by drying the stone, combing the fibres, smothering them with talcum powder, painting in some features and tying on a ribbon, and Hey Presto, you had your own little pet lamb or guinea pig!).

Edith Stiffle née Lloyd-Marrow, a senior at MHS when I was there, has reminded me that on Sundays there was the 3 pm 'Bun Bell' signalling the end of the rest period on our beds (in silence), when we would all line up in the Quad to receive a fruity bun.

But apart from official treats, we would organise our own dietary supplements. Edith would assuage her constant hunger with a half pound of 'baker's biscuits' and a tin of condensed milk from Hafiz's shop up the hill. Hafiz's shop was our unofficial tuck shop, and when we were flush with cash we could buy all manner of tinned goods, including frankfurters, sardines and tinned fruit. He also sold some delightfully squidgy Indian sweets, as well as 'gram' (early progenitor of those spicy mixes of cereal, pasta, nuts and pulses available in Indian and wholefood shops in Britain today. My favourite is 'Bombay Mix', which beats Western nibbles hands down.) Edith also helped a friend to consume the cakes she received from an ardent admirer, even persuading her to continue the association for the sake of his love offerings, long after the loved one had lost interest in her swain. She would also slip the 'Burra Bearer' 4-6 annas for an 'aloo' chop or cutlet from the teachers' dining room whenever a teacher was out for a meal. And some of us had our own primus stoves, on which we would make fudge or chips, the sale of which would also help to bump up our pocket money. Today, with much more awareness of fire hazards, this would probably be forbidden, but in the old days we pumped away at our primuses with no fear of prohibition.

In conclusion, 'school-kids' all over the world have always complained about school 'grub', and will go on complaining, even when shovelling it down! Hill school children were no exception, but they invariably arrived at their homes in the plains for their three-month winter holiday looking rudely healthy. Could it be that 'a little of what you don't fancy, does you good ?'

Entrance to Oak Grove School, Mussoorie

Oak Grove School, Mussoorie
Mr Watts the Principal on Prize-giving Day 1939

Oak Grove School, Mussoorie
Prize winners 1939 watched by the topee wallahs!

17

The Same Only Different

Most of the memories of old students at India's hill boarding schools reveal many similarities with their counterparts at Home, upon which they were so assiduously modelled.

Their curricula differed little, with the Cambridge exams: Junior Cambridge and Senior Cambridge (the Cambridge School Certificate) forming the educational goals, all papers being sent back to Britain for marking and assessing, and many schools offering a college department for higher education; discipline was largely based on that practised in similar schools at Home; organised games and athletics were the same – with perhaps an even greater adherence to *mens sana in corpore sano* in India!

Indeed, most schools were relentlessly British despite the majority of their pupils never having set foot in England, Ireland, Scotland or Wales, a typical example being the Oak Grove Schools (Boys', Girls' and Mixed Juniors) set up in Jharipani, Mussoorie, for the children of East Indian Railway officials, the majority of whom were Anglo-Indian. The Anglo-Indian Community were very loyal to the British and revered the Union Jack and all it stood for. 'Les' Paul recalls his time there from 1942 to 1948 and still remembers the words of the Oak Grove school song, the fifth verse of which declared, in his day: *Though far from Britain's shore/We're British children true/We'll serve our God whom we adore/Our Queen and Empire too.* To-day, with a predominantly Indian student body, such jingoistic sentiments are dated and out of place and the verse has been replaced with the following more appropriate words, which are displayed at the school entrance: *We love this school of ours/We're Oak Grove's children true/We'll serve her in her darkest hours/And in her glory too.*

But differences there were, differences which set such schools apart and gave them their own ethos. Obviously the surroundings were unique. Even we, in our limited experience of the wonders of nature, marvelled at the grandeur all around us in the mountainous foothills and plateaux. Our diet, too, was unusual, to say the least, and the kindly ministrations of Indian servants throughout our daily lives reminded us that we were far from Home.

Amongst these differences lay bonuses not to be found elsewhere. One prime example is the 'Sunshine Holiday. This was the sudden treat sprung upon us after weeks of torrential rain during the June to September monsoon period, when a sparkling, sunny day might dawn. The Principal would declare a 'Sunshine Holiday' at assembly, sometimes of his or her own accord, and sometimes at the special request of pupils via a prefect or a teacher. And then it was a quick change into our holiday clothes with a whole free day in front of us to roam the forests or just hang about the school doing what we liked. Bliss it certainly was to be alive! And the day literally sparkled, with the sun glinting on the mica chips embedded in the road surfaces, a feature in many hill stations.

The ceaseless, pounding rains of the monsoon were a constant reminder that we were in a very different environment. One ex-student at a school in the Nilgiri hills of South India remembers terrific thunderstorms rolling round the mountains, and hailstones at least as big as cherries. When she was at school in England and all around her were hiding under their bedclothes during a storm, she wondered at their fear. 'To me it was a slight drizzle.' During our walks along the Cart Road into Darjeeling we were often caught in cloudbursts, and arrived back at school drenched and shivering, with the additional hazard of pulling off the leeches which had sucked their fill of our blood even through our terrible black, woolly stockings. But such walks were rare in the monsoon and we were usually imprisoned in the gym, where we could roller skate or the assembly hall, where we raced about in games of tag, or moped around until the next meal provided a diversion.

Another little girl at a convent school in Kotagiri in the early 1940s would take fire flies and glow worms to bed in a match box to light up the dark of the dormitory. She, too, recalls that the elements in Southern India made themselves felt in spectacular fashion, and remembers a meteor coming through an open window, hovering over her and finally shooting out through the windows behind her.

As has been recorded in many an old 'koi hai's' memoirs, the monsoon wreaked enormous damage to personal possessions and household goods. On fine days we would go out on to the balcony of the Senior dormitory and brush our mildewed clothes and shoes, or check our books for the voracious silverfish which had taken up residence during the damp season.

With the arrival of the better weather came the repairing of the roads. Teams of coolies would set about filling in pot holes and rolling out bumps. In Kurseong, Dow Hill schoolgirls would sit on their school wall cheering the panting workers on as they struggled with the heavy roller round the tortuous bends in the winding road.

I don't remember a raincoat featuring in my school wardrobe, merely a warm, navy blue overcoat, but it must have been on the uniform list. However, as a boarder at St Hilda's Girls' school in Ooty in 1925, Veronica Westmacott (Mrs Downing) and her fellow pupils had to wear 'curious waterproofs proofed with wattle (mimosa) gum during the monsoon.' St Hilda's was established in 1892 by the Sisters of the Church, Kilburn, later to be run by the Clewer sisters under the administration of the Madras Diocesan Board of Education with its governing body made up of the Church Committee of St Stephen's Church, Ooty. The school was for 'pure Europeans only and in his tract entitled '*Our English Church Schools in India*', published in 1934, Bishop Eyre Chattetton has this to say about St Hilda's:

> 'As, however, both teachers and pupils must be English by birth, the number of pupils is limited to 40, and the fees are high. Such a policy in the new India seems to be open to question.'

By the time Miss Phyllis Deane was there as a Matron in 1956, the school was taking pupils of all nationalities, 'including two Indian princesses'. Miss Deane, too, recalls compulsory protective clothing for pupils during the monsoon. She used to take the little ones for afternoon walks in the rain when 'they wore sou'westers, gum boots and oilskin coats, and there was nowhere to dry clothes, there being no sun or other heating.' This lack of heating was a feature at most hill boarding schools, including my own. The opening and closing months of the school year could be extremely cold and neither classrooms nor dormitories were heated. Some teachers had coal or

OUTFIT FOR BOARDERS

1 voile or silk frock (white not cream) and dress hat.
1 pair white shoes.
3 pairs white stockings.
2 navy blue best costumes for special occasions, one may be of velvet.
1 velour hat.
3 navy blue pleated serge skirts.
4 navy blue cotton pleated skirts (poplin).
6 warm white viyella jumpers.
4 silk jumpers.
10 cotton jumpers.
  Jumpers are to have turned over collar with
  navy blue tie, long sleeves with cuffs.
3 warm navy blue knickers.
3 cotton navy blue knickers.
1 Gymn costume.
2 Sola hats.
1 navy blue woollen cap for daily use.
2 flannel petticoats.
6 cotton petticoats.
4 heavy vests.
3 light vests.
6 pairs warm stockings black or tan.
6 pairs Lisle thread stockings black or tan.
  The same in socks for juniors.

4 warm and 9 cotton combinations for Juniors.
12 cotton knickers for gown girls.
3 flannel night gowns.
4 cotton night gowns with long sleeves.
1 warm and 1 cotton dressing-gown.
6 sheets, 6 pillow cases.
1 pillow.
2 pairs of blankets.
1 rug (nota rezaia).
1 pair of/felt bed-room slippers.
2 doz. handkerchiefs.
18 pinafores with pockets for juniors.
6 Towels. 3 Bath towels.
12 serviettes with ring initialled.
4 pairs strong black boots.
2 pairs shoes for best wear.
1 Holdall, Waterproof, Umbrella all absolutely necessary.
  Dressing-case furnished with sufficient toilette
  Requisites Hair-ribbon etc. for the year.
1 clothes-brush.
1 small workbox furnished.
1 Tennis racket and ball.
  Each article must have the owner's name marked in full.

All possible care will be taken of the clothing, but the authorities will not hold themselves responsible for the fast wear or loss of clothing. It is of absolute importance that each child be provided with a complete outfit in good condition.

No jewellery is allowed except a watch and brooch for the elder girls.

Two girls of Loreto Convent, Darjeeling, in their 'No.1s' – 1925

218

wood fires in their rooms (and no doubt electric fires), and there was a fire in the teachers' common room-cum-drawing room. But we poor kids were often freezing cold and sat in our coats during class. At Mount Hermon there was hot running water for baths and showers, so there must have been a boiler room somewhere. No one had the foresight to run pipes to radiators in the early days, but this method of central heating was probably in its infancy and considered an unnecessary luxury anyway. We rarely had snow down in our valley, but higher up in Jalapahar the St Paul's schoolboys experienced snowfalls at the end of the school year. In Murree there was frequently deep snow, as St Denys ex-students can testify.

In pre-World War Two days, many schools were still lit with oil lamps. Until 1937 Dow Hill had its 'Butti Wallah' (light man), who would be in charge of the hurricane lanterns used throughout the school. And before the girls went into the hall for night study, the 'Butti Wallah' would pump away at the Petromax lamps hanging overhead, light them with a match and go on his way. As they bent over their books the girls would hear their hiss and splutter, and on dark Sunday nights they would walk to and from Church for evening service by the light of hurricane lanterns.

At St Denys in Murree in the early 1930s, the school had its own electric generator while the town itself was still lit by gas. Their generator was a very precious possession and lighting was never wasted. 'At 10.50 at night the lights blinked twice, a warning to start putting away any work we were doing', remembers a young student teacher. 'Then it was torches or hurricane lanterns. Ahmed was the electrician and we always prayed for good health for him. No one else understood the eccentricities of that noisy little chug-chugging engine.'

At night time, instead of traffic, the young boarders tucked up in bed would hear the howling of jackals, or the squealing of bagpipes and banging of drums signalling a local 'tamasha' (social event) in a nearby village. Eva Obree née Mackenzie at Hebron, Coonoor, in the 1920s, used to be awoken by a local singing at the top of his voice as he passed through the tea bushes, swinging his lantern, trying to scare off evil spirits. Victoria schoolboys in Kurseong were adept at imitating the cries of jackals, and Dow Hillians were hard pressed to decide whether the calls were animal or human. The silence in the study hall at night was often broken by this howling, and excitement mounted if it was known that the boys would be on the prowl on a particular night.

Even in church, as Enid Tod recalls from her schooldays at Nazareth Convent, Ootacamund, India was never very far away.

'Every Friday at 5 pm we celebrated Stations of the Cross... Every child, of whatever denomination, attended church... there was one child there from one of the Indian princely states. She had a male escort, smartly uniformed and turbaned, who went into church with her and stood to attention throughout the service.'

A highly publicised incident in Britain recently regarding the right of young Muslim girls to adhere to their religious traditions by wearing scarves over their heads while attending a British school, is echoed in the memories of a schoolboy at BCS, Bangalore, of over 60 years ago. He remembers that a boy named Reza, a member of the Persian Royal family, was the only boy allowed to wear his national head dress while his school fellows sported their topees. (Incidentally, as many old India hands will know, the wearing of topees died out during the Second World War and this practice has never been revived. Army doctors discovered that sunstroke was not caught from the beating down of the sun upon the uncovered head, but rather the neck. I can still recall the taste of my topee's leather strap as I sucked away at it while out in the noonday sun!)

Some aspects of being educated in India brought searingly sad memories. Dow Hillians of the late 1930s had their lives rudely shattered, when, all unsuspecting, they made pets of the many stray dogs who had found their way up to the school. They missed their beloved pets left down in the plains, and encouraged the strays into the school compound, feeding and petting them and enjoying the affection they received in return. Rabies was a constant danger and an ever-present fear in India, so much so that the Commissioner of Police ordered the school's new canine boarders to be rounded up. The girls heard of the order and desperately tried to save their pets by driving them away, but the dogs had grown used to the pampering they had received and would not go.

Whilst in class, the girls heard a commotion outside with much shouting of orders and the sound of running feet. To their horror this was followed by the crack of rifle shots and they leaned out of the windows to see their dead pets being dragged away. Denise Coelho remembers that 'it didn't help to be told by some teachers that we were entirely to blame for the destruction of the animals.' A besotted animal lover myself, I think I would have been beside myself with grief .

Before becoming a boarder at St Peter's Boys' School, Panchgani, the little 7 year-old Zbyszek Plocki was given a puppy whose mother had been carried off by a tiger. He remembers later looking out from school into the valley and seeing the flames of fires which villagers had lit in order to trap the beast. Life was very different for the young Pole and bore no comparison to the life he had left behind in war-torn Europe. For one thing he was becoming indoctrinated with those very English traditions, the operettas of Gilbert & Sullivan and Lamb's 'Tales from Shakespeare'. And on the health front he was dosed with castor oil and first heard of 'Carter's Little Liver Pills' when the Headmaster would shout that a boy was in need of them! But the study of Urdu in class was a reminder that the school was in India.

World War Two also brought its share of sorrow to some of the children being educated in the East. School magazines of the mid and late 1940s contain harrowing accounts of the suffering experienced by children who had trekked with their families from Burma to India at the time of the Japanese occupation of Burma and their gradual encroachment upon India's borders. The horror continued during and after Indian Independence in 1947, and as late as 1952, the Headmistress of Bishop Cotton Girls High School in Bangalore was murdered at the school on the day of the Queen's coronation.

Schools in India's hill stations in wartime did not give much thought to the possibility of air raids from Japanese aircraft, even supposing that 'planes could fly that high above the mountains in those days. But the nuns at Pamela Humphreys' convent school in Kotagiri told their young charges to hide under their beds if a bomb dropped. 'Very stupid', thought Pam, 'who wanted the ceiling and the bed on top of one?!' This instruction was later amended and the pupils were told to rush into the woods. In the event, neither ploy was found necessary as the dreaded Japanese aircraft never materialised.

Another major feature in school life since their establishment in the 19th century right up to the present day was the lurking danger of landslides and earthquakes. Peggy Coldwells remembers that at Loreto Convent in Shillong there were earthquake drills as opposed to fire drills. And in Shillong there appeared to be no fire brigade as such in the 1930s, the lack of which resulted in the burning down of the Roman Catholic and Clerics College next door to the Convent.

On a happier note, one thing that we 'Indian-educated' kids could boast about to anyone from Home trying to lord it over us, was the fact that we knew our 16 times table. There were 16 annas to the rupee, so we needed this recherché information! Today, such a skill is not considered essential. Even the smallest school child has access to a pocket calculator.

School hobbies would sometimes reflect the 'Indianness' of its location. Apart from the popular 'Gooli Danda' referred to previously, boys would enjoy themselves hugely in the ancient Indian pastime of kite fighting. The kite strings would be coated with a mixture of powdered glass and crushed leaves, and the kite flyers would do their best to ground their opponents' kites by cutting the others' strings with their own – a skilful feat. Cecil Wilkins remembers doing this at BCS, Bangalore, as well as the keeping of quails and training them to fight, a hobby to which the staff turned a blind eye.

At American-run coeducational Woodstock at Landour, Mussoorie, in the 1940s, David Little looks back now on what he realises was a very serious attitude by the school authorities towards academic work, with night and morning study strictly supervised. But unlike schools in England, during David's time at Woodstock the school held no exams, with students' progress being assessed daily in class instead. However, if grades were not maintained, boys and girls were kept back and not promoted until the required standard had been reached. And Gordon Hostetler, son of American missionaries, looking back at his time at Woodstock and comparing it with schooling in the US, realises that much more homework was set in Mussoorie. Later, he sent his own son and daughter to Woodstock from the States for their third year of High

School, a wonderful experience for both of them which included a tour of India during the winter vacation. Like her father before her, his daughter is still in touch with the friends she made at Woodstock.

Many ex-students recall the friends they made among their Indian schoolfellows, some of whom were to become 'illustrious alumni'. Old Boys proudly record the names of Indian friends now holding high office in Government, Medicine and the Services, with Old Girls able to do the same about their erstwhile classmates, especially in the healthy attitude towards female emancipation which has arisen in post-Independent India.

Loreto Juniors

Going Home Day at Dow Hill School, Kurseong,
by Denise Coelho

18

Going Home Day

Many memories of schooldays may fade, but the one forever etched into the psyche of every hill school child must be 'Going Home Day'. Our school year lasted from early March until late November or early December – nine long months away from our loved ones. Where else in the world did school children get to know their fellows and teachers so intimately? But despite the forging of life long friendships and the advantages of living in the healthy climate of India's magical hill stations, going home was the only thing that counted for most boarders.

David Little, however, an old Woodstock boy, says he really used to miss school once the initial excitement of being home again was over: 'After all, one spent the greater part of the year with friends and classmates and they became one's family.'

'Old Gallian' John Walker echoes this oft-repeated sentiment: 'I am quite sure that what binds people who attended schools in India, was the comradeship. We were together for nine months of the year, longer than with our parents, so our family for those nine months were our teachers and our friends...'

From as early as October, 'Going Home Day' fever would start. There were tear-off calendars to be made, with the nightly ritual of ripping off each day, and most schools organised events as signposts to the eventual parting. Some had bonfire nights, where the cheekier pupils manufactured effigies of their teachers to be consigned to the flames. But the 'guys' chosen took this in good part, and were almost as popular as the eponymous Mr Fawkes. There were Farewell Banquets, where the food was several cuts above the meals dished out during the year. I seem to remember roast chicken at our Banquet and have a vivid recollection of Mrs Brewster, one of our Matrons, rolling her eyes heavenward and muttering, 'The inevitable chicken.' It may have been inevitable to her in the teachers' dining room, but to us it was very heaven. Witty speeches were delivered by teachers on these occasions, with would-be witty replies from their students, and the proceedings closed with resounding choruses from our repertoire of Going Home Day songs. Some of the tunes of these songs were common to all schools, in particular 'Riding down from Bangor' and 'The Camptown Races'. At Mount Hermon both melodies had been joined to form a most effective whole as 'Going Home Day has come at last'. In the few weeks prior to the great day, GHD songs were sung at every possible occasion, including morning assemblies. Some of the songs were poignant reminders that schooldays were nearly over for a few alumni. Our saddest offering was 'Old Walls are Friendly Walls', composed by Charles Swan. Tears shone in many a senior's eye, boy or girl, as we sang the poignant words, a phenomenon regarded with suspicious astonishment by the younger ones, for whom school was to go on for another hundred years, or so it seemed.

Another annual fixture was the special dinner laid on by the Pre-Seniors (Class 8) for the Seniors (Senior Cambridge Class), which was held in the teachers' drawing-room. Everyone dressed up in full evening fig, and I can remember having a long dress specially made by the school durzi when I was a Pre-Senior. My friend 'Pete' (Betty Peterson), helped me to give instructions to this purveyor of colonial haute couture at the first fitting, and her immortal words still ring in my ears: 'Miss-sahib bahut patli-walli' (the Miss-sahib is a very thin person), an observation designed to remind him to put plenty of fullness into the bust. The Miss-sahib wasn't just a thin person, she was pint sized and downright skinny. The finished creation was entirely up to my expectations. I loved that blue taffeta dress and it says much for the dear old durzi's expertise that it camouflaged all the skinny bits and made me feel at least 21.

Before Going Home Day arrived, there was much to be done. Money was needed for the purchase of the regulation paraphernalia connected with the journey home, part of which was a malacca cane for waving joyfully through the train windows. At Mount Hermon, our primus stoves came in handy. Those of us who did not own our own would hire them from a big wheel in the Senior Dormitory who knew a good bit of business when it came her way. We would buy potatoes and ghee from our friend Hafiz up the hill and make chips to sell; we would sacrifice treasured tins of condensed milk hoarded from our tuck parcels and deny ourselves the pleasure of sucking it straight out of the tin, our usual practice throughout the year. Now it was boiled up on our stoves for saleable fudge. My mother would respond to my pleas for extra money by sewing the odd rupee coin into the leaves of a paperback book and post it up to me, a brilliant ploy which always seemed to outwit the Indian postal service.

The malacca cane was popular with homeward bound children from the majority of hill schools, as were water pistols and little paper bombs. The Nepalese people who gathered at the little halts on the Darjeeling Himalayan Railway, as well as the railway officials themselves, took a terrible beating from the jubilant train loads. Apart from the drenching they received from the water pistols, or the fright they got when a bomb exploded at their feet – frequently a stink bomb to lend an added touch of hilarity – they had to take cover from the stinging swish of a malacca cane. These handy implements would also be used to rattle along the banks of the hillside through the toy train windows, or to flick at the mules and their drivers plodding along the Cart Road adjoining the narrow gauge track. An added hazard might be the sting of a missile launched from a catapult. Dow Hill girls were furnished with some very superior models by their Victoria School boy friends, the 'Y's burned, sanded and polished to perfection by their adoring swains and finished off with lengths of black rubber called 'Simla squares' purchased from the bazaar.

But there was much to be done before these devilish pleasures could be indulged in. Trunks had to be packed under the Matrons' supervision, and then there was the arcane pursuit of label-making to be completed. The manufacture of home-made labels provided much innocent pleasure, with artistic proclivities given full rein. The labels were lovingly decorated with mountain scenes entwined with greenery, and stuck down with flour and water paste, many of which did not survive the journey. Fortunately, most school trunks had their owners names stencilled on in white paint, which was all that was needed when they were reclaimed at journey's end. But this label-making figures in many a student's reminiscences and was part and parcel of the annual ritual, as was the regulation homeward bound banner emblazoning the front of the big train. Every school in Darjeeling and Kurseong carried its own banner and if there was more than one 'batch' from each school, every 'batch' made its own banner. And what splendid creations these were. Some bore the school crest, and all had the words 'Homeward Bound' prominently displayed. Budding young artists were allowed to use their own imaginations in the design of these banners, and parents waiting on the platforms could see their offsprings' handiwork as the train steamed into the terminus. Henry Swan remembers his mother's heartfelt cry on seeing her son's creation, 'And he's even spelt it right!' The banners were usually reserved for fixing on to the big train at Siliguri, the all-change terminus between alighting from the toy train and boarding the Calcutta express. Some schools chose to fix their banner on at a halt during the early hours of the morning, and Dow Hill girls would get up early when the train stopped at Ranaghat for their ritual fixing.

This school seems to have been extremely well-organised regarding the traditional rites of GHD. Win Ballantine recalls the preparation of a feast for consumption during the homeward journey, when the school butler, Gillan Singh, was given orders for the menu required by some of the senior girls, who all chipped in at Rs 1/- a head. Baskets were labelled and filled with tinned herrings in tomato sauce, 'a cooked hump' (from which animal I ask myself?), tinned crab, tinned butter and cheese, cooked chicken, bread galore, hundreds of oranges and lemonade. And throughout the school's history, there was the ritual purchase of delicious Darjeeling oranges as presents to take home for parents. These cost Rs 1/- per 100 and were packed into hessian-lined local baskets, labelled and despatched to Kurseong station where the owners would take delivery of them on boarding the toy train.

But not every child joined the main school party on its jubilant way down to the plains on the official Going Home Day. Some had to stay up at their empty school for 'Cambridge Week'. The week actually ran into ten days to a fortnight, and was designed for students to sit their Junior and Senior Cambridge exams in peace and quiet. I was a Junior Cambridge student in 1942 and well remember when we used to drag our empty tin trunks on to the balcony, wrap ourselves up (winter had set in by now) and curl up in our trunks with a stack of books and revise for the next day's exam. We JC candidates had the heady experience of mixing with our exalted seniors (only two forms up) almost as equals. I can recall wearing a beautifully embroidered Nepalese hat for most of the time, in imitation of an American boy taking his SC exams, whom I was sweet on.

There were other occasions, too, when homeward bound students did not form part of the main 'batch'. Lawrence Swan, of the legendary Swan clan in the Twenties and Thirties, made his descent to Siliguri on a trolley of his own manufacture, similar to those used by gangs working on the line. And Ray Raymond remembers being in a small 'batch' sent down in a multi-seated trolleylike conveyance used by the DHR, in order to catch up with the original school 'batch'. To this day she marvels at the Headmistress's insistence at subjecting her young charges to such a hair-raising ride instead of waiting for a later DHR express which would coincide with a scheduled train leaving from Siliguri. What a picture those passengers must have presented, with the little girls' plaits flying at every bend! And one wonders if the intrepid solo trolley rider got punished when he arrived at his destination.

Rosemary Fletcher née Hudson was at Mount Hermon in post-Independent India and has cause to remember a 'Going Home Day' which lengthened into several days in November 1962. This was at the time of the Sino/Indian conflict concerning the border. Transport was being commandeered for Indian troops and Darjeeling was considered as a vulnerable target for possible bombing, a situation which prompted the school authorities to evacuate the children ahead of schedule. As a result, what should have been a well organised operation by people well-versed in such homeward bound journeys, turned into a series of nightmares for all concerned. Train after train was commandeered for the Indian Army, with the children taken on and off at short notice. After several such train journeys, including a journey by ferry, the young passengers were forced to spend a night sleeping in an empty train because of a missed connection. The party finally arrived in Calcutta 24 hours late, much to the joyful relief of their waiting parents, not all of whom had seen the notice put in 'The Statesman' newspaper by the school authorities warning them of the delay. Station masters along the route were hard pressed to provide enough food for the hundred or more children who arrived unannounced, and the staff in charge of the party must have wondered when the nightmare was going to end.

To broaden these reminiscences of the Going Home Day saga, it is interesting to read Eric Tyndale-Biscoe's account of the Sheikh Bagh boys' return journeys from Kashmir to the plains during the 1940s. The one hundred or so boys would rise at 5.30 am, warmly wrapped up in overcoats and balaclavas, and set off in a convoy of buses at 7 am to wind their way through the Jhelum Valley Gorge.

Their destination was the railhead at Rawalpindi and the journey took two days. They stopped at Dak bungalows on the way and had to contend with the delays involved in the checking of bicycles at Customs points inside and outside the Kashmir border. Such checks were needed so that the bikes could be re-imported at the beginning of the next term without further Customs duties being levied. Some of the school party experienced another type of delay in 1940 when heavy snow caused a bus to get stuck in a drift on a narrow mountain road, until a shovel was sent for – a basic necessity not carried by the driver! As the buses crossed the Jhelum Bridge into the British India of those days, the boys would set up a chorus of 'Beef, beef!' in anticipation of their change of diet – Kashmir was a Hindu State where cattle are sacred. The buses would forge their way down the long descent of Murree Hill, a distance of 4,000 feet in 20 miles, and having passed Murree, the Punjab plain was spread out before them in the distance. Two hours later the boys would arrive at Rawalpindi after a journey packed with incident, enlivened also by their tooting the horns of the buses to summon the sleeping bus drivers after an overnight stop. The resultant cacophony brought the drivers rushing back, not so much because they were late but rather because they were afraid the batteries in their old bone-shaking vehicles would be run down. Anyone who has travelled in these unreliable conveyances will know what a flat battery on a lonely mountain road can do to spoil a journey in India.

The majority of old students at the Darjeeling schools from my era cannot claim to have experienced any truly hair-raising journeys to and from school. But our memories of our journeys home are as vivid today as they ever were. We shall always remember the thrills we experienced at travelling across the subcontinent in those wonderful Indian trains by night, with the particular smell of the village fires which pervaded the carriage, mixed with the aromas of spicy foods being cooked. Unlike those thoughtful Dow Hillians, I had no basket of oranges in the luggage van as a present for my parents. My greedy little self was more concerned with feeding the inner man during the journey, to which end my companions and I had stocked up with supplies such as tinned sardines, Indian sweets and fruit, most of which was consumed in the toy train as the little puffing engine of the DHR (Dirty Hardup Railway) pulled us down the winding track. The fact that we were to be given dinner at the Siliguri restaurant in the evening before boarding the big train did nothing to spoil the pleasures of our hors d'oeuvres.

In between stuffing ourselves, we leant out of the windows and felt the wind on our faces, heedless of the smuts being blown from the engine. As night fell, we'd peer into the thick jungle all around us by the light of the flare fixed to the engine. Every little engine had its cow-catcher on the front, and some said that trains had been known to halt because of elephants or tigers lying on the track and refusing to budge.

Once on the big train, we hardly ever slept all through the night and lay in our bedding rolls listening to the sounds of India so close outside, or giggled and chattered with excitement as the turning of the wheels brought us closer and closer to home. When we stopped at the larger stations we heard the familiar cries of the platform vendors, hawking their 'Pan, bidi cigarettes', their 'gurram cha' (hot tea) or their 'Singapore pineappul'. With the dawning of the new day, our chota hazri would arrive on trays passed through the window at a convenient stop. Dow Hillians remember some of their friends hurling their topees into the muddy waters of the Hugli River as the train clattered over Hardinge Bridge, a practice echoed by British troops and other old India hands as they steamed out of harbour on their journeys home to Blighty. On my last train journey home from Mount Hermon, it wasn't our topees we threw out of the window, just our breakfast trays, cups, saucers and all. Sheer vandalism, some would say, but they've never experienced the delirium of going home after a childhood spent under the old school topee.

The famous St. Paul's weathervane

'Going Home Day has come at last'
(Mount Hermon version)

Sung to tune of 'Camptown Races'

Going Home Day has come at last, doo dah, doo dah,
Going Home Day has come at last, doo dah, doo dah day.
We travel all the night, we travel all the day
We spend our money on the DHR, doo dah, doo dah day.

Sung to tune of 'Riding down from Bangor'

Down from old Mount Hermon on a small toy train
After nine months' mugging back to home again.
Teachers are so rosy, children are the same,
Everybody's happy, waiting for the train.

Ghoom, Sonada, Kurseong,
All are left behind,
Though our journey's very long
I'm sure we do not mind.

When we reach Sealdah
Hail it with a shout,
"Pan, Bidi, cigarette"
Hop the beggars out!

OLD WALLS

Old walls are friendly walls
Friendly walls, farewell!
Old walls hold memories
That breathe a kindly spell.

Breathe then your benison
On me as I depart,
I'll keep your memory
Warm in my heart.

Old shadowed arches grey,
Long have we been friends.
We can no longer stay
Where your kind shade extends.

Breathe then your benison
On me as I depart,
I'll keep your memory
Warm in my heart.

Old friends are loyal friends,
Friends of happy days.
Now we must say goodbye
And go dividing ways.

Breathe then your benison
On me as I depart
I'll keep your memory
Warm in my heart.

Appendix A

Who are the Anglo-Indians?

I first heard the term 'Anglo-Indian' as a 10-year old 'evacuated' to India during the early years of World War II. It hadn't impinged upon my infant consciousness during our earlier sojourns in India.

Such remarks as 'chi-chi' and 'fifteen annas' were occasionally bandied about and the meanings of these strange phrases were eventually made clear. 'Chi-chi' referred to the sing-song, almost Welsh, accent of some of the British people who'd lived in India for generations, 'Domiciled Europeans' as they were called, and, in particular, to 'Anglo-Indians', whose ancestors were both Indian and British.

Talking with a 'chi-chi' accent was a sin, as I soon learned in the school holidays after my first 9 months' incarceration at a European boarding school in the hills. On quizzing my father with the words, "Are you go-ING now?" as he walked through our compound towards the gate of his conveniently adjoining office, he spun on his heel with a "WHAT did you say? Don't dare to speak in that sing-song, 'chi-chi' way. Now say it again, properly." All I'd done was to swoop up about an octave on the syllable 'ing' – a superbly interrogative inflection which sounded entirely natural to me.

Even to-day I find the so-called 'chi-chi' accent attractive to my ears. It is not to be confused with the English spoken by some Indians and Pakistanis, which is altogether more guttural, matching the guttural consonants of their own vernaculars. I am convinced that 'chi-chi' is first cousin to Welsh. The Royal Welsh Fusiliers were sent to India in John Company's early days, and, in their voluble way, must have imprinted their accents all over India. Why, some people speaking 'chi-chi' – mainly men and boys – even used to preface their sentences with "C'mon Mun" or "I say, Mun", just like the Welsh! In fairness to the thousands of Anglo-Indians who have never said "Mun" in their lives, I should add that such expressions sprang mainly from the lips of the young, and adults who should have known better. 'Nice people' didn't use 'em... Another possibility is that many of the early missionaries sent out to India were Welsh, but I have yet to research both these rather shaky theories.

'Fifteen annas' was a joke for not quite *pukkah* or one hundred percent pure, for didn't everyone know that sixteen annas made one rupee?

To escape the heat of 'the plains', my brother and I were sent to school in Darjeeling, I to Mount Hermon, a co-educational boarding school run by American Methodist missionaries, and he to St. Paul's School for Boys. My schoolfellows came from a wide spectrum of nationalities. My parents could not have chosen better to fit their daughter for adulthood had they planned it. But the school had been chosen quite unconsciously. The mundane fact of the matter was that the daughter of a colleague of my father's had been there.

I worked, played, quarrelled, ate and slept in the company of English, Scottish, American, Anglo-Indian, Scandinavian, Parsee, Indian, Bhutanese, Tibetan, Australian, Anglo-Burman, Armenian, as well as Austrian refugee children, to name dozens. I learned who was Anglo-whatever and who was not. I can still hear my piping treble declaring, "But I'm not colour 'prejadiss' Ching-Chang, really I'm not." This to the quaintly nick-named Persian girl who'd got into a fight with a group whose leaders happened to be English. Her only line of defence was to shriek, "You're colour-prejudiced, that's why you're being so nasty to me." As a member of the gang I hotly refuted this, none too clear as to the meaning of 'prejadiss'.

The European child said good-bye to Anglo-Indian chums, rarely to see them again until the school departure on the railway platform for the following 9-month stint. With hindsight, I'm amazed that we accepted this state of affairs without question. (I refer, of course, to children living in the same city. Many Anglo-Indians coming from remote up-country stations or railway colonies were out of reach of their English schoolfriends in any case.) Mummies and Daddies belonged to certain clubs where Anglo-Indians were not allowed, and it just wasn't done to play with them in the holidays. In fact, some of the clubs had committees to look you over before you joined in case you were marked with the visible taint of colour. I have since heard this charade described by a bitter victim who was rejected, as 'the shade card test'.

On a later sojourn in Calcutta as an 18-year old I can remember having to undergo this scrutiny. My pedigree and skin tones adjudged O.K., I was admitted to the Calcutta Swimming Club. In later life, such a performance would have received the lash of my liberal tongue, but then I accepted it – along with my parents – as the norm. Nevertheless, I did have a few Anglo-Indian friends during that period. One was a fellow secretary at 'The Statesman' newspaper office, several years my senior and working for the Managing Director. Another, whom I met at a party, would come with me to the cinema occasionally. They were never my guests at the Swimming Club... To give them their due, they never expressed a desire to be accorded this doubtful privilege.

On the other side of the coin, an Anglo-Indian school friend of mine and still one of my best friends, remembers that prejudice was not so marked in the government circles in which her parents moved. Her Anglo-Indian father and his family were readily received as friends by his British colleagues at dinner parties and other social functions in Dacca. They were also members of the Dacca Club.

In fairness to my parents, they were not of the hide-bound, Blimpish variety. Restricted though they were within the social barriers of the day, they numbered several 'country born' and Anglo-Indian people as their friends, despite their inability to entertain them at the Club. But too much overt fraternisation was frowned upon and, indeed, could present a serious hazard in the long climb up the promotional ladder. *Burra sahibs* (bosses) could make things very sticky for employees who strayed, unwittingly or not, beyond the strictly laid down social path.

08⊱0

We have treated all Indians with kindness
This Country we've made it our own,
For this reason our children get nothing
Because they have never been home.

'Thus runs a petition in verse demonstrating discriminatory treatment of Anglo-Indians, written about 1875 by Captain Hearsey, Anglo-Indian son of General Sir John Bennett Hearsay.'
(From 'Hostages to India' by Herbert Stark)

Apart from the people of mixed origins who grew up in and around the East India Company's settlements, particularly Madras, as a result of deliberate Company policy, nothing could have stopped the natural gravitation of Englishmen, not to say any European man, towards Indian and Eurasian women in the ensuing years. The 17th and 18th century settlers were well and truly cut off from their homeland, Company regulations preventing Englishwomen from boarding the East Indiamen sailing ships without special permission and a certain amount of money, and this ban lasted until the renewal of the Company's Charter in 1833. As Stark points out in his 'Hostages to India', marriages therefore took place between British officers or Company officials and high-born Indian women just as frequently as those contracted between the humble soldiery and lowlier born Indian women. Wives were obtained by treaty with Indian acquaintances, as well as from the many Muhammedan widows left on the battlefields, to say nothing of slave girls among the camp followers.

It is widely held that until the closing years of the 18th century, prejudice against such mixed marriages or liaisons and the resulting progeny was not universally practised. But the rot does seem to have set in before this according to S. C. Ghosh in his book, 'The Social Condition of the British Community in Bengal 1757-1800', who states that 'irregular unions' with Indian women were accepted as inevitable in 18th century Bengal, but that is not to say, however, that they were socially acceptable... Anglo-Indian wives of members of the Company's military or civil services were never fully accepted in European society in Bengal.' He quotes the redoubtable Captain Thomas Williamson, who published the two volumes of his 'East India Vade Mecum' in 1810 after fifteen years' service in India as a bible for the British who followed him out there. Williamson writes that despite being natural daughters of high-ranking men in the King's or Company's services, 'they (as Anglo-Indians) were never invited by the Governor-General to public assemblies or entertainments.'

Most of the descendants of illustrious mixed marriages or liaisons were eventually lost to the Anglo-Indian community when they were sent Home for their education and never returned to India's shores. Such siphoning off of the elite of mixed parentage has always been a matter of some regret to the leaders of the Anglo-Indian Community in India, who feel that its history might have been different had more pride in the Community's dual heritage been inculcated, in some measure by the 'staying-on' in the country of its 'top drawer' sons and daughters

In Britain to-day, many families from the aristocracy to the 'working class' could probably trace their ancestry back to an Indian great-great-great-grandmother, and, if she were a princess, would be only too pleased to publicise the fact. It is the Indian and Anglo-Indian ancestors further down the social scale whom their descendants are reluctant to acknowledge, demonstrating that colour *per se* is not such a blot on the family escutcheon as having the wrong social background. The same reluctance is often maintained regarding male ancestors in India, many of whom were privates and NCOs in the British and Company armies. A large number of ex-soldiers chose to retire in India and went on to carve out remarkable careers both in Government service and in private commercial enterprise. In Angus Wilson's 'The Strange Ride ot Rudyard Kipling', the late Sir Terence Rattigan reveals that his grandfather, who rose to be a member of the Governor-General's Legislative Council, was the son of an illiterate Irish Private in the Indian Army who had to make his mark on his enlistment papers. Such refreshing honesty about humble forbears is rare in people with Indian connnections – centuries of snobbery have proved only too effective a gag.

The early Luso-Indians and Portugese were lost to the Community by their gradual merging with the Indian nation, and the remainder became the Anglo-Indian Community as we know it, with the enormous depletion of its numbers in India through the mass emigration of thousands of its members to Britain and Commonwealth countries at the time of Indian Independence in 1947 and after.

It is useless to deny that in the good old days of 'John Company', the period had its share of illicit liaisons. When the practice of marrying Indian women fell into disfavour by the end of the 18th century, many Englishmen defied convention by resorting to concubinage or, to use Herbert Stark's picturesque phrase, 'setting up a seraglio'. They preferred to do this rather than to 'lower' their social status by marrying an Indian or a girl of mixed parentage. The men involved were usually the higher officials and wealthier merchants and planters. Tea planters carried on the tradition into the 20th century. It was for their little destitute and abandoned offspring that the famous Scottish missionary, Dr Graham, established his Kalimpong Homes in the Himalayas in 1900. (See Appendix B)

On the whole, the soldier classes were, *force majeure*, of a more moral frame of mind. Even if the men in the ranks had wanted to kick over the traces, they were not afforded much opportunity to do so under the beady eye of the Chaplain or the Commanding Officer. Any irregular unions formed between humble rankers and Indian women were usually brief, the children born to them abandoned with their mothers, who brought them up as Muslims and Hindus.

Army officers used the excuse that the constant moving about the countryside from camp to camp precluded the possibility of their having wives in the legal sense, and many an officer's bungalow had a *bibi-khana* or *beebeeghar* (mistress's apartment) attached for the use of his Indian concubine or, in rare cases, wife.

The taint of illegitimacy is another bogey which prevents some Anglo-Indians from 'coming out'. This has been a recurring theme in novels down the ages, with many authors portraying the 'Eurasian' as wily, cunning, not to be trusted and usually illegitimate. Somerset Maugham is a prime example, and many Anglo-Indians are none too keen on John Masters for his portrayal of the unfortunate Anglo-Indian girl, Victoria, who, in his best-seller, 'Bhowani Junction', appears to divide her favours between men of both races. As Cedric Dover writes in his 'Cimerii? or Eurasians and Their Future', published over sixty years ago and long before 'Bhowani Junction', 'Novelists have never been kind to the Eurasian. But novelists reflect the opinions of their age and race. And the ordinary European generally believes that Eurasians are the result of temporary weaknesses in an unaccustomed climate. While he is not entirely wrong, he is certainly not right.'

With marriage to Indian women dying out, wives for the ever increasing number of Englishmen in India continued to be sought from among the girls of mixed parentage. But the lifting of the ban on Englishwomen coming out to India with the 1833 Charter Act, coinciding a couple of years later with the opening of the overland route to India via Suez, brought out more and more potential wives from 'Home', heralding the arrival of the archetypal *memsahib* and the beginning, according to some historians, of racial and social prejudice. While this may have been true of some *memsahibs*, there were hundreds of Victorian women missionaries, teachers and doctors who came out to India bent only on improving the lot of people of all shades and religions, and upon whom the slur of racial prejudice is a canard. Others, like Sir Henry Lawrence's 'so beloved Honoria', were their husbands' strong right arms during long and arduous careers, sharing the same hardships of climate and ever present dangers of disease, never complaining, trusting always to a Divine Providence and light years away from Kipling's frivolous, languid, spiteful and racially prejudiced Mrs Hauksbee and her ilk.

And in fairness to those Victorian ladies and their sisters of successive generations who did practise social and racial discrimination, were they not obediently emulating their menfolk? Britain itself was very socially compartmentalised from the mid 19th century right up to the Second World War. Life in India was merely an extension of the social mores existing at Home, only more so.

But before developing the *memsahib* theme, let us chart the progress of the Anglo-Indian Community before her arrival on the scene. Herbert Stark points out that the East India Company relied heavily upon the sons born to their English soldiers and factors and their Indian wives to defend the Company's wealth against 'bandits and outlaws, invading armies and harrassing Marathas... These were bound by a common bond of interest to the Company in which their fathers served... Those of them that had attained to manhood were of greater value than imported soldiers and writers. They cost nothing to bring out to India. They were acclimatised, and did not readily fall a prey to the inclemencies of the Indian sky. They were not under the necessity of learning the vernaculars, and they well understood the commercial morality and practices obtaining in the markets. They were familiar with the details of business, the class of goods in demand by Indians, and the time to buy and sell. Nor was this all. Their trading instincts had been quickened and given an edge amid the sudden call to arms, the dashing onslaught, the desperate defence.' He concludes: *But for the presence in India of successive generations of those sprung from British fathers and Indian mothers, it may well be questioned whether in India England would ever have passed from the market place to the forum, from the factory to the council chamber, from merchandise to empire, from Company to Crown.* (My italics.)

During the 18th century, posts in the Company's service were freely open to 'Eurasians', and those whose fathers were wealthy enough were sent to England to be educated, returning to India to take up jobs in the company's covenanted and commissioned services. Those not fortunate enough to go Home to school were nonetheless considered sufficiently educated to fill positions in the uncovenanted civil service as warrant officers and artificers in the Company's army. 'Eurasians' were called up or volunteered for active service and fought in many battles under Clive, including campaigns against the French. Some perished in the Black Hole of Calcutta in 1756 and many were massacred with their English comrades in the Company's frequent battles against Indian rulers. They were ferociously loyal to the Union Jack and were always lumped together with the British when their physical assistance was required in adverse times.

Such loyalty had always been amply rewarded. But by the end of the 18th century Anglo-Indians outnumbered the British in India and the shareholders at Home grew jealous of their standing with the Company, coveting such positions for their own sons and nephews in England. Putting their heads together, they evolved the first step in a plan to take away the rights of Anglo-Indians as the Company's time-honoured employees. This took the form of an order by the Court of Directors in 1786 preventing the orphans of British military officers at the Upper Orphanage in Calcutta from being sent Home for their further education.

The banner of home-grown nepotism was unfurled. Another safeguard towards its unhampered flight was a Standing Order in 1791 precluding all those with Indian blood from holding positions as officers in the civil, military or marine services of the Company. This repression of the Anglo-Indian Community conveniently coincided with the revolt in 1791 of the mulatto and black population against their French and Spanish masters in Haiti, culminating in the establishment of its Black Republic. Siezing eagerly upon this dramatic *coup d'état* as a warning of things to come, the Court of Directors compared the mulattos with the 'Eurasians', who might, they declared, just as readily join forces with the Indian population to crush the British! Such scare tactics had the desired effect and the next repressive measure was a resolution to the effect that all persons not of 'pure' European descent were disqualified from army service except as fifers, drummers, bandsmen and farriers. Thus, a 'Eurasian' couldn't even serve as a private in the Company's army.

The ingratitude of the British towards a people who had worked, fought and died for the Company for over a century left the Anglo-Indian Community stunned and resentful. British fathers of 'Eurasian' sons destined for the Upper Military Orphanage in the event of their fathers' deaths, sons who would no longer have the automatic privilege of being sent Home for their education, were outraged when they were told the reason for the cutting off of what they had considered a right. *'The settlement and education in England of such orphans,'* ran the cruel and inaccurate rationalisation, *'involved a political inconvenience because the imperfections of the children, whether bodily or mental, would in process of time be communicated by intermarriage to the generality of people in Great Britain, and by this means debase the succeeding generations of Englishmen'* ! (My italics).

But even when authority classed him as 'English' the Anglo-Indian could not win: under Company law Englishmen (in this instance including Anglo-Indians) were neither allowed to own land nor to reside further than ten miles away from the nearest Presidency town or Company settlement without written permission from the Chief Secretary. As a result Anglo-Indians were denied the opportunity to take up farming or private commerce. The Company was their life-line and with that life-line snatched from their grasp they were totally unequipped for any other calling.

The soldiers among them decided to join the ranks of the armies of the Indian Chiefs. There was nothing unusual in this. Many officers, both British and 'Eurasian' already in such regiments, had quit the King's or the Company's armies after some punishable misdemeanour, or to attain the promotion not forthcoming in their own units. But there was worse to come. In the opening years of the 19th century the Company issued another proclamation recalling all 'Eurasians' to serve in its own regiments against the warring Marathas! The mercenaries who had gone over to the Maratha and other private armies raised by Indian Princes were warned that if they failed to rejoin the British ranks they would be treated as traitors.

As Stark proudly records, 'They heard the call of their blood, and obeyed it with alacrity'. The offer of bribes as well as threats did nothing to shake their patriotism, and Stark recounts the oft-repeated tale of an Anglo-Indian Colonel named Vickers who, together with two of his Anglo-Indian comrades, Dodd and Ryan, was beheaded in 1803 by Holkar, the Maratha Maharajah in whose army they had enlisted, for refusing to fight against the British. Their heads were mounted on lance points and exhibited in front of Holkar's camp.

Many other Anglo-Indian authors championing their Community's cause have quoted Stark's version of this heroic tale to demonstrate the unquestioning loyalty of the Anglo-Indians to the ungrateful British. They become incensed when British writers and historians use the blanket term 'British' or 'English' to describe such heroes, and wryly note their punctilious use of the term 'Eurasian' or 'Anglo-Indian' when reporting misdemeanours of any kind on the part of a member of the Community.

It must be said, however, that Stark may have been overstating his case. In his book, 'A Particular Account of the European Military Adventurers of Hindustan 1784-1803', (Fisher Unwin 1892), Herbert Compton refers only to Major Vickers as a 'half-caste', adding that he was an exceedingly gallant young soldier. Major Ryan is referred to as an Irishman commanding a battalion in Holkar's service, 'whose only claim to fame was that he was beheaded with Dodd and Vickers'. Compton describes Dodd as an Englishman commanding a brigade in Holkar's service, and one of the 'British' officers beheaded by Holkar in 1803 for refusing to fight against their countrymen.

Another intriguing historical footnote comes to light in Jac Weller's 'Wellington in India', (Longman 1972), in which he tells the story of an East India Company Lieutenant William Dodd stationed in Seedesegur who beat a goldsmith to death. Dodd was also involved in 'financial irregularities' resulting in his court martial and dishonourable discharge. Wellesley, intent on stopping the spread of crimes by *all classes of European* against Indians, made moves to try Dodd for murder in a civilian court, but Dodd got wind of this and fled to 'safety and fortune in the European officered Battalions which served the Mahratta princes and got away in spite of efforts to apprehend him.' If this was Dodd, the heroic 'Eurasian' of Stark's much-quoted polemic, some of the gilt comes off the gingerbread...

Despite the patriotism displayed by some Anglo-Indian men in returning to fight the Marathas, the Company's only reward was an order from the Commander-in-Chief in 1808 discharging them from the many British regiments now stationed in India. Since its inception there was always rivalry between the Company's (Indian) Army and the King's (British) Army, to say nothing, later, of a great deal of snobbery on both sides. In his book, 'Britain's Betrayal in India', Frank Anthony is scathing in his comments about fair-skinned Anglo-Indians who slipped into the British Army during World War II, while their darker- skinned kith and kin – sometimes from the same family – were acceptable only in the Indian Army. I believe the R.A.F. was more democratic, making no distinctions between the two.

To return to the 19th century, having made certain that the Anglo-Indian Community was made up of what would now be dubbed 'second class citizens' – and if you tell people they are inferior and go on doing so at regular intervals, inferior they become – the Company introduced another villain to thicken up its sorry plot. He was Viscount Valentia, commissioned by the Court of Directors in London to visit all the Company's possessions. This lordly globe-trotter wrote a diary of his travels published in 1811 as 'Voyages and Travels to India, Ceylon, the Red Sea, Abyssinia and Egypt in the years 1802-1806. Like many a globe-trotter before and since, the noble lord came, saw and made snap judgments on the people and places he fleetingly visited.

About the 'Eurasians' he was explicit and inaccurate. After a sojourn in Calcutta he wrote: 'The most rapidly accumulating evil of

Bengal is the increase of half-caste children. They are forming the first step to colonisation by creating a link of union between the English and the natives.' He goes on to raise the bogey of Haiti and the Black Republic, and continues... 'this tribe may hereafter become too powerful for control. Although they are not permitted to hold offices under the Company, yet they act as clerks in almost every mercantile house; and many of them are annually sent to England to receive the benefit of an European education. With numbers in their favour, with a close relationship to the natives, and without an equal proportion of the pusillanimity and indolence which is natural to them, what may not in future be dreaded from them?'

As Herbert Stark proudly counters, what indeed? In the Indian Mutiny of 1857 Brendish saved the Punjab; Hearsey saved Calcutta; Forgett saved Bombay; the La Martinière boys defended the Lucknow Residency. All were Anglo-Indian metamorphosed into 'Englishmen' by later historians, much to the wrath of the Community and its leaders.

Viscount Valentia ends his tirade against the 'Eurasian tribe' with a suggestion put forward to solve the 'problem: *'I have no hesitation in saying that the evil ought to be stopped; and I know of no other way of effecting this object, than by obliging every father of half-caste children to send them to Europe prohibiting their return in any capacity whatever.'* He was obviously unaware of the previous rationalisation by the Court of Directors to British fathers whose sons were debarred from travelling to England for their further education because *'the imperfections of the children would debase the succeeding generations of Englishmen'!*

At this point in their history, some of the better educated Anglo-Indians decided to make a bid for the improvement of their lot. Some had fortunately entered the higher echelons of the Company's service before the dates of prohibition but would not be succeeded by their sons. And in 1813 a lakh (100,000) of rupees had been sanctioned by the Court of Directors for spending on education, but not a single pie (lowest value Indian coin) had been allocated for use in the setting up of Anglo-Indian and European schools, the whole amount earmarked exclusively for Indian education. However, the forces of adversity wrought their usual magic and one young man emerged to speak and write about his down-trodden community in an attempt to goad its members into action. He was an 18 year-old 'Eurasian' poet, Henry Derozio, whose slim volume of poems published in 1828 attracted critical acclaim in London and Calcutta. He became sub-editor on 'The Indian Gazette' and later taught in the Hindu School in Calcutta founded by David Hare, where he was much revered by his Indian pupils. He also established 'The East Indian' newspaper in which he published articles championing the Anglo-Indian cause.

He and others of similar parentage and like opinions – some men considerably older than himself – would meet at each other's houses to discuss their plight. To all the meetings came Mr J W Ricketts, who was eventually deputed to present a petition to Parliament in London setting out the East Indians' political, social and economic grievances. The term 'East Indian' was the designation chosen by the 'Eurasians' of those days. Ricketts presented the petition in 1830, a particularly unpropitious year in England. Many pressing domestic issues, to say nothing of the repercussions following the French Revolution, totally eclipsed any interest there might have been in the petition, and, to cap everything, George IV died in June 1830. Ricketts did, however, manage to present the petition to both Houses before the King's death and seemed to have been received sympathetically. Parliament was dissolved, reassembled and dissolved again within a few months of his return to India in March 1831. The first petition appeared to have sunk without trace, followed soon after by a second. The East Indian Movement was short-lived, lasting only from 1827-1830, its prominent members dying a few years later.

But someone in England must have taken note, for under the renewal of the Company's Charter in 1833 which removed the last vestiges of Company power as the sole trading body in India and opened up commercial trading to any British subject, 'no native of the said territories, nor any natural born subject of His Majesty's residents therein, shall by reason of his religion, place of birth, descent, colour, or any of them be disabled from holding any place, office, or employment under the said Company.' Fine words indeed, but Company posts in the higher echelons were still available only by recruitment in England. The Anglo-Indians continued to be subtly elbowed out and relegated to the more lowly, uncovenanted posts unless they could afford to go to England for education and eventual recruitment.

The question of an acceptable designation for people of mixed blood continually exercised the Community until its final official adoption of the term 'Anglo-Indian' in 1911, sanctioned by the then Viceroy, Lord Hardinge. In earlier times they had been called 'Indo-Briton', 'East Indian' and 'Eurasian'. They particularly disliked the latter, which had always been applied in a derogatory sense. Somewhat confusingly many of the 'pure' British in India referred to themselves as Anglo-Indian, and continued to do so both in conversation and in literature, well into the 20th century. Indeed, the term is still used to-day in reminiscences of the British Raj to describe the British temporarily based in India.

The sad and desperate cleaving of 'Eurasians' to the word 'Anglo' was graphically demonstrated by one of the Community's former leaders, Dr J R Wallace, in his inaugural speech to the newly formed 'Imperial Anglo-Indian Society' in 1898 when he declared, "Britishers we are and Britishers we ever must and shall be. Once we relinquish the name (Anglo-Indian) and permit ourselves to be styled 'Eurasians' or 'Statutory Natives of India' we become estranged from our proud heritage as Britishers." Later generations of Anglo-Indians are scathing about what they consider as Wallace's pathetic insistence on the Britishness of Anglo-Indians, pointing out that 'Eurasians' are the result of the mixed marriages of many European nationalities with Indians and other Asians. Such logic is impeccable. How can people born of French, German, Dutch or Scandinavian ancestors be called Anglo anything? How could the child of a French father and a Burmese mother be called Anglo-Indian? 'Franco-Burman' would be the accurate description, and 'Eurasian' fits the bill even more neatly. Eurindian, Euro-Burman, Euro-Malaysian would all be equally appropriate and not unpleasant to the ear. But what's in a name? 'Centuries of prejudice' would be the reply of many Anglo-Indians.

Another group of people often lumped together by officialdom with the Anglo-Indian Community was that of the Domiciled Europeans. This quaint appellation was given to people said to be of unmixed European descent, generally British, from families whose members had been born, lived and worked in India for generations, not even going home to Britain or Europe for either education or retirement.

Training his beady, legal eye upon the subject, Frank Anthony, in his book "Britain's Betrayal in India", is vociferous in his condemnation of the designation 'Domiciled European'. In his estimation the term has always been a misnomer as persons of European descent domiciled in India could be domiciled Indians but not domiciled Europeans. He goes on to accuse British officialdom of practising discrimination between the so-called Domiciled Europeans and Anglo-Indians by granting the 'DEs' preference where jobs were concerned. In my own day I can remember the term 'country born' as referring specifically to Domiciled Europeans, and the majority of the British were as snobbish towards them as they were to Anglo-Indians, denying them, in some cases, entry into their clubs.

Ever on the alert to crush any delusions of superiority on the part of Domiciled Europeans and, for that matter, 'true Brits' over Anglo-Indians, Anthony quotes the official definition of an Anglo-Indian under an Article of Independent India's Constitution (in effect a reproduction of Article 366 (2) of the British Government of India Act 1935), which states:

An Anglo-Indian means a person whose father or any of whose other male progenitors in the male line is or was of European descent but who is domiciled within the territory of India and is or was born within such territory of parents habitually resident therein and not established there for temporary purposes only.

(A strangely woolly definition which pays no regard to the nationality of the mother.) Needless to say, such official edicts did little to lessen the discrimination practised against Anglo-Indians, regardless of their social or educational standing, and the arrival of the British *memsahib* did everything to exacerbate the situation. She, and later generations of her type, were quick to notice that the majority of Anglo-Indian girls were extremely attractive. The lonely ex-patriate male fell easy prey to such charms, and vigilance had to be exercised by *memsahibs*, commanding officers and employers alike lest such young men 'lowered' the tone of society by consorting with or – worse – marrying a 'half-caste'. This attitude prevailed right up to 1947 with the exodus of the British from India. Many *memsahibs*, in their sere and yellow age, must now regret their cruel, unthinking prejudice towards the Anglo-Indians who crossed their paths during their Raj days.

Scientists have long exploded the myth that people of mixed parentage exhibit the worst traits of both races, and have proved that environment plays the most important role in the formation of character. Sadly, the less privileged Anglo-Indians have proved the environmental theory only too exact, brought up as they have been in an atmosphere of poverty and deprivation, the label of inferiority applied to them since birth. Some are still existing – rather than living – in the slums of Calcutta and other Indian cities, marooned between two cultures and deserted by both. But the many who came from more privileged backgrounds or had the tenacity and talents to rise above the cruel stigma of inferiority demonstrated that their dual parentage proved no hindrance to them, as the eminent writers, doctors, scientists, lawyers, sportsmen, soldiers, teachers, musicians, actors and ordinary respectable human beings among their ranks will testify. And in the India of to-day, many Anglo-Indians who stayed on after 1947 have learnt to accept with pride their status as responsible citizens of India, thereby gaining the respect and admiration of Indians themselves.

It will always be a blot on the pages of Britain's colonial history that as rulers they failed to emulate the Dutch who cultivated a 'Eurasian' race in their colonies who were proud of their dual nationality, accepting its attendant rules and privileges as their birthright. In the eyes of the Dutch there was no stigma attached to inter-marriage and when they relinquished their East Indian colonies after the last war, members of the 'Eurasion' community were given the opportunity of 'repatriation' to Holland if they chose – unlike the British after Indian Independence in 1947, who left Anglo-Indians to sink or swim unless they had applied for citizenship under the 1948 U.K. Citizens Act, a procedure calling for documentary proof of British nationality on their fathers' side.

With the dawning of the 20th century life for the Anglo-Indian Community did improve as far as employment was concerned. The advent of the Railways and the Post and Telegraph Departments in the 1850s had already made thousands of jobs available to Anglo-Indians and many other Government Departments opened their doors as successive governments proved more liberal. The Indian

Railways would never have become successful without the devoted pioneering service of Anglo-Indian supervisors and track layers through India's swamps and jungles, as well as the thousands of drivers, stokers and engineers who kept the trains running. The Railways virtually became an Anglo-Indian preserve for 100 years until Indian Independence, with many subordinate posts in the Post & Telegraph Departments also reserved for them alone. Indeed, where would the British in India have been without those life-lines, particularly the Telegraph Department, during the Indian Mutiny? The Port Commissioners and Customs Services, too, provided them with sources of employment, as did the Indian Medical Department, the 'junior' wing of the prestigious Indian Medical Service, where they could enter as uncovenanted Assistant-Surgeons.

At the same time the more adventurous among Anglo-Indian men had severed the umbilical cord traditionally binding them to Government service and had carved out successful careers in mercantile firms, tea-planting and the legal, medical and teaching professions, although it must be recognised that some employers still discriminated against 'country born' and Anglo-Indian personnel by paying them derisory salaries compared with those earned by their colleagues recruited from Britain.

One of the most famous Anglo-Indians ever to emerge during the Community's history was Sir Henry Gidney, who began his medical career in the Indian Medical Department and, after passing the requisite exams in England, rose to be a most brilliant specialist in Opthalmic surgery in the prestigious Indian Medical Service. He entered politics and represented the Anglo-Indian Community in the Imperial Legislative Assembly in India, becoming their spokesman. By 1931 he had been knighted. Gidney did much for the Community's morale and once admonished its members, 'If there is one thing which you must completely eradicate from yourselves, it is the retention of superiority and inferiority complexes; and you should bring about their replacement with a complex of equality.' He died in 1942 and his mantle as leader of the Community was assumed by Frank Anthony, then a brilliant young lawyer, who died in 1993 aged 84. The current President of the Anglo-Indian Association is Major General Robert Williams.

During my schooldays in India – perhaps understandably – I was never aware of the existence of a united 'Anglo-Indian Community' and it is only in recent years that I have discovered that there was an Anglo-Indian Association in the important cities of India, fighting for the rights of its members. Now, all these years later, I am forced to conclude that not all Anglo-Indians wished to be associated with such a group and never heeded its still, small voice.

By
H. A. Stark.

By the 20th century, careers for Anglo-Indian women, too, were burgeoning. There had always been a nursing career open to them since Lady Canning founded the Calcutta Hospital Nurses' Institution in 1859. They became the country's first nurses as India's rigid caste system precluded its own women from doing such work. Anglo-Indian girls have been renowned ever since for their devoted services to the medical profession as both nurses and doctors – a fact not unnoticed by the many British women who worked with them in Indian hospitals during the Second World War. They also became extremely efficient secretaries and excellent school teachers, and thousands of them served in the famous W.A.C.(I) [Women's Auxiliary Corps (India)] during the Second World War while their menfolk were serving in the British and Indian armies.

The catalogue of the various roles played by Anglo-Indians during the British Raj and after is a lengthy one and not within the scope of this book. But their very existence was the catalyst – if one can apply this rather explosive epithet to a largely quiescent group of people – which brought about the establishment of schools for their children as well as those of the British living and working in India who couldn't afford or, more importantly, did not want to send their children across thousands of miles of ocean to school in Britain.

ഗ৪০

I wrote this chapter in a white heat of indignation at what I learned during the early stages of my research for this book, and am indebted to the late Herbert Stark for much of the history of the Anglo-Indian Community contained in his 'Hostages to India', first published in Calcutta in 1936 and reprinted by BACSA in 1987. In the event, 'Who are the Anglo-Indians?' was deemed as not germane to the main theme of 'Under The Old School Topee' by the editors of the original imprint in 1990 and was consequently deleted. I recognised the wisdom of this decision at the time, but now feel bound to include the edited chapter as an appendix in this revised reprint in the hope that readers will find the history of people of mixed race in India as much of a revelation as I did.

The children and grandchildren of the Anglo-Indians who became the new Canadians, Australians, New Zealanders, Americans and Britishers – or citizens of whatever country in the West they chose to settle in – will have listened with delight to their parents' and grandparents' stories of 'the good old days' in the India of over 50 years ago. Some of those sons and daughters will also have been puzzled and hurt by their elders' tales of the prejudice and slights they suffered. But as citizens of a more enlightened era they feel no inferiority themselves and neither should they. Nor, happily, do most of them see the need to fight old battles. To the young the past is the past, and the future beckons.

HMC April 1996

Dr. Graham's Kalimpong Homes

*The school buildings with the
Katherine Graham Memorial Chapel
in the background*

*School cadets, boy scouts and cubs in
front of their cottage*

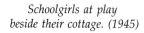

*Schoolgirls at play
beside their cottage. (1945)*

254

Appendix B

Dr John Graham of Kalimpong
Champion and Benefactor of Needy
Anglo-Indian Children

John Anderson Graham was born in 1861, the second of the four sons of Scottish parents living in West Hackney, London. The family eventually returned to Scotland and as a young man John Graham was ordained as a minister of the Church of Scotland. In 1899 he married his beloved wife, Katie, and went out to Kalimpong in what was then known as British Sikkim as a missionary of the Kirk. While primarily appointed by the mission to bring Christianity to the native people of Kalimpong, i.e. the Lepchas, the Bhutias and the Nepalese, during his travels Graham became aware of the plight of the Eurasian children born of liaisons between Englishmen and Indian women, many of whom were abandoned together with their mothers. Like Bishop Cotton before him, he realised their desperate need for refuge and education and as a result in 1900 he founded the St. Andrew's Colonial Homes in Kalimpong, re-named Dr Graham's Homes in 1947. I am indebted to Mrs Pat Hardie, one time Hon. Secretary of the old students' association for the following account of the world famous 'Kalimpong Homes'. Readers may also like to know that the biography, 'Dr Graham of Kalimpong', published in 1974 by the late James R. Minto (Principal of the Homes from 1961-1970) is now available in paperback @ £5.99 including postage from The Secretary, Miss V Cassie, 21 Balmoral Place, Edinburgh, EH3 5JA.

A BRIEF HISTORY OF ST ANDREW'S COLONIAL HOMES, KALIMPONG, RE-NAMED DR GRAHAM'S HOMES IN 1947

Founded in 1900 by John Anderson Graham, a missionary to the Church of Scotland mission in Kalimpong in the Eastern Himalayas.

The first home was a rented cottage with 6 children from the Assam tea gardens. Graham was motivated by the plight of the lighter skinned children he had seen on the tea estates in Darjeeling and neighbouring areas – children of liaisons between British tea planters and local women – children who were often rejected by the communities of both parents.

Graham was a visionary, but a deeply practical man of boundless faith. His decision to build a "children's city" for impoverished, orphan and destitute European and Eurasian children he had seen in the cities of India as well as the tea estates, was not well received by the Mission Guild in his native Scotland. So he went to the thriving business houses of Calcutta and to Government officials of British India with his begging bowl. His enthusiasm for this ambitious project and his personal charisma softened the hardest hearts. Between 1901 and 1930 a bare hillside on a ridge overlooking the mighty Eastern Himalaya mountain range was transformed into his children's city, providing home and education to 600 children from all corners of India. Some 20 cottages, a babies' nursery, school buildings, a school assembly hall with clock tower, hospital, farm, swimming baths and staff houses were built during that period with the financial support of numerous benefactors from British India and Britain. The beautiful Katherine Graham Memorial Chapel was opened in 1925, built in memory of Graham's wife and helpmate who had died in 1919. The kindergarten school block was opened in 1938. The names of the cottages and the foundation stones in the many buildings commemorate the generous individual donors or groups from a particular region. In the early years the Homes Board of Management read like a "Who's Who of British India", such was the support he received.

The cottages each housed 32 children ranging in age from 5 to 18 years, with two staff members. This created the essential family atmosphere intended by Graham. Until 1954 all the cottage staff as well as many of the teaching staff were recruited from overseas, at first from Britain – mainly Scotland – but later from Australia, New Zealand and other western countries. The cottage staff, with their missionary zeal, instilled a strong Christian ethic into the children. Some devoted their entire working lives to the Homes. The concept of cottage living was unique in India, and the staff were called 'aunties' by the children. The children did all their own domestic work in the cottages on a weekly rota system. This, too, was unique to boarding schools in India.

The education system was that enjoyed by all Anglo-Indian schools in India, up to Senior Cambridge (School Certificate) level. In addition sports, games and swimming were compulsory for all, with fierce competition between the cottages for trophies. The annual Sports Day and Swimming Gala were highlights of the school year. Thus the children received an all-round education. Vocational training was also introduced for the less academic students – farming for the boys and child nursing for the girls. Discipline was strict and punishment could be severe, in keeping with the times. The school motto 'THOROUGH' was strongly upheld.

An interesting feature of the Homes was that the children went barefoot. This custom, introduced by Graham, lasted until 1962. Graham felt this was healthy, particularly during the monsoon, and it also saved a great deal of money. The Homes became known as the insitution where the children did not wear shoes. In 1962 the wearing of shoes was introduced by James Minto who had been appointed from Scotland as Headmaster of the Homes in 1959 and became its Principal in 1961. The wearing of shoes made a dramatic impact on the morale of the children who could now consider themselves on the same level as all other Anglo-Indian boarding schools. Minto retired from the Homes in 1970 and was awarded the OBE the following year. In 1974 he published his biography of Graham, 'Graham of Kalimpong'.

John Anderson Graham was deeply beloved by his 'bairns' as he called the boys and girls in his Homes. Since many did not know their fathers, it was natural that he should be called 'Daddy' by them, and he is still universally thought of by former students in this affectionate way.

The loyalty and bonding to the Homes by former students (OGBs, or 'Old Girls & Boys' as they prefer to be called) is extremely strong. At the regular old school reunions held in London, Edinburgh, Sydney, Melbourne and other private gatherings, the camaraderie spanning generations is commented on by outsiders.

In the early years many children, on leaving the Homes, were sent to New Zealand to work on farms or as domestics. This practice ceased after World War I. Australia was less receptive to receiving Graham's 'bairns', the government there insisting on the children's parentage being at least three quarters white, which was in effect a question of colour. Graham was deeply disappointed by this attitude.

In a changed and changing India, the Homes, as they near their centenary, have also changed, but great efforts are made to uphold the principles and traditions laid down by their Founder. The number of underprivileged Anglo-Indian children now being educated there are in a minority. Much of the funding for these children is provided by overseas sponsors, who in turn make their commitment through overseas committees in Scotland, Australia, New Zealand and Canada. Many former students also sponsor children. The committees raise funds, much of these going towards the constant maintenance of ageing buildings in a harsh climate.

Dr Graham's children, and now grandchildren and even great-grandchildren have continued to take an interest in the running of the Homes.

With ever increasing costs, the Homes are now a largely fee-paying school, students coming from all parts of India as well as the neighbouring countries of Nepal and Bhutan. A number of Tibetan refugee children have also been given an education and status in the Homes since the 1950s. The number of boarding students is considerably swelled by day scholars in a burgeoning Kalimpong population. The Principal, Howard O'Conner, is an Anglo-Indian, and all cottage and teaching staff are also Anglo-Indian, Indian or Nepalese, many of them former Homes students.

Memorials in the Homes to their saintly founder include the sculpted words in the school assembly hall: 'DR GRAHAM, WHO LOVED CHILDREN, FOUNDED THESE HOMES 1900', and the moving epitaph on the grave he shares with his wife in the little cemetery, which reads: 'THE CHILDREN RISE UP AND CALL THEM BLESSED'.

Pat Wilsone Hardie
OGB 1943-1952

ೞ

USEFUL ADDRESSES

All India Hermonite Association
Pratap Singh Rai
Mount Hermon School
North Point P.O.
Darjeeling
West Bengal 734104
INDIA

Auckland House School, Simla
Mrs Janet Chapman
3 St. Michael's Close
Rough Common
Canterbury
KENT CT2 9BN

British Ancestors in India Society
Mr Paul Rowland
2 South Farm Avenue
Harthill
SHEFFIELD S31 8WY

Kalimpong Homes
Editor: Kalimpong Newsletter
Miss Lorraine French
80 Shoot up Hill
West Hampstead
LONDON NW2 3XJ

Kodaikanal Woodstock
International
K.W.I.
159 Ralph McGill Boulevard NE
Room 408
Atlanta
GEORGIA 30308, U.S.A.

La Martinière College (Boys)
Dilkusha
Lucknow 226001
Uttar Pradesh
INDIA
(For copies of 'Bright Renown – La
Martinière College, Lucknow 1845–
1945')

MHUSA (Mount Hermon U.S. Alums)
Mrs June Dewsberry
1906 Quail Trail
Lee's Summit
MO 64081
U.S.A.

Mount Hermon Alumni Association
Nepal
Bachan Gyawali
P.O.Box 1357
Kathmandu
NEPAL

Mount Hermon (Calcutta)
Sajan Singhania
Hermonite Association, Calcutta
Chapter
175 Jodhpur Park
Calcutta 700068
INDIA

Oak Grove Association
Mr Maurice Van Ristel
664 Prince Avenue
Westcliff on Sea
ESSEX SSO OEY

Old Cottonians Association
(BCS Bangalore)
Mrs Pat Mamprin
27 Osborne Court
Cowes
ISLE OF WIGHT PO31 7QS

Old Cottonians Association
(BCS Simla)
Mr Tony Sinha
189 Grosvenor Avenue
Hayes
MIDDLESEX UB4 8NW

Old Gallians
(Lawrence College, Ghora Gali)
Hon. Secretary
Mr John Walker
16 Elm Grove
Farnham
SURREY GU9 OQE

Old Lawrencians (Lovedale)
Mr Alan Hipwood
36 Radford Drive
LEICESTER LE3 3DR

Old Martinians Association
Mr Ibrahim Ali Khan
Sheesh Mahal
Durga Devi Marg
Lucknow 226003
INDIA

Old Martinians (Australia)
Mr Clayton Roberts
34 O'Grady Way
Girrawheen
WESTERN AUSTRALIA 6064

Old Martinians (Calcutta)
Mr Donald Alney
Principal
La Martinière for Boys
11 Loudon Street
Calcutta 700017
INDIA

Old Martinians (France)
Madame Amalia Abad
Fondation Claude Martin
9 rue des Arguetins
69001 Lyon
FRANCE

Old Paulite Association
Mr S B R Naidu
c/o Blue Print
1 Old Court House Street
Calcutta 700 069
INDIA

Old Sanawarian Society (U.K.)
Mrs P Curry
106 Cranley Gardens
Muswell Hill
LONDON N10 3AH

OMHSA (U.K.) [Old Mount
Hermon Students' Association,
U.K.]
Contact: the author

Presentation Convent, Kodaikanal
Mrs Jane Turner
Monkshatch
Hog's Back
Guildford
SURREY GU3 1DG

Raj Connections
The Newsletter and Contact Maker
Editor: Mr Patrick O'Meara
1 Oakhill Grove
Surbiton
SURREY KT6 6DS

St Denys, Murree, Pakistan
Mrs Lee Just
16F Kent Road
Gravesend
KENT DA11 0SY

St Joseph's College, Coonoor
Mr Bill Douglas
29 Bush Grove
Sudbury
SUFFOLK CO10 7HH

St Joseph's College, North Point,
Darjeeling
Mr Basil La Bouchardière
1 Blackbridge Court
Blackbridge Lane
Horsham
WEST SUSSEX RH12 1RH
(Mr La Bouchardière was a student
1922-29)

St Mary's High School, Mount Abu
Mr Patrick O'Meara
1 Oakhill Grove
Surbiton
SURREY KT6 6DS

Sherwood College, Naini Tal
Mr Malcolm Johnson
104 Norbury Avenue
Thornton Heath
SURREY CR7 8AF

South India Association
Hon Secretary
Mrs Jane Turner
Monkshatch
Hog's Back
Guildford
SURREY GU3 1DG

The East Indies Telegraph
(A Newsletter providing a point of
contact for those interested in
Anglo-Indian family history)
Ms G Charles
68 Greenway Close
Friern Barnet
LONDON N11 3NT

The Foothill Hermonites (Siliguri)
Jagjit Singh
Tera Hotel
Sevoke Road
Siliguri 734401
INDIA

The Hermonites, Delhi
Shyamal Bhattacharjee
c/o Mr Krishan Goenka
307-308 Magnum House II
Community Centre, Karampura
New Delhi 110015
INDIA

VADHA (Victoria & Dow Hill
Association)
Hon. Secretary
Mrs Grace Pereira
20 Merton Hall Gardens
Wimbledon
LONDON SW20 8SN

Select Bibliography

Anglo-Indian Education   A. A. D'Souza, New Delhi, 1976
A Particular Account of the European
  Military Adventurers of Hindustan,
  1784-1803   Herbert Compton, London, 1892
Britain's Betrayal in India   Frank Anthony, New Delhi, 1969
British India   Michael Edwardes, London, 1976
British Social Life in India,1608-1937   Denis Kincaid, London,1938,1973
Cimerii? or Eurasians and their Future Cedric Dover, Calcutta, 1929
Country Born   James R. Staines, London, 1986
Darjeeling Past and Present   E.C. Dozey, Calcutta, 1922
Dr Graham of Kalimpong   James R. Minto, 1974, 1995
Heaven's Command   Jan Morris, London, 1973
Hostages to India   H.A. Stark, Calcutta, 1936,
     reprint BACSA, 1987

India Britannica   Geoffrey Moorhouse, London, 1983
Ladies in the Sun   J.K. Standford, London, 1962
Life of Claude Martin   S.C. Hill, Calcutta, 1901
Merle   C. Higham & R. Moseley,
     London, 1984
My Thirty Years in India   Edmund Cox, London, 1909
Orchids and Algebra, The Story of Dow Hill School
     Denise Coelho, 1982
Pax Britannica   Jan Morris, London, 1973
Plain Tales from the Raj   Charles Allen, London, 1975
Railways of the Raj   M. Satow & R. Desmond,
     London, 1980
Simla Past and Present   Edward J. Buck, Calcutta, 1904
The Anglo-Indian Vision   Gloria J. Moore, Melbourne, 1986
The British Army in India   Julius Jeffreys, London, 1858
The East India Vade Mecum   Capt. T. Williamson,
     London, 1810

The Eurasian Problem constructively
  approached   Kenneth E.Wallace, Calcutta, 1929
The Games Ethic and Imperialism   J. A. Mangan, London, 1986
The Good old Days of John Company W.H. Carey, London, 1882
The Last Days of the Raj   Trevor Royle, London 1989

The Nabobs   Percival Spear, London, 1963
The Promotion of Learning for early
    Settlers in India   N.N. Law, London, 1915
The Public School Phenomenon   J.Gathorne-Hardy, London, 1977
The Social Condition of the British
    Community in Bengal 1757-1800   S.C. Ghosh, Leiden, 1971
These are the Anglo-Indians   Reginald Maher, Calcutta, 1962
The Strange Ride of Rudyard Kipling   Angus Wilson, London, 1977
Travels in India   Oscar Browning, London, 1903
Two Monsoons   Theon Wilkinson, London, 1976,
                                              1987
Up the Country   Emily Eden, London, 1930, 1978,
                                              1983
Wellington in India   Jac Weller, London, 1972

PAMPHLETS

The Anglo-Indian Community and
    their Romantic History   Bishop Eyre Chatterton,
                                         SPCK, London, 1937
Our English Church Schools in India   Bishop Eyre Chatterton,
                                         SPCK, London, 1934
Guide to Murree   E.P. Peacock, Lahore, 1883, India
                                         Office Library & Records (IOL&R)
Mussoorie – Queen of the Hill
    Stations   Mrs K. Agarval, Delhi, 1977
                                         (IOL&R)
Hills in the clouds (A guide to
    Kodaikanal)   Zai Whitaker, Madras, 1993

MANUSCRIPT SOURCES

Report of Committee upon the Financial Condition of Hill Schools
    for Europeans in Northern India, 1904, (IOL&R)
    Ref. V\26\86\Pt.I & Pt.II.
Report on the existing schools for European and Eurasian children
    throughout India, 1873 (IOL&R) Ref (1) 1483
Lawrence Asylum, Sanawar – being a brief account of the past ten
    years of existence and progress of the Institution established in
    the Himalayas by the late Sir H.M. Lawrence, KCB, for the

orphan and other children of European soldiers serving or
having served in India (IOL&R)

Rules of the Lawrence Military Asylum (IOL&R) Ref. P | T 5107

Papers and correspondence concerning the Lawrence Asylum at
Ootacamund (IOL&R) Ref. Madras N. Series, 83A – 86

Correspondence between Sir H.M. Lawrence and Commanding
Officers of Honourable Company Regiments (IOL&R)

Correspondence between Brevet Major H.M. Lawrence and
Officiating Sec. to Govt. of India Military Department (IOL&R)

The Hill Stations in Colonial Urban Development, Anthony D.
King, in *Social Action*, New Delhi Ref. Vol. 26, No.3, 1976 (IOL&-R)

'Our Journals' (Mussoorie School) 1867, Society of Genealogists
Ref.AC 252170.

Government of India Home Department Proceedings
(correspondence between Government and D.P.I. Punjab re
Bishop Cotton School) (IOL&R)

N.B. The India Office Library and Records (IOL&R) is now known
as the Oriental & India Office Collections (OIOC) and is part of
The British Library.

Alphabetical Index